Margaret Thatcher

Margaret Thatcher

Life After
Downing Street

Peter Just

\Bᵇ\
Biteback Publishing

First published in Great Britain in 2025 by
Biteback Publishing Ltd, London
Copyright © Peter Just 2025

ISBN 978-1-78590-920-7

10 9 8 7 6 5 4 3 2 1

A CIP catalogue record for this book is available from the British Library.

Set in Adobe Caslon Pro and AWConqueror Didot

Printed and bound in Great Britain by
CPI Group (UK) Ltd, Croydon CR0 4YY

FSC
www.fsc.org
MIX
Paper | Supporting
responsible forestry
FSC® C013604

For my grandmother, Ivy Mary Just, with whom I used to discuss Margaret Thatcher, and for my father, Derrick Hugh Just, with whom I used to 'debate' her.

Contents

Preface

The immediate genesis of this book was a paper I presented at a conference in the House of Lords in September 2023, organised by Professor The Lord Norton of Louth, the Centre for Legislative Studies and the Centre for British Politics. The conference was on Margaret Thatcher's life, work and legacy. My presentation covered her time as a former Prime Minister following her resignation in 1990. It focused on her (after) life, (continuing) work and (emerging) legacy.[1]

The book's gestation, however, has been much longer. My conference paper was based on postgraduate research I undertook under Lord Norton's supervision at the University of Hull in the 1990s into what prime ministers do after they resign. That research had been inspired by my undergraduate dissertation on Margaret Thatcher and her 'ism' post-Downing Street.

As a northern, working-class child of the 1970s, Margaret Thatcher and Thatcherism, and people's reactions to both, have been a significant feature of my life. Some of my earliest memories are of Lady Thatcher. One of these was the Conservatives' victory in the 1983 general election. I can still recall getting up, going downstairs, picking up the newspaper, what was then the *Daily Mirror*, and seeing the news that Lady Thatcher would still be Prime Minister. Another memory is one of my uncles criticising Lady Thatcher to my paternal grandmother. This was about the poll tax. At the conclusion of his diatribe, Grandma, then in her eighties, replied, 'Well, she's very clever.' End of. This only added to my uncle's irritation. Adding to a man's irritation itself surely being a Margaret Thatcher kind of thing to do.

The day Lady Thatcher announced her resignation was the day of one of my mock A levels. I still remember the reaction of my politics teacher, Chris Robinson, when the news broke. I also remember seeing first hand the reaction that Lady Thatcher continued generating after No. 10. This was when I worked for Iain Dale at Politico's, the Westminster bookshop, in the early 2000s. During the 2001 general election, our 'Bring back Maggie' badges sold out. We could not keep up with demand. That was certainly not the case for the badges of the then party leaders.

Then there were the occasions on which I met Lady Thatcher while working at Politico's. First at a speech in her former constituency. We talked about how 'exciting' politics was – the former Prime Minister's word, naturally. Then at a lunch event celebrating the portrait of Lady Thatcher by Richard Stone used on the cover of this book. She was wearing a blue coat dress. I wore a dark suit with purple shirt and purple tie. Waiting to be photographed with Lady Thatcher, I said to her, 'I wish I had worn blue.' Lady Thatcher looked at what I was wearing, looked at what she was wearing, and replied, 'No, it wouldn't have been quite right.' The last time I met Lady Thatcher was the evening before the Queen Mother's funeral. It was at a launch at the Savoy for her book, *Statecraft*. We talked about the statement she had issued, and the coverage it had and had not got.

When Lady Thatcher died, I was living and working in Rome. Walking down Via Ostiense, almost at Via del Porto Fluviale, I received a text message: '*Margaret Thatcher non è più con noi.*' But, as we will see, although Lady Thatcher was no longer with us, Margaret Thatcher was. She still is. Some may wonder if she will ever *not* be with us. Cue Sir Keir Starmer's comments about her in late 2023, the reaction to them, and Starmer's subsequent recantation. As Madam Deputy Speaker, Dame Eleanor Laing, said during Prime Minister's Questions on 6 December 2023, 'There is understandable excitement about the mention of the name.'[2] Why excitement? And why understandable? This book helps to explain.

After Lady Thatcher's death, the flag at the British Embassy flew at half-mast. A book of condolence was opened. The Cardinal Secretary of State, Tarcisio Bertone, sent a telegram on behalf of Pope Francis to David Cameron: '…the Holy Father invokes upon all whose lives she touched God's abundant blessings', it concluded. Lady Thatcher's death had political aspects too. An Italian friend posted a photograph of her on Facebook. Their message read, '*In Italia ci vorrebbero persone come Margaret … Forse così le cose andrebbero alla grande.*' ('In Italy if we had people like Margaret … maybe things would be great.')

Interestingly, entertainingly, or perhaps both, during my time in Rome, there were regular transport strikes. They always seemed to happen on a Friday. The only time they had any actual impact on my life was the Friday after Lady Thatcher died. Was it a sign? What was also interesting when I lived in Rome was that, after Queen Elizabeth II and Diana, Princess of Wales, the person Italians asked me about most often was Margaret Thatcher.

Given the nature of both my work and the Italians with whom I worked, our conversations invariably turned to politics. When they touched on Germany, I always commented, 'You sound like Margaret Thatcher' – as the Italians did when they talked about the single currency. There was a meme entitled 'For those who have forgotten…' that frequently did the rounds. It featured photographs of Lady Thatcher and Romano Prodi, the former Italian Prime Minister. Lady Thatcher's quote read: 'The euro is a danger for democracy, it will be fatal for the poorest countries. It will devastate their economies.' Prodi's read, 'With the euro we will work one day less, earning as if we worked one day more.' No doubt you can guess which opinion the meme creator thought was the correct one.

After 1990, Lady Thatcher did more than just provide quotes for Italian memes. In addition to visiting the country, both for work and on holiday, she intervened in Italian politics – including by supporting Silvio Berlusconi in the 2001 election.[3] She was also called in aid by various figures. Ahead of the 1994 election, Antonio Martino, a member of Berlusconi's *Forza Italia*, proposed a reform programme that was, he said, 'more radical than that espoused by Margaret Thatcher in 1979.'[4] After *Forza Italia* won the election, Lady Thatcher sent Martino congratulations. When he called to thank her, she gave him 'her usual pep talk: "You must do for Italy what I did for Britain."' Martino explained why Italy was at a disadvantage compared to Britain. He then added, 'However, we have something which you didn't have.' 'What's that?' Lady Thatcher asked. Martino replied, 'Your example.'[5]

Martino revealed another important part of Lady Thatcher's life after 1990: simply being Margaret Thatcher. During a break at a conference in Fiesole, Tuscany, in 1991, he and Lady Thatcher were walking along the hotel's portico. The countryside 'looked magnificent'. Lady Thatcher said to Martino, 'Yours is a beautiful country, with a rotten government.' Martino replied, 'My dear lady, the opposite would be much worse.' At the conference, Lady Thatcher commented, 'Civilisation is the exclusive prerogative of

English-speaking peoples.' Martino was the only non-English, non-American person present. He looked at John O'Sullivan, who was sitting next to him. O'Sullivan smiled and said, 'You have been consigned to barbarism!'

Lady Thatcher continued to be called in aid after her death, too. Following disturbances between Napoli and Eintracht Frankfurt fans in March 2023, the Napoli owner, Aurelio De Laurentiis, said, 'Now politics must face the problem and I hope that [Prime Minister Giorgia] Meloni will do like the only prime minister who has had the courage: the English one, Margaret Thatcher.'[6] Meloni has also been compared to Lady Thatcher, including by Rishi Sunak. In December 2023, he said, 'I can only guess what first attracted Giorgia to the strong female leader who was prepared to challenge the consensus, take on stale thinking and revive her country both domestically and on the international stage.'[7]

This calling in aid and being compared to Lady Thatcher was a defining feature of her life after Downing Street. It was and is one of the hallmarks of and central reasons for her continued and continuing influence in British politics. As seen above, it did not just happen in the United Kingdom. It happened in other countries, too. Examples of this are detailed in files in the National Archives about Lady Thatcher's post-prime ministerial travels. All this could be taken to demonstrate, adapting some words of President Macron's about the Queen, that to us she was our Prime Minister, while to them she was *The* Prime Minister. How The Prime Minister lived her life, continued her work and witnessed her legacy emerge after Downing Street is the story this book tells.

It has been written largely during visits to Rome, which is fitting, for the Italian capital was the stage for one of Lady Thatcher's most indelible post-prime ministerial appearances, certainly of her last years. This was when she met Pope Benedict XVI in St Peter's Square in May 2009. The image of the Pontiff and the Prime Minister was iconic. Naturally, it generated press coverage. But then, as we will see, what didn't with Lady Thatcher after No. 10? The *Daily Mail* headlined the story: 'Iron Lady grants the Pope an audience'.[8]

In his magisterial official biography of Lady Thatcher, Charles Moore writes movingly about this meeting and its aftermath. The anecdote highlights another aspect of Lady Thatcher's life after Downing Street: performance. That too was, and is, central to her legacy, and to her continuing political relevance. The crowds in St Peter's Square had recognised Lady Thatcher and were clapping. While heading to her car, someone told her that people wanted to photograph her. Having removed her mantilla and adjusted her hair, Lady Thatcher 'gave a regal, all-embracing wave, to loud applause.' Moore concluded, 'She had performed brilliantly.'[9]

If not Lady Thatcher's final public appearance, this was surely one of her last performances, however fleeting, on the world stage. That it should have been in Rome is also fitting. For if all roads lead there, as this book shows, then Lady Thatcher's premiership was the starting point from which all subsequent premierships began. In large part that was due to her post-premiership, and to how, after 1990, people responded and continue to respond to Margaret Thatcher's life after Downing Street.

Introduction

Margaret Thatcher concluded the first volume of her memoirs, *The Downing Street Years*, with the following sentence:

> I waved and got into the car with Denis beside me, as he has always been; and the car took us past press, policemen and the tall black gates of Downing Street, away from red boxes and parliamentary questions, summits and party conferences, budgets and communiqués, situation rooms and scrambler telephones, out to whatever the future held.[1]

What did the future hold for Lady Thatcher[2] as she embarked on her new life as a premier emeritus, a former Prime Minister who no longer holds any ministerial or party office?

Some may be forgiven for thinking that Lady Thatcher did not have much of a future at all. Indeed, Caroline Slocock wrote that her life seemed to 'fall apart when she left No. 10'.[3] Books about her have tended not to devote much space to her life after Downing Street. Just 15 per cent of the final volume of Charles Moore's official biography was about Lady Thatcher's post-1990 life, covering 'The lioness in winter', 'Stateswoman – and subversive', and 'The light fades'. Other biographies, such as those by Robin Harris, Jonathan Aitken and John Campbell, have followed a similar pattern.

Reviewing Harris' book in 2013, Andy Beckett wrote of 'the

empty, sad quarter of a century that unfurled for her' after 1990.[4] That quote encapsulates the general, largely negative, view of Lady Thatcher's post-premiership. Indeed, a participant at the Margaret Thatcher life, work and legacy conference in September 2023 described it as 'a failure'. In 2005, Andrew Roberts said that her post-1990 career had been 'almost unbearably poignant and frustrating'.[5] Charles Moore wrote that while her interventions in UK politics after 1990 were 'usually right in principle', they were 'sometimes ill-judged in practice'.[6] 'I don't think she's had anything useful to do,' Sir Bernard Ingham said in 1999, and spoke of a 'singularly empty existence' compared to her time as Prime Minister.[7]

That said, in the same article as Ingham's comments, Lady Thatcher's private secretary, Mark Worthington, spoke of her being in the office every day. She had a huge overseas travelling schedule, visiting the United States five or six times a year, and the Far East almost the same amount. 'There is an awful lot of preparation for her speeches and she is in continual meetings with people from here and overseas,' Worthington commented.

So, there clearly was a life for Lady Thatcher after 1990. To date, it has been under-researched and largely misunderstood, if not actively misrepresented. As a result, its long-term effect has not been fully appreciated. This book, the first full-length examination of Margaret Thatcher's life as a former Prime Minister, attempts to rectify that.

Making extensive use of material from the National Archives, the testimony of key players and more detached observers, as well as contemporary media reports and material from the Margaret Thatcher Foundation, we show that rather than having an 'empty, sad quarter of a century', Lady Thatcher in fact had a full life, filled with incident, at least up to 2002. Her time from then until her death in 2013 was characterised by appearances, silent but present, ever less physically, and seemingly ever more psychologically.

Beyond that, we also reveal the long-term, continued and continuing impact of Lady Thatcher's post-prime ministership. Without a proper understanding of Lady Thatcher's ex-premiership and, perhaps most of all, people's reaction to it, it is impossible to understand British politics today. That is why, while Lady Thatcher's last quarter of a century could not compare with the one preceding it, it is worthy of study.

At the outset, it is important to note the context of Lady Thatcher's life after Downing Street.

First, the amount of material about it is vast. It might not be too much of an exaggeration to say that, before Lady Thatcher, never in the field of the ex-premiership had so much been written about one former Prime Minister over such a long period of time in such depth.

Masses of newspaper articles about Lady Thatcher after 1990 have been published, up to and including today. For all her mastery of detail, Lady Thatcher was also always a headline type of person, and she continued generating them long after her departure from Downing Street – long after her death, even. Two of Lady Thatcher's books, *The Path to Power* (1995) and *Statecraft* (2002), provide rich material. So do the books that have been written about her. Other political actors' biographies, autobiographies and diaries also contain information about her premier emeritus years. There are also recordings of Lady Thatcher after 1990, including speeches, interviews, Q&As and footage of her campaigning in general elections, many of which are available online,[8] as well as the observations of participants and other witnesses, some captured in documentaries, some in academic interviews.

Then there are the archives – specifically material held in the National Archives. The Prime Minister's Office records largely deal with Lady Thatcher's role in UK politics after 1990 and provide insight into her relationships and interactions with John Major and Tony Blair. Foreign Office records detail Lady Thatcher's travels abroad as a former Prime Minister and tell us more about her global role, the impact and influence she had in the countries she visited. They also show how what Lady Thatcher said and did in those countries could have an effect back in the UK. As well as the archives of other countries, and other individuals, there is Lady Thatcher's own archive: the Margaret Thatcher Foundation website provides substantial information about her post-premiership. It is both an invaluable resource for any student of Margaret Thatcher and a remarkable achievement. This is largely due to the site being run – as Sir Julian Seymour, the director of Lady Thatcher's office, noted – 'to the highest scholastic standards' by Christopher Collins. As for Lady Thatcher's private papers, Seymour noted her 'generosity' in donating them to Churchill College in Cambridge.[9] While the extensive papers relating to her life after Downing Street are closed, the Margaret Thatcher Archive Trust is currently focused on strategies to provide access to them. Andrew Riley, the archivist of Lady Thatcher's papers, has said that this will be a major project. He estimates there will be many hundreds of thousands of pages to process.[10]

It is, therefore, important to note that our understanding of former Prime Minister Margaret Thatcher may develop further over time as more material becomes available and, given the amount of currently available material, what follows is not an account of everything Lady Thatcher did after Downing Street, but a sketch of just some of it.

When writing that story, it is necessary always to distinguish between Margaret Thatcher the person and Margaret Thatcher the persona. After 1990, we learnt more about both. With regard to the latter, the character that was Margaret Thatcher, and the way Lady Thatcher played her after Downing Street, was crucial to her legacy. It helps to explain why, in her centenary year, she persists in British political consciousness, arguably as potent now as an idea as she was as a person between 1979 and 1990.

We must also recognise that, as important as *what* Lady Thatcher did after No. 10 was the *way* she did it. Speaking in 2000, a member of the shadow Cabinet said, 'There's as much showbusiness as ideology in her performance.'[11] At times after 1990, people could be forgiven for thinking they were witnessing a production of *Carry On Maggie*.

It must be stressed, however, that when Lady Thatcher was playing the character that was Margaret Thatcher, she was true to herself. Her performance was authentic and was played with conviction. The character that was Margaret Thatcher was simply the dramatic persona that gave voice to Margaret Thatcher's beliefs and illuminated her character. As Chris Patten wrote, 'One of Margaret Thatcher's commendable virtues, though it rattles the chandeliers in chancelleries and embassies the world over, is always to be herself.'[12]

As is the case with most subjects, nuance is required when examining Lady Thatcher's post-prime ministership, a requirement also stressed by Sir Julian Seymour.[13] This is especially the case with Margaret Thatcher the person, though less so with Margaret Thatcher the persona. As with her premiership, there is a danger of viewing Lady Thatcher's life after 1990 through the prism of what she and what others *said* she did, rather than what she *actually* did and did not do. If she was a more nuanced Prime Minister than many, including herself, might claim, she was also a more nuanced ex-premier than has been appreciated.

Lady Thatcher's years as a former Prime Minister fall into two distinct, but connected, phases, which are of almost equal length. The first, from 1990 until 2002, we call the 'siren' years. The second, from 2002 until Lady Thatcher's death, are the 'symbol' years. During the former, Lady Thatcher's active political work took place, while in the latter, she demonstrated that you do not always need to speak in order to communicate.

Lady Thatcher's life after office is the story of 'a powerful personality now operating in more adverse conditions.'[14] After 1990, Lady Thatcher's life was about attempts at influence, rather than the making of decisions. We see her trying to make a difference; and we see her navigating, or perhaps ignoring or not recognising, the difficulties and challenges of doing so.

That said, Lady Thatcher's post-Downing Street life is as much about others' – mainly men's – reactions to her as it is about herself. As Moore wrote, 'The effect on others of her extraordinary personality, made greater by the fact that she was a woman operating in a world of men, is often the story itself.'[15]

The post-prime ministerial effect of Lady Thatcher's personality on others is clear from the observations of many of her political contemporaries. Her personality had a wider effect, too, after Downing Street, including on non-political contemporaries and across the globe. This is revealed in files released by the National Archives since her death. These records, especially those about her post-prime ministerial travels, pulsate with Lady Thatcher's personality and the reaction it, and sometimes the reaction her name alone, excited in others, both in anticipation and in actuality. The use of exclamation marks in the files is telling, as are handwritten comments on formal documents.

If her being a woman is key to understanding Lady Thatcher's premiership, it is also key to understanding her post-premiership. Throughout her time as a former Prime Minister, Lady Thatcher spoke about being a woman. She also faced (or perhaps more accurately, she continued to face) certain judgements because she was a woman. Long after Lady Thatcher's resignation, one of her Cabinet ministers, reflecting on her behaviour towards Geoffrey Howe, commented, 'She spoke to Geoffrey like no man should be spoken to by a woman.'

Not unrelated to that, men seemed even less sure how to respond to Lady Thatcher after Downing Street than they did before. Indeed, it might be argued that Lady Thatcher spent her premier emeritus years winding men up. Or, rather, men spent Lady Thatcher's premier emeritus years being – and allowing themselves to be – wound up by her.

'Irritating', 'irritated' and 'irritation' are words that run through much of the commentary, at least the contemporary commentary up to 2002. Some (men) probably felt that, after 1990, Lady Thatcher became the most irritating person in British political history, if she was not already. She may have taken this as a badge of honour. Launching her *Collected Speeches* at Hatchards bookshop in 1997, she spoke of 'speeches delivered to barely disguised fury since leaving office', adding: 'And just so no-one gets any wrong ideas: be warned – I intend to keep on talking!'[16] We can almost hear the (subversive) pleasure in her voice, can't we? What might have added to the irritation, and to Lady Thatcher's pleasure, is that, as she no doubt would have argued, events generally turned out to prove her right – and the men wrong.

Finally, as with almost everything else to do with Margaret Thatcher, her premier emeritus years are contested and full of myth, though given her personality, and others' reactions to it, how could it be otherwise?

Judgements about both the myth and reality of Lady Thatcher's (after Downing Street) life, (continuing) work and (emerging) legacy have varied, but have often been coloured by three things: first, how the people making them think former prime ministers in general do and should behave – and how they think this former Prime Minister should have behaved – rather than how premiers emeritus have historically behaved and do behave;[17] second, people's views of how Lady Thatcher compares as a premier emeritus to other former prime ministers; and third, what might be called the effect of Lady Thatcher as a premier emeritus.

We will, therefore, conclude by assessing these existing judgements about Margaret Thatcher's life after No. 10. By doing so, we will determine whether they remain valid or whether it is time for fresh perspectives on her premier emeritus years – perspectives that tell us something new about former Prime Minister Margaret Thatcher and that require us to reframe how, to date, we have seen her life after Downing Street.

Part I

Margaret Thatcher's (after) life

Like all ex-premiers, Margaret Thatcher lived three lives after No. 10: private, public and political. From each of these lives, we learn more about both the character of and the character that was Margaret Thatcher.

While the whole of Lady Thatcher's life after Downing Street is under-researched, this is especially so when it comes to her private and public lives during this period. Studying them, however, is crucial. To adapt Walter Bagehot's phrase, while in her political life we witness Lady Thatcher attempting to be efficient, in her private and public lives we see her being dignified. This provides often over-looked insight into Margaret Thatcher the person and Margaret Thatcher the persona.

More importantly for our purposes, elements of Lady Thatcher's private and public lives also contributed to her continued and continuing political significance. They generated reactions in others. They excited media coverage. They kept her in the public eye. They, on occasion, had contemporary political impact. They helped Lady Thatcher burnish what Charles Powell has described as her 'deliberately cultivated image of battling Maggie'.[1] And all of this was to have consequences for Lady Thatcher's (emerging) legacy, as was her political life after Downing Street. About that, as we shall argue, existing views need to be revisited. That is so we can better understand both what happened after Lady Thatcher resigned, and why even today she continues to have political relevance.

Chapter One

Private life

As with every aspect of Margaret Thatcher's life after Downing Street, her private life had political significance. Sometimes this was purely contemporary, impacting on the politics of the day, and sometimes it had a longer-term effect, affecting how Lady Thatcher was, and is, viewed.

Family

As a family, the Thatchers provided good copy. For better or worse, throughout her premier emeritus years, Lady Thatcher's relations found themselves in print or on television, and even, on occasion, in files now held in the National Archives.

Sometimes this played up to the character that was Margaret Thatcher. After Carol Thatcher's victory in *I'm a Celebrity... Get Me Out of Here!* in 2005, Lady Thatcher said she was 'immeasurably proud' and 'absolutely thrilled to bits' to see her daughter win. Carol had displayed 'True Thatcher spirit'[1] – this, no doubt, being both the spirit of 'battling Maggie' and a winner.

As for Lady Thatcher's son, Mark Thatcher, at times he played a controversial role in her life after 1990. As will be seen in Chapter Five, this included the 1994 Conservative Party conference, where his business dealings overshadowed her attendance. Her son's activities could also have political consequences for the government, and were sometimes raised in Parliament.[2]

Sometimes Mark's involvement in Lady Thatcher's overseas trips caused issues for her office, and for officials in the UK and the countries she was visiting, either because of his role in organising them or because he accompanied Lady Thatcher when she visited. An FCO telegram to Britain's ambassador to China towards the end of August 1991 highlights examples of this regarding her September 1991 visit. The telegram concludes, 'Clearly much of the above is extremely sensitive.'[3] In September 1991, the high commissioner to Brunei, Adrian Sindall, reported that Mark Thatcher had arrived some days before his mother, noting that the Ministry of Foreign Affairs had 'smartly sent him down to the High Commission to see me.'[4] In 1992, the British ambassador to the United Arab Emirates, Sir Graham Burton, reported Mark Thatcher arriving and being 'instantly into the role of Private Secretary and programme checking and amending.'[5]

As well as controversy, coverage of Mark Thatcher could also generate sympathy for Lady Thatcher. In March 1995, John Major wrote inviting Lady Thatcher to a seventieth birthday dinner at Downing Street later that year. Referring to the continued scrutiny of her son's activities, Major commented on how upsetting it must be for her and reflected on similar treatment of his own son's private life.[6]

Sometimes Lady Thatcher's family found itself in the media because she talked about it in pieces with wider political content, and this was the case in a June 1991 *Vanity Fair* profile by Maureen Orth[7] and an August 1998 interview with *SAGA Magazine*.[8]

Health

If Lady Thatcher's family life became, or remained, political after 1990, so did her health.

Extensive coverage greeted the announcement on 22 March 2002 that Lady Thatcher was giving up public speaking following a series of small strokes.[9] Much of this was obituary-style in content and tone. The cover of *Private Eye*'s 5–18 April edition was headlined 'Thatcher shock'[10] and featured an empty speech bubble coming out of her mouth.

From 2002 on, bouts of ill-health were reported in the press, both broadsheet and tabloid. On occasion this too was obituary-like in content and tone. Coverage of Lady Thatcher's arrivals home and departures from hospital – her 'entrances and exits' – gave a nod to her career. All this contributed to what we might call the iconography of illness, and it played up to and helped to cement a particular image of Lady Thatcher in our political consciousness. Even in a medical context, the character that was Margaret Thatcher took centre stage.

In March 2008, for example, there was significant coverage of Lady Thatcher leaving hospital. The *Sunday People* spoke of 'Maggie OUT!',[11] the *Sunday Telegraph* ran with 'The lady returns to health',[12] and the *Sunday Mirror* 'Maggie Maggie Maggie, Out Out Out of hospital'.[13] A *News of the World* leader, 'An Iron constitution', reflected that although Lady Thatcher may be frail, 'she still has more steel than the rest of us',[14] while the *Sunday Telegraph* opined that she had 'proved herself indomitable once more, making a characteristically regal exit'. It spoke of her taking 'as commanding a place in the spotlight as she ever has.'[15]

In June 2009, Lady Thatcher had a shoulder operation. When she returned home, she wanted to talk to a group of journalists outside her house. She was persuaded by her aides not to do so, with Andrew Pierce reporting one saying, 'You know what Lady T is like. She would have told the reporters not to make a fuss about her and would have demanded to know from them what has been going on in the real world while she has been in hospital.'[16]

In 2010, illness forced Lady Thatcher to miss her eighty-fifth birthday reception at Downing Street. She sent a statement to be read out, 'I hope that you will appreciate that on this particular occasion I have had to accept that the Lady is not for returning.'[17]

When Lady Thatcher left hospital, it was front-page news in the *Daily Telegraph* under the headline, 'The Iron Lady returns home'.[18] Directly below *The Sun*'s story was an article revealing that Tony Blair had donated £27,000 towards David Miliband's leadership bid.[19] On the same day as Lady Thatcher left hospital, Gordon Brown delivered his first speech in the House of Commons since resigning as Prime Minister.[20] Yet, of the three ex-premiers, it was Lady Thatcher who still seemed the most newsworthy, almost twenty years after her resignation.

When overtaken by illness, both Lady Thatcher herself and people's reactions to her tended to reinforce the Margaret Thatcher persona. She seemingly went on and on despite her ill-health, giving the impression of having taken to heart Winston Churchill's injunction to 'never surrender'. In October 2022, Henry Kissinger commented, 'I continued to call on her on every trip to London, even in the years after illness had clouded her mind. During our final meetings, I saw a leader who had faced down life's trials with courage and grace.'[21]

Speaking after her death, Ed Miliband said, 'As a person, nothing became her so much as the manner of her final years'. Speaking of Lady Thatcher's 'utmost dignity and courage', he said he would always 'remember seeing her at the Cenotaph in frail health but determined to pay her respect to our troops and do her duty by her country.'[22]

The wider context of what was and was not known about Lady Thatcher's health in her siren years should be noted. By the twenty-first century, Lady Thatcher's mental powers were in decline, but when the decline had started was disputed.[23]

It is difficult to judge, therefore, to what extent, if any, Lady Thatcher's health affected her (continuing) work, at least until 2002. Writing in 2005, John Sergeant said he thought 'it would be a mistake to believe that declining health was a factor in her approach to important issues.'[24] We share that view.

Chapter Two

Public life

In June 2007, Tony Blair was asked what he would be when he resigned as Prime Minister. When 'ex-politician' was suggested, Blair replied, perhaps tellingly, 'No, I'll be a former celebrity.'[1] While Lady Thatcher was not a 'former' type of person, she did acquire celebrity status after Downing Street. As Matthew Parris wrote, 'as a famous personality she became a source of national entertainment.'[2] While this may have started before 1990, it intensified afterwards.

Lady Thatcher's post-office public life involved formal state and public occasions, as well as attending, and sometimes taking part in, less formal events. Sometimes, Lady Thatcher's comments at functions found their way into the press. For example, at the launch of Sir Bernard Ingham's *The Wages of Spin* in March 2003, Lady Thatcher placed her finger over the 'p' in the word 'spin' on the front cover. 'It's amazing they ever put that letter in,'[3] she observed 'witheringly'.

As this anecdote illustrates, Lady Thatcher's public appearances revealed more about her character, and we also saw her performing the character that was Margaret Thatcher. As with her private life, coverage of Lady Thatcher's public life kept her in the public eye and tended to reinforce the 'battling Maggie' image, which shaped how people viewed and continue to view her. Equally, Lady Thatcher's public life also had political consequence, both contemporary and longer-term. The dignified aspects of Lady Thatcher's life supported the efficient.

This could be seen in the judgements that continued to be made about Lady Thatcher's appearance. Much of the commentary about her after 1990, particularly by sketch writers, referenced how she looked and what she wore. Lady Thatcher would not necessarily have disapproved of this, since, as Charles Moore wrote in 2005, 'She dresses and makes up and has her hair done with the greatest elegance and care. She is dignified and beautiful, believing that she must look her best. It has always been an iron law with her that she must not let people down, and she obeys it still.'[4]

Although it was the case that she experienced this judgement because she was a woman, nevertheless, Lady Thatcher's appearance gave her a visual advantage over her male colleagues in getting her message across on television and in photographs used in newspapers and magazines.

Throughout her time as a premier emeritus, Lady Thatcher's wardrobe featured in the media. In January 2000, the *Daily Telegraph*'s fashion editor, Hilary Alexander, noted that she was 'emerging as the year's most unlikely fashion icon.'[5] In May 2004, *The Times*' fashion editor, Lisa Armstrong, wrote of 'the Maggie look'.[6] That November, the American fashion designer Marc Jacobs was reported as saying, 'This season is all about finding the Margaret Thatcher look sexy.'[7] After her death, reflecting on Lady Thatcher's prime ministerial attire, Vicki Woods wrote an article for the *Daily Telegraph* headlined 'Margaret Thatcher, the Iron Lady, used her wardrobe as a weapon'.[8] Arguably, she used it in the same way after 1990. She consistently looked the part and was always dressed for impact.

This was seen most clearly at funerals and memorial services. In his nineties, Harold Macmillan described the latter as the 'cocktail parties of the geriatric set',[9] and Lady Thatcher was assiduous at attending these, going to over 100 after Downing Street. At such events, biographer Charles Moore notes, she 'cut a striking figure, carefully and formally dressed, wearing elegant hats'.[10]

Lady Thatcher was at her most striking at Sir Denis Thatcher's funeral and memorial service. At both, iconic photographs of her were taken, capturing what might be called the look of loss, constituting some of the most arresting images of her after 1990.

Those services aside, Lady Thatcher's most important attendance at the 'cocktail parties of the geriatric set' was after the death of President Reagan in 2004. In what the Thatcher Foundation calls 'her last important public statement',[11] she delivered a eulogy at Reagan's funeral, via pre-recorded video.[12] She was the first non-American to do so at a President's funeral. Lady Thatcher also attended Reagan's burial and was photographed next to Arnold Schwarzenegger. 'The Terminator meets The Iron Lady', reported the *Sunday Telegraph*,[13] while the *Sunday Times* went with the headline: 'Shoulder to shoulder: The Terminator and Lady T'.[14] There had been an earlier iconic image too. As Reagan lay in the Rotunda, Lady Thatcher placed her hand on his coffin. Having done so, she curtsied.[15]

Aspects of her life being brought to screen reinforced Lady Thatcher's iconography. This included *Margaret Thatcher: The Long Walk to Finchley* in 2008, and *Margaret* in 2009. Reviewing the latter, Quentin Letts wrote of 'the maddening, impossible, but ultimately great and dramatically irresistible figure of Margaret Hilda Thatcher, the Gloriana of the suburbs.'[16]

Then, in 2012, *The Iron Lady* was released. Although criticised because of its focus on Lady Thatcher's illness, there was, however, praise for Meryl Streep's performance. Matthew d'Ancona described the film as 'a profoundly important revisionist tract', noting: 'It is curious to reflect that the main political event of the first week of 2012 is a film about a Prime Minister who left No. 10 more than 21 years ago.'[17] Dominic Sandbrook wrote in similar terms, arguing that 'Margaret Thatcher still dominates British politics'. He went on, 'More than any of her rivals, she has become an icon, a cultural and political symbol.'[18]

After Lady Thatcher's death, Michael Dobbs wrote, 'Some 30 actresses have portrayed her on screen, few have come even close to getting her right.'[19] Arguably, that is because the only actress capable of getting the character right was, in fact, Margaret Thatcher herself. 'She used to say to me, "I'm not an actress",' remembered her speech writer, Ronald Millar, 'but she certainly became one.'[20] In 1992, the former Conservative Cabinet minister Lord Cockfield commented, 'I have always said that Margaret envisages herself as Laurence Olivier playing the part of Henry V before the Battle of Agincourt.'[21] Sir Gerald Kaufman, former Labour minister and one-time chair of the Select Committee on Culture, Media and Sport, noted after Lady Thatcher's death that 'her international significance was emphasised … when, almost twenty-four years after she had stopped being Prime Minister, an actress in Hollywood could win the "best actress" Oscar for portraying her almost as well as she used to portray herself'.[22]

Lady Thatcher's skill as an actress was seen throughout her premier emeritus years.[23] Although a deeply serious person, not known for her sense of humour, when it came to timing, Lady Thatcher's hardly ever failed her after 1990. Her ability at the great dramatic performance was to be seen in *Thatcher: The Downing Street Years*, the television series accompanying the first volume of her memoirs, while her skill at broad, almost end-of-pier performance was witnessed in the 1992, 1997, and 2001 general election campaigns.

As well as portrayals in film and television, photographs and paintings of Lady Thatcher after Downing Street also tended to emphasise the character that was Margaret Thatcher.

In 2008, for example, she was photographed by Mario Testino for a *Vogue* feature entitled 'Tempered Steel'. When the Peruvian praised her for creating a Britain devoid of socialism, Lady Thatcher replied, 'Yes, you're right! People wouldn't let you spend your own money. We chucked that all out!'[24]

The artist Richard Stone painted Lady Thatcher six times after Downing Street.[25] One of those portraits was for her former study at No. 10, known as the Thatcher Room, and it was offered to Lady Thatcher by Gordon Brown when she visited him in 2007. Describing it as 'a classic, historic portrait', Stone reflected that it was 'an extraordinary act of homage by the Prime Minister'[26] and considered it the most important painting he had been asked to do.

'Statesmen usually have to wait till they are dead before they are immortalised in bronze or marble,' notes John Campbell.[27] Lady Thatcher was an exception, seeing herself immortalised in both.

Sculptor Neil Simmons produced an eight-foot marble statue of the former Prime Minister, complete with handbag and weighing 1.8 tonnes.[28] Unveiling it in May 2002, Lady Thatcher said, 'I'm not bound to say anything but you can't stop a woman, can you? I think it is marvellous.' Setting the piece in its historic context, she noted: 'It's a little larger than I expected but that's the way to portray an ex-Prime Minister who was the first woman Prime Minister.' In character, Lady Thatcher noted that the statue had a 'good, big handbag'.[29] In July 2002, it was decapitated with a cricket bat and iron bar. *The Times* headlined the story, 'The Iron Lady loses her marble head' and reported that a man had been arrested for criminal damage.[30]

On 21 February 2007, a bronze statue of Lady Thatcher by Antony Dufort was unveiled at the House of Commons. Traditionally, the honour of a statue was bestowed posthumously, after ten years, though Speaker Michael Martin reflected, 'It is right and fitting that Lady Thatcher's period in office as the first woman Prime Minister should be celebrated while she was still alive'.[31] 'I might have preferred iron,' she said at the unveiling ceremony, 'But bronze will do. It won't rust,' adding: 'This time, I hope, the head will stay on.'

Chapter Three

Political life

Private and public life aside, the focus of this study is Margaret Thatcher's political life. As Jonathan Freedland said after her death, 'Let's talk politics: it's what she'd have wanted.'[1]

Five themes

Lady Thatcher lived her political life largely within what we might call the infrastructure of the Office of Prime Minister Emeritus. In *After Number 10: Former Prime Ministers in British Politics*,[2] Kevin Theakston highlighted five themes that are relevant to Lady Thatcher's time as a premier emeritus: returning to office, health and age factors, honours, putting pen to paper, and money matters.

Returning to office

Some former prime ministers have returned to government after leaving Downing Street, most recently David Cameron when he was appointed Foreign Secretary in November 2023. This, however, was never a realistic possibility for Lady Thatcher. Nor was an official international role. Lady Thatcher recognised this. She received a private suggestion that she might become secretary-general of the United Nations,[3] but ruled this out publicly, saying, 'My views are far too strongly held for that.'[4] In 1994, General Sir John Akehurst, former Deputy Supreme Allied Commander in Europe, reflected on a suggestion she might become NATO secretary-general: 'She would get headlines,' he judged, 'but not consensus.'[5]

Health and age factors

Theakston noted that 'longevity and good health are essential ingredients for a successful post-premiership'.[6] Lady Thatcher certainly had the former, living over twenty-two years after leaving Downing Street. Her life up to 2002 was by any measure one of intense activity, and had illness not forced her effectively to retire from political life, it is likely this would have continued. It is also arguable, however, that in Lady Thatcher's case, her ill-health helped to make her post-premiership even more successful than it would otherwise have been. Rather like when a relative dies, their family tend to remember only the good things about them, it was really in the years after she was silenced that Lady Thatcher's mythological status reached its peak.

Honours

Lady Thatcher both proposed and received honours after ceasing to be Prime Minister. Her resignation Honours List was published in December 1990. She was awarded the Order of Merit the same month and the Garter in 1995.

Lady Thatcher was granted a peerage in 1992. She had decided to stand down as an MP in June 1991. This followed debate among her friends and supporters, some of which had been in the public arena. In March 1991, a *Times* leader, 'Mother of the House', argued that she belonged in the House of Commons. It described her as 'the mother of the mother of parliaments.'[7] In an 'Open letter to an Iron Lady' in *The Spectator* on 29 June 1991, Paul Johnson also urged Lady

Thatcher to stay on as an MP.[8] At the end of May, Cecil Parkinson[9] and Sir Bernard Ingham[10] had publicly advised her to stand down.

Lady Thatcher herself later wrote that she felt 'ill at ease' on the back benches. 'The enjoyment of the back benches comes from being able to speak out freely,' she said. 'This, however, I knew would never again be possible. My every word would be judged in terms of support for or opposition to John Major. I would inhibit him just by my presence, and that in turn would inhibit me.'[11] In his diary on 13 February 1991, Michael Spicer recorded, 'We discuss Margaret Thatcher's future as an MP. I say it's selfish but we need her as a rallying point. She repeats "rallying point"! Then she says, "The only problem is I hate coming into this place now", meaning the Commons.'[12]

That said, Lady Thatcher wished to retain her connection with Parliament. Speaking to Woodrow Wyatt in January 1991, she said, 'I couldn't not be connected with the Houses of Parliament.'[13] In June that same year, she commented, 'Whether from one house or another – I shall be there. I shall be there.'[14]

The day after the announcement that she was standing down, *The Guardian* published a leader, 'And now we can all get on'. It opened with one word: 'PHEW!'[15] Ahead of an interview with Michael Brunson on 28 June, there was a photocall outside Lady Thatcher's office. This provided a stage for her to play the character that was Margaret Thatcher. When asked about her energy, she responded that she had 'tons of energy left'. Speaking to the journalists, she added, 'I hope you have some'.[16] Cabinet ministers were said to be 'beaming with relief' as they paid tribute to her.[17]

Until David Cameron's elevation in 2023, Lady Thatcher was the last former Prime Minister to go the Lords. Once there, as in the

Commons, she intervened rarely. In fact, she intervened in Parliament only fifteen times after Downing Street, making her one of the less parliamentary active ex-prime ministers. In comparison, her immediate predecessor as Prime Minister, James Callaghan, has to date been the most parliamentary active premier emeritus in British history, intervening almost 500 times.

As much of the commentary on Lady Thatcher's speeches in the Lords makes clear, she was not temperamentally suited to the Upper House. One of her ministers observed to this author, 'She needs the sort of clubbing to stir her up', while a former member of her Cabinet reflected to us in 1999, 'I suspect she didn't really find the House of Lords very congenial, having a much more kind of seminar-like setting.' Lady Thatcher herself alluded to this in a letter to John Major following her introduction to the Lords in June 1992, writing, 'I only hope that proceedings in their Lordships House will sometimes be as exciting as question time in the Commons!' Ever practical, she added, 'scarlet and ermine is not the most appropriate clothing for a hot summer's day'.[18]

Whether suited to the Upper House or not, Lady Thatcher was never not herself, both in the Chamber and in the Lords' more informal spaces. Once, upon meeting Lord Richard, one-time Leader of the House of Lords and a former European commissioner, in the Lords' bar, Lady Thatcher 'complained loudly' that there were 'too many ex-commissioners in the Lords'. To which Lord Richard responded, 'Some people might say there are too many ex-prime ministers.'[19]

As this anecdote demonstrates, Lady Thatcher was always able to generate a reaction in others. She had done this in the Commons, too. In her diaries, Edwina Currie recorded that in December 1991, Lady Thatcher had turned up in the Commons for the first day of a debate on Maastricht and there was 'quite a kerfuffle over where she was to sit'. The next day, Peter Tapsell 'made a point of coming into Prayers and took his seat'. On his Prayer card, he wrote, 'Tapsell – in case M. Thatcher wants to sit here'. 'Silly boys, all of them,' Currie concluded.[20]

Lack of temperamental suitability was allied, and perhaps related, to a lack of understanding of the ways of their Lordships' House. To this author, one of Lady Thatcher's ministers observed, 'The thing about Margaret Thatcher was she never understood the House of Lords all the time she was Prime Minister and still doesn't.' Lord Richard said the same thing, commenting to us, 'She does not understand this House.' He shared an anecdote too. 'She turned up once to vote. She dashed into the Lobby which I was in, looked at me and said: "Oh, am I in the right Lobby?" So, I said: "Yes." She said: "Now, as a man of honour, am I in the right Lobby?"'

Though speaking rarely, Lady Thatcher did attend the Lords for votes. In 1999, the former Leader of the House of Lords, Baroness Young, reflected on Lady Thatcher's turning up for her amendments on the age of consent. Commenting to this author, Lady Young said, 'I think people were pleased to see her. I was both pleased and to a certain extent surprised, because she hardly ever comes.'

When she did attend, her appearances generated a frisson. In June 1999, a former Labour Cabinet minister, Lord Merlyn-Rees, said to this author, 'She's in today. Everybody said: "What's she doing here?" She never comes; she's entitled not to come. I wonder why she's here today. I've just no idea.' What is fascinating is that a political opponent should be interested in, and seemingly care about, what Lady Thatcher was doing. In April 1999, a Labour frontbencher, Lord McIntosh of Haringey, commented to us, 'Even when she comes in order to take part in an important vote … she doesn't actually say anything. She just sits there and glares, the Gorgon, stone-faced.' Lord McIntosh had earlier reflected, 'She walks in, stony-faced, sits down, stony-faced, and leaves, stony-faced.'

Curiosity about motive was matched by awareness of Lady Thatcher being what Lord Norton of Louth has described to this author as 'a presence'. This was something to which the shadow Leader of the House, Baroness Royall of Blaisdon, referred in her tribute in April 2013: 'As increasingly frail as she became, as a result of [her] enormous impact, her appearances in the House at key moments and on key Divisions were electrifying.' Lady Royall spoke of being 'mesmerised by this frail but still powerful woman'.[21]

Baroness Royall also noted another important aspect of Lady Thatcher's later parliamentary career, namely the assistance she received from Michael Forsyth when she attended the Lords. Lady Royall spoke of 'the real, caring support' he gave her.[22]

Putting pen to paper

After resigning as Prime Minister, Lady Thatcher also put pen to paper, writing two volumes of memoirs: *The Downing Street Years* in 1993 and *The Path to Power* in 1995. Both generated considerable controversy, as did the supporting documentaries and interviews that were done in conjunction with their release. She also recorded audio versions of her books and undertook extensive promotional tours.

Not only did the content of *The Downing Street Years* generate coverage, but so did people's reaction to the book around the world. The *Wall Street Journal* spoke of 'Thatchermania'. In Washington, people waited six hours for a book-signing session.[23] Peter Riddell said Lady Thatcher had 'become a marketing phenomenon', noting the response of most ministers being 'muted irritation'.[24] On 22

October 1993, *Private Eye* renamed itself 'Private Hype', devoting its cover to the book.[25] Matthew Parris spoke of the British public being 'well and truly lassoed', arguing that Lady Thatcher's 'great success, elevating her above every postwar British politician since Churchill, has been to appear, for some time, larger than politics.'[26]

Reflecting on *The Downing Street Years* in *The Path to Power*, Lady Thatcher commented, 'I wanted to give encouragement to those who thought and felt as I did, the next generation of political leaders and perhaps even the ones after that, to keep their gaze fixed on the right stars.'[27] In February 1991, she had told Charles Moore that she wanted her memoirs to be 'a historical version of Hayek's *Constitution of Liberty*'.[28] People could, perhaps, be forgiven for being reminded of Tallulah Bankhead, who once claimed that the two greatest books ever written were the Bible and her own autobiography.[29]

Of the television series accompanying the memoirs, Charles Moore wrote that Lady Thatcher 'dramatized them better than any play could have done',[30] while the series executive producer, Hugh Scully, commented, 'There are Shakespearean overtones to the whole story. The series is documentary but plays like drama, and that's the magical thing about it.' Having described Lady Thatcher's description of Geoffrey Howe's resignation speech as 'probably the most gripping piece of television I have ever seen,' Scully concluded, 'The series is beyond doubt the most fascinating project I've worked on in thirty years as a broadcaster.'[31] Denys Blakeway, the series producer, found Lady Thatcher 'extremely professional at rehearsing and delivering lines. She delivered her words with her "tremendous theatricality" and sometimes even set up her own shots.'[32] 'The sheer force of her words made great television,' Moore concluded, 'but, as so often, injected too much drama for her own good.'[33]

Ahead of the first episode being broadcast, *Daily Mirror* TV critic Simon London and political editor John Williams commented, 'It's an X-rated political drama, a cross between *Night of the Living Dead* and *Jurassic Park*, starring the only politician who ever made John Wayne look a wimp.'[34]

As with almost everything else about Lady Thatcher's life after 1990, while bringing triumph for Lady Thatcher, *The Downing Street Years* also generated turbulence – for her and for the government. Some of this was in the public arena, as will be seen below, while some remained behind the scenes, as detailed in files in the National Archives.

Some two years and more before her memoirs had even appeared, their prospect had caused a stir within government. In May 1991, John Major's principal private secretary, Andrew Turnbull, had sent a memo to Major about Nicholas Ridley's memoirs.[35] Turnbull noted that critics of the government would be able 'to make a great deal of use' of the book and, given his criticisms of them, some of Ridley's former colleagues might be 'goaded into retaliation, creating an impression of disunity in the Conservative Party.' He presented Major with options of what might be done, one of which was for Major to raise the matter with Lady Thatcher, whom Major was due to meet shortly thereafter. Turnbull thought that she 'might be prevailed upon' to persuade Ridley to tone down the text, though he admitted: 'I am not too hopeful of this', since on various issues, for example, the 'pre-Madrid ambush' (when in 1989 Nigel Lawson and Geoffrey Howe attempted to force her into giving an undertaking that Britain would join the Exchange Rate Mechanism (ERM) and specifying a date for doing so), Ridley 'says things she would love to have said but has either not dared to or not got round to writing.' At the top of the memo, Major agreed about the government's critics and the impression of Conservative disunity. He went on, 'This book is the trailer to the main feature as your last para. implies. I will not demean myself – or put myself in debt – by asking for changes.'

The prospect of Lady Thatcher's memoirs also stirred activity in one of her former colleagues, Nigel Lawson. In April 1993, Alex Allan, John Major's principal private secretary, wrote to Terence Burns, the Permanent Secretary at the Treasury. The letter was headed, 'LORD LAWSON'S AND LADY THATCHER'S MEMOIRS'.[36] Lawson had contacted Allan about the background to the interest rate cut of 17 May 1988, as word had reached Lawson that Lady Thatcher's version of events was 'somewhat different' to his. Noting this would 'become quite a focus of debate' when Lady Thatcher's memoirs were published, Allan said he was conscious of the rather tricky issue of proprieties raised in trying to resolve this in one direction or the other'.

There was a further 'rather tricky issue' when, in line with the Radcliffe recommendations on ministerial memoirs, Lady Thatcher submitted the draft of hers to the Cabinet Secretary, Sir Robin Butler.[37] She accepted one of Butler's comments on national security grounds and also made some changes about discussions with Chancellor Kohl and President Mitterrand on German reunification. On 30 June, however, Butler explained to John Major that Lady Thatcher had not complied with all his comments on that section. Noting that what she had written might cause offence to the French and Germans, Butler reflected that, nevertheless, 'her attitude on these matters is, after all, well known'. On 'disclosures destructive to confidential relationships', Lady Thatcher 'resisted deleting or further modifying' passages. These related first to discussions with Francis Pym on the American peace plan for the

Falklands; second, to Major's contribution to a speech on the community charge, and exchanges on the ERM and European Monetary Union (EMU); and third, differences with Malcolm Rifkind on schools and the community charge. Butler presented Major with three options: they could do nothing; Butler could go back to Lady Thatcher on Major's behalf; or someone else could contact Lady Thatcher, either John Major himself or somebody acting for him. Butler suggested they pursue the second option and then consider option three. He concluded, 'Lady Thatcher can only say "no" – although she probably will!'

In a covering note to John Major on 30 June, Alex Allan commented, 'It would probably be better to get someone else to approach Lady Thatcher – I am sure you should not do it yourself.' Allan wrote that one of the points Lady Thatcher made – her claim that Major was slow to grasp how essential it was to provide poll tax reliefs – was 'slightly awkward, if it is seen as you being resistant to helping her solve one of the issues that brought her down'. Next to this, Major wrote, 'It's <u>not</u> <u>true</u>.'

Butler wrote to Lady Thatcher on 1 July. Responding on 6 July, the second sentence of Lady Thatcher's letter read, 'I note that the only points on which you and the Prime Minister are still pressing for changes relate to passages concerning him and Malcolm Rifkind.'

Nevertheless, she did concede some further changes. About Major, she amended the wording that he 'tended to drift' to 'was drifting' with the intellectual tide, making the point specific rather than general. However, she refused to remove or amend other passages, including those critical of Rifkind. Another she refused to remove was on discussions she had had with Major over what became Maastricht. She said this was 'crucial to showing how the difference' between Major and her was evident 'from well before I left office'. As Moore commented, 'This was, of course, exactly the point which Major did not want revealed.'[38]

On 7 July, Butler reported back to Allan on Lady Thatcher's reply. He said he had 'now shot my bolt under the Radcliffe procedure', adding, 'The Prime Minister will no doubt want to consider whether there is any other leverage which he can apply to Lady Thatcher.' Sending the note to Major, Allan handwrote, 'Only a very little movement. I hope Charles Powell will, in particular, have a go at "drifting with the tide" and persuade her to remove it.' A letter to Allan from Powell dated 8 July revealed that Powell had tried and failed. While Lady Thatcher would make some changes, Powell apologised for not having done better.

This is an illustration of Charles Powell's importance to Lady Thatcher's post-premiership. Files in the National Archives highlight the central role he played in supporting the ex-premier, and in supporting, and on occasion acting on behalf of, those – usually ministers and advisers – who were attempting to influence her to do something, or mostly to *not* do something. For Sir Julian Seymour, Powell was 'the single most important person of all' after Downing Street.[39] To this author, Seymour said that he could not have done his job without Powell's advice.[40] Rather as Lord Cockfield was a go-to person when Lady Thatcher was in office – with Lord Baker of Dorking recollecting that as Prime Minister she would say, 'we must send for Arthur'[41] – it appeared that Powell performed a similar function when she was out of office, with people saying, 'we must send for Charles'.

Mirroring what happened with *The Downing Street Years*, the second volume of Lady Thatcher memoirs, *The Path to Power*, published in 1995, also generated extensive media coverage and its fair share of controversy – as well as yet more work for government officials.

As part of her promotion of the book, Lady Thatcher gave an interview to David Frost, who opened by asking if she sometimes felt a bit like Norma Desmond – a case of '"I still am big", it's the politics that have got small'. 'Not in the least,' Lady Thatcher replied. 'I wasn't a Hollywood star. I was a mere politician.' A reviewer reflected that, rather than Norma Desmond, Lady Thatcher more resembled Dame Edna Everage.[42]

Of a Hatchards book-signing in June 1995, Alan Hamilton noted, 'The faces were expectant, reverent, beatific even, as though they were about to receive Communion.' The story was headlined 'The lady grants her fan club an audience'.[43] Interviewing Lady Thatcher at the time, Henry Porter wrote, 'She talks as if geared up to fight an election, not go on a book tour.'[44]

In 2002, shortly before she retired from public speaking, Lady Thatcher published *Statecraft: Strategies for a Changing World*. This too generated controversy, as will be seen, though whatever else may be said of its contents, there is no denying it contains insights into Lady Thatcher's travels after 1990 – the description of her 1992 trip to Taiwan being a prime example. While she was relaxing in the whirlpool bath in her hotel suite, there was an earthquake. The room swayed. Each tremor resulted in soapy water slopping over the sides of the bath. Lady Thatcher stayed in the bath until the earthquake stopped and wrote of the event, 'Neither I, nor the hotel, nor, as far as I know, the rest of Taipei was the worse for it.'[45] To paraphrase Lord Carrington about the bus, surely the earthquake wouldn't dare?

Money matters

As a former Prime Minister, Lady Thatcher received a pension and use of a car. She also received police protection. Her unique contribution to the development of the Office of Prime Minister Emeritus was an increase in public expenditure. In response to the tens of thousands of letters she received after resigning, new support was introduced for ex-premiers from April 1991, the Public Duties Cost Allowance (PDCA).[46]

The background to this is contained in files released by the National Archives in 2020 and 2023. In these files we see Lady Thatcher fulfilling a new role, that of a shop steward for former prime ministers. Throughout her time as an ex-Prime Minister, Lady Thatcher would speak about the dignity of the office of former Prime Minister. Ever practical, early in 1991 she also sought to ensure that she, and thereby other existing and future former prime ministers, received government support to help with the duties that they continue to carry out.

On 4 January 1991, Cabinet Secretary Sir Robin Butler had 'a long talk' with Lady Thatcher.[47] She was 'anxious to establish what help she could call on', and they discussed three issues. First, secretarial help, on which Butler 'acknowledged that there was a case for providing help at public expense for former Prime Ministers, in acknowledgement of the public duties which they were called on to continue to perform by virtue of being former Prime Ministers'. Second, access to official papers from her period as Prime Minister. Third, the continuing provision of information. Butler suggested to Andrew Turnbull that the two of them, together with Gus O'Donnell, Major's press secretary, chat about what help they could provide her. He noted, 'The provision of any No 10 papers will of course need to be approved by the Prime Minister.' Lady Thatcher had also raised help in relation to travel and accommodation, although Butler did not agree with her views on those.

Butler and Turnbull discussed the issue at a meeting on 23 January, also attended by another official, Mrs Case. Subsequently, a Treasury official put a submission together.[48] This was discussed at a meeting on 6 February. Butler highlighted what he saw as the need for both transitional and continuing secretarial help to be provided to former prime ministers.

On 22 February, Butler sent a memo to John Major on 'Assistance to Former Prime Ministers'. Setting out his proposals to the Prime Minister, Butler noted, 'This offer may not entirely satisfy Mrs Thatcher, who has requested assistance also with accommodation and with travel.' In January, Major 'had welcomed the suggestion that officials should look at the options for providing assistance to former Prime Ministers'.[49] By February, he did not seem so sure. On Butler's memo, he wrote, 'Not sure. Why now? "Am I going"… jokes?'[50] In a subsequent meeting with Butler, Major said there was 'some awkwardness about putting forward proposals from which he stood to benefit. He could be represented as preparing the ground for his departure from office.' Major, nevertheless, agreed to Butler's proposals.

On 5 March, Butler wrote to Lady Thatcher advising her of them. On 19 March, Butler wrote separately to each of the other surviving former prime ministers, Lord Home of the Hirsel, Harold Wilson, Edward Heath and James Callaghan. In addition to the formal text about the allowance, each letter contained a short, tailored message. Those to Wilson, Heath and Callaghan were in Butler's own hand. To Heath, he said he hoped the allowance would be 'helpful'. On Callaghan's letter, he wrote, 'I remember your saying to me, after the provision of cars for previous Prime Ministers, that help with secretarial expenses was the other thing needed.' Butler added, 'I am sorry it has taken so long!'

The allowance was announced via written question on 27 March.[51] The next day, in *The Times*, Richard Ford reflected, 'Having provided cash to ease poll tax bills and to help haemophiliacs infected with the Aids virus, the prime minister yesterday found another deserving cause on which to shower largesse.' Ford described the ex-prime ministers as 'the latest beneficiaries of John Major's efforts to show that Conservative governments really do care.'[52]

In terms of earnings, Lady Thatcher took a consultant role at Philip Morris. She also followed the precedent set by some previous premiers emeritus, and followed by others since, of delivering lectures. Many of these are available on the Thatcher Foundation website.

From 1990 to the early 2000s, Lady Thatcher spoke all over the world. As Moore noted, 'She was a natural at this form, being a born preacher and, by careful training, a uniquely forceful public performer.'[53] When Harris wrote about Lady Thatcher's preparation for, and delivery of, her speeches, he could have been writing of an actor learning and performing their lines. 'Her audiences,' he said, 'above all those in America, were spellbound.'[54]

Sir Julian Seymour recalled that Lady Thatcher would not as a rule accept payment for speeches made in the United Kingdom or in Hong Kong and China. There were exceptions, however. One of these included a speech made to the American Bar Association in London. She had been advised by the tourist authorities that if she spoke to the association, many more lawyers would attend, and thus a lot of money would be generated for them.

Seymour also noted that Lady Thatcher's lecture tours abroad were not part of a 'grand farewell tour' or undertaken for 'altruistic reasons'. They were a means of earning money. He estimated that 90 per cent of her engagements outside America were for personal gain, and in America 70 per cent, with the remaining 30 per cent designed to raise funds for the Thatcher Foundation.[55]

Lady Thatcher's speeches had a range of political consequences in the UK. These could be negative for her successors as Prime Minister and Conservative Party leader, and this was especially the case when they generated press coverage because they were critical of or were seen to be critical of or at odds with government or party policy. What is less well known, because it was not covered in the UK in the same way, was when Lady Thatcher used her speeches to promote British interests, commercial and/or political, in the countries she was visiting, with positive impacts for the UK.

The extent to which she 'batted for Britain' while on her travels abroad, and her impact and the reactions she generated when doing so, is revealed in files that have been released by the National Archives since her death. What these also reveal is the sheer amount of work that Lady Thatcher, and her speeches, could generate for ministers and officials.

Her speech in Fulton in March 1996, marking the fiftieth anniversary of Winston Churchill's 'Iron Curtain' speech, is an example. Entitled 'New threats for old', it warned of 'rogue states',[56] highlighting the vital importance of defence technology and ballistic missiles and how to create a free and orderly world out of the disorderly chaos left by communism.[57] Describing Lady Thatcher as 'Churchill's representative on Earth', Andrew Roberts said the speech was a 'tour d'horizon'.[58] President Bill Clinton was invited to accompany Lady Thatcher to Fulton and introduce her.[59]

The speech was delivered on 9 March, and two days before, on the 7th, Julian Seymour sent an advance copy to Downing Street.

On the 8th, an official from the Ministry of Defence (MoD) sent a note to an official in No. 10. It followed a request from Downing Street for briefing on the issues Lady Thatcher covered. After that initial request, it was further agreed that it would also be helpful to have lines to take on the other points Lady Thatcher raised which were at variance with government policy. In truth, it might have been easier to list the areas with which Lady Thatcher was *not* at variance with government policy, for the MoD official listed defence preparedness, the United Nations Special Commission (the United Nations mission designed to destroy Iraq's weapons of mass destruction after the first Gulf War), the former Yugoslavia and NATO enlargement as areas where Lady Thatcher differed with the government. The briefing note for Downing Street runs to eleven sides of A4.[60]

Other themes

There are other themes not delineated by Theakston that are relevant, and some of these may increase in relevance over time if the current trend continues for ex-premiers to leave office younger and live for longer than many have in the past. These include institutional infrastructure, birthdays and personal anniversaries, political anniversaries and explaining themselves.

Institutional infrastructure

In addition to the PDCA, Lady Thatcher's post-premiership saw another innovation: the establishment of the Margaret Thatcher Foundation in 1991, 'to advance the cause of political and economic freedom'.[61] Even before its formal establishment, it had generated press coverage. Its story has been variously told, including in an article by Tom Baldwin in *The Times* in 2006.[62]

Lady Thatcher talked about the foundation in her June 1991 interview with Michael Brunson. She said, 'It is going to embody all of those things I have explained and believed in. How to roll forward the frontiers of freedom, how to bring it about, educating people about what it is all about, giving practical help to the people in Eastern Europe who are trying to do it.' She concluded, 'we must have a Foundation to make certain we have a centre through which it can continue. That is what I will do. The best of Britain to the best of the world.'[63] It was not clear if Lady Thatcher was referring to herself or the Foundation at this point.

Today, the Thatcher Foundation provides 'the largest contemporary history site of its kind' and offers 'free access to thousands of historical documents relating to the Thatcher period'.[64] This study, for one, owes it a debt.

Birthdays and personal anniversaries

Lady Thatcher's seventieth, seventy-fifth, eightieth and eighty-fifth birthdays were all marked.

The first of these, her seventieth, was celebrated with several parties. These included one at Downing Street and one at Claridge's – the latter attended by the Queen. In his speech at this event, Bill Deedes quoted from Psalm 90: 'The days of our age are three score years and ten, and though some be so strong that they come to four score years, then is their strength only labour and sorrow.' According to Jonathan Aitken, Lady Thatcher had not known the source of those words and demanded to know who had written them. When Aitken explained that it was King David in the Psalms, Lady Thatcher responded, 'Well, he got a lot of things wrong, as kings in the Middle East still do!' Aitken concluded that

Lady Thatcher 'could have been back at the despatch box at Prime Minister's Questions'.[65]

As ever with Lady Thatcher after 1990, the birthday proved political. This had consequences for Downing Street, including for officials' workloads.[66] In May 1995, there was discussion regarding the guest lists for the parties, Alex Allan noting, 'there is the opportunity to split the guest list between the two, with those whom it might be awkward to invite here [Downing Street] being invited to Claridge's instead.' Officials also discussed the funding of the party and what the government's public line would be on it. In response to Allan's note, another official, Roderic Lyne, said that it would be helpful if some invitations could be passed through him. He wanted 'to make political capital out of them', and cited the invitation to Lee Kuan Yew, which would 'soften a refusal to see him in early June'. So, not all the political consequences of Lady Thatcher were negative for the government. She and her name could also be of help.

Officials initially tried to persuade John Major that he did not need to go to the Claridge's party. In a memo to him on 31 August, Allan commented, 'I had tried to persuade you that there was no need to accept.' Allan argued that Major would be tired, there would have been the Downing Street dinner and 'the cast list is not that attractive'. Allan added that after discussion with others, however, the 'consensus was that you *should* go', since it would be 'well received' by the party and, if declined with no other engagement, 'it would look like a snub, notwithstanding your own dinner'. After Major decided to go, Allan alerted Arabella Warburton, Major's PA. In his own hand, Allan wrote, 'Arabella, Both PM & Norma will go (groan!) Alex'. A handwritten note to Allan dated 30 August opens with, 'Can we really not decline this one?' Highlighting the dinner was the Monday after party conference, the memo concludes, 'Lord knows what games she'll be playing there. GRRR!!!' In a note to Major on 29 September about the seating arrangements, Allan suggested that in 'the spirit of healing', Major might like to sit between Rosemary Lamont and Christine Hamilton. He added, '<joke!>' Next to it, in his own hand, Major wrote, '<u>Bad one.</u>'

Lady Thatcher's eightieth birthday was marked with a reception, also attended by the Queen. This inspired a *Have I Got News For You?* greetings card in 2006 featuring a photograph of Her Majesty and Lady Thatcher looking at one another outside the Mandarin Oriental Hotel, where the reception had been held. The card's caption reads: 'Following an argument over who sits at the head of the table, two dinner guests decide to sort it out in the car-park.'

Lady Thatcher's birthdays also generated media coverage, especially the eightieth. As so often with coverage of Lady Thatcher after 1990, some of this was obituary-style in content and tone, spanning the range of views about Lady Thatcher. Andrew Roberts' article in the *Daily Express* was headlined 'Happy birthday to a fearless Iron Lady',[67] while Kevin Maguire's, in the *Daily Mirror*, read: 'The old witch'.[68]

Obituary-style profiles also marked Lady Thatcher's career anniversaries, including those of her election as Conservative Party leader, her appointment as Prime Minister and her resignation. In April 2008, the *Daily Telegraph* ran a series entitled 'Portrait of a Leader', offering perspectives on Lady Thatcher's life, work and legacy, including after Downing Street. In 1999, the *BBC* had done something similar headed, 'Thatcher – 20 Years On'.[69]

Indeed, this living in a state of almost permanent obituary had started before she formally resigned as Prime Minister, and was the tone of much of the contemporary coverage. In *The Path to Power*, Lady Thatcher wrote of reading 'obituary-style assessments'.[70] In addition, the National Archives holds the letters that she received in response to those sent to heads of state and heads of government telling them of her resignation.[71] Again, ever practical, the letters Lady Thatcher sent stated, 'I shall of course remain in charge of the Government until my successor has been appointed.' No doubt this was intended to 'reassure' the recipients. The responses Lady Thatcher received invariably paid tribute to her, in terms of her ideas, her leadership and her style. What the impact on the recipient might have been, given their content and tone, is only to be imagined.

Political anniversaries

Throughout her time as a premier emeritus, Lady Thatcher marked anniversaries of the Falklands War.

Reporting from the Falklands in June 1992, John Ezard commented, 'it has been Margaret Thatcher's weekend. No modern politician, not even Churchill, has been as loved in Britain as she is here.'[72] Ahead of a trip to Argentina by Sir John Coles, the Deputy Under Secretary of State, Asia and the Americas at the Foreign Office, defensive points to make had been prepared for him about Lady Thatcher's visit.[73] At the start of 1992, the first Margaret Thatcher Day had been instituted. The chosen date was 10 January – the day on which Lady Thatcher received the freedom of the islands during her visit in 1983.[74] She also had a peninsula on South Georgia named after her, as detailed in the National Archives' file, called 'Mount Thatcher'.[75]

In 1997, Lady Thatcher gave 'an emotional address' to thousands of veterans and their families at a ceremony in Gosport. She also unveiled a plaque honouring those who had died or were injured during the war.[76]

As part of twentieth-anniversary commemorations in 2002, Lady Thatcher was guest of honour on the *QE2*, which had taken part in the conflict. She made a few remarks and, in full Margaret Thatcher character, opened with, 'Now, as you will know, my doctors recently advised me to give up all public speaking – that just goes to show how little men understand women. But I just happen to have a few words at the ready and I promise that if you don't tell, I won't!'[77]

To mark the twenty-fifth anniversary in 2007, Lady Thatcher undertook 'a taxing programme of engagements'.[78] Dr Colin White, the director of the Royal Naval Museum in Portsmouth, described her as 'the war's most senior veteran'.[79] After Lady Thatcher's death, Sir Gerald Howarth recalled her attendance at an anniversary dinner at the Painted Hall in Greenwich. 'When Margaret Thatcher got up to leave, there was the most astonishing roar from men who had been maimed, cheering their warrior leader who had instructed them to go into battle and they wanted to pay tribute to her.'[80] Lady Thatcher also made a broadcast through the British Forces Broadcasting Service. In it, she sounds almost otherworldly.[81]

Ahead of the thirtieth anniversary in 2012, the *Evening Standard* quoted Whitehall sources saying that 'concerns' about Lady Thatcher's 'failing health' meant it might be the last one she could mark.[82] As it was, she was too frail to attend any commemorations, with Andrew Pierce reporting that she had declined 'a clutch' of invitations.[83]

Explaining herself

In December 2015, the *New Statesman* published an article entitled 'Tony Blair's second career: explaining his first'.[84] Its author, Kevin

Meagher, stated: 'Once, what went on in government stayed in government. Now, the decisions they take in office are starting to follow them out of Number Ten's famous black door.'

Like other ex-premiers before her, Lady Thatcher faced some of this herself. As will be seen, her actions as Prime Minister on the Single European Act were quoted against her during the passage of the Maastricht Bill.

Beyond that, Lady Thatcher gave evidence to the Scott Inquiry into arms for Iraq on 8 December 1993. It was one of her most memorable, if not to say in parts entertaining, post-prime ministerial interventions, and featured all the key aspects of her life after Downing Street: extensive media coverage, some of it factual, some of it commentary, some of it sketch; Lady Thatcher being herself; Lady Thatcher performing the character that was Margaret Thatcher; and others' reactions to her.

Ahead of her appearance, Lady Thatcher had sent written material to the inquiry on 3 December. She opened with, 'I have been asked to make a preliminary statement to the Inquiry.' At the end of her six sides of A4 statement, she noted, 'As regards my meeting with King Hussein on 31 August 1990, I was very severe with the King about reports that defence equipment destined for Jordan had been diverted to Iraq.'[85]

As for Lady Thatcher's oral evidence, the transcript runs to 49,284 words. Given from 10 a.m. to 5:15 p.m., with an hour's break for lunch, the Thatcher Foundation notes it 'constitutes her longest public testimony of any kind in the course of a fifty-year career'.[86] During her testimony, she made 464 comments, responding to 370 listed questions.

Opening, Lord Justice Scott told Lady Thatcher that the inquiry counsel, Presiley Baxendale, would be asking most of the questions, but that he might come in and ask a few himself. The sparring between Lady Thatcher and Baxendale formed a substantial part of the reporting of Lady Thatcher's evidence, and in 2014 she was described as having 'skewered' Lady Thatcher.[87]

At the time, *The Independent* headlined a story, 'Thatcher entangled in icy battle of wills'.[88] John Mortimer, author of *Rumpole of the Bailey*, penned an article in the *Daily Telegraph* analysing the 'courtroom techniques of inquisitors and witness'. It was headlined 'Thatcher pursued by a smiling huntress'.[89] Mortimer noted that Lady Thatcher treated Baxendale 'in a patronising manner' and at various points in her evidence, rather than respond to Baxendale's questions, Lady Thatcher replied instead to Lord Justice Scott. She used the words 'My Lord' fifteen times, 'Your Lordship' twelve, and 'My Lordship' once.

Paul Callan's sketch in the *Daily Express* was headlined 'Eye to eye with Medusa',[90] and in it he wrote of Lady Thatcher stabbing 'tetchily at the air with a fierce forefinger'. He also noted that she 'knew how to use her dark pink spectacles with skill'. This was, he said, 'a dramatic technique of its own'. Having explained how Lady Thatcher used her glasses, Callan concluded, 'It was all quite magnificently theatrical.' He also recorded that there was 'laughter all round' when Lady Thatcher responded to Lord Justice Scott asking if she had received a document the previous day, by saying, 'I had a meeting, quite a long meeting, with Mr Gorbachev yesterday and then I was speaking later in the evening.'

As suggested by Callan's piece, parts of the media coverage were themselves 'magnificently theatrical', as so much of the response to Lady Thatcher was after 1990. In an article headlined 'It is no good asking me, I was only Prime Minister', Matthew Engel wrote, 'Her performance was part Nixon, who took the responsibility but not the blame, part Reagan, who remembered nothing, and part Ceaușescu, who regretted nothing and how dare they?'[91] Joe Joseph spoke of Lady Thatcher having attended the inquiry 'in the manner of a celebrity who has been persuaded to appear on a rather naff game show only because it is being filmed for a worthy charity.'[92]

Perhaps the most revealing part of Lady Thatcher's evidence – revealing both about her and about people's (mainly men's) reaction to her – was the final exchange with Lord Justice Scott. He told Lady Thatcher that a transcript would be sent to her, and the inquiry would be very grateful if she would add anything she wished to add or correct anything. Lady Thatcher replied, 'I fear there will be much grammar to be corrected.' Possibly betraying something of the irritation that Lady Thatcher seemed almost uniquely capable of exciting in men, Lord Justice Scott responded, 'Never mind grammar, that is the least of the problems.' Lady Thatcher responded, 'Thank you very much.' The hearing adjourned.

Despite this, Lady Thatcher took the inquiry sufficiently seriously to speak on its findings in the House of Lords in February 1996.[93] Another ex-premier, Lord Callaghan, also took part in the debate. Strongly supporting the government, Lady Thatcher concluded, 'Finally, amidst the mass of detail we should remember that at the end of the war to liberate Kuwait, in which the British government and Armed Forces played such a proud role, no British lethal equipment was found among Iraqi supplies on the battlefield.' Can we detect a tone of 'so there'?

Part II

Margaret Thatcher's (continuing) work

When she arrived at her Dulwich home on 28 November 1990, a journalist asked Margaret Thatcher what she would do now. She replied, 'Work. That's all we have ever known.'[1]

There was never any doubt that that work would be political. Everything she did politically after 28 November 1990 could either have been foreseen or was advertised, either just before her resignation, or not long after it, including by Lady Thatcher herself.

As John Campbell noted, Lady Thatcher 'could no more walk away from politics than she could stop breathing'.[2] Writing in 2019, Gyles Brandreth remembered meeting her in South Africa while she was holidaying with Mark Thatcher. 'She was being driven around looking for things to do and people to meet. There were no members of the South African government available that day, so she was delighted to see me, not because it was me, but because we had both been MPs and she could talk politics. That's all she wanted to do.'[3] In a 1995 profile, Lesley White recorded, 'Before we met it was made clear that she would not enjoy a light, soft-focus interview; she would talk politics and that was that.'[4]

The workaholics' workaholic, as Tim Bell said, Lady Thatcher was 'not a hobby person'.[5] Proposed non-political activities were not met with approval. Seeing Lady Thatcher after her resignation, Richard Wilson, former Head of the Economic Secretariat in the Cabinet Office, suggested she take up golf. Looking at him 'with mock horror', Lady Thatcher replied, 'Oh, no, Mr Wilson. I don't like little balls (gesture with finger and thumb), I like playing with the globe (huge expansive gesture)'.[6]

More than that, Lady Thatcher loved politics and was passionate about practising it. In May 1993, one of her friends commented, 'It has to be said that she comes alive when there is a whiff of gunfire in the air. It perks her up no end. When she expresses that rage and despair about the latest mess, one cannot help noticing a certain spring in her step.'[7] A month later, Matthew Parris wrote, 'Show her a good scrap and the decades fall away.'[8]

In 2013, Baroness Buscombe recalled one evening when she divided the House of Lords seven times on the Licensing Bill. 'Others were nudging me slightly, saying, "Peta, when is this going to end? Margaret Thatcher has a party. She is here and she's missing her own party".' Lady Buscombe went to speak to Lady Thatcher, saying, 'I'm so sorry, Margaret, but I'm so glad you're here support-ing my amendments'. Lady Thatcher replied, 'My dear, it's marvel-lous. I'm really enjoying myself. This is just like old times.'[9]

The impact of the loss of office was traumatic for Lady Thatcher. In his biography of her, Iain Dale has noted: 'It is no exaggeration to claim that, following her ousting as Prime Minister, Margaret Thatcher underwent some sort of PTSD-related psychological ex-perience.'[10] Lady Thatcher alluded to this herself. When Michael Brunson interviewed her at the end of June 1991, she became vis-ibly upset, dabbing her eyes with a handkerchief, when speaking of her resignation. 'You are thinking back to traumatic things,' she replied when Brunson said it was affecting her.[11] In the 1991 *Vanity Fair* profile, Lady Thatcher reflected graphically, 'It's like throwing a pane of glass with a complicated map upon it on the floor and all habits and thoughts and actions that went with it and the staff that went with it ... You threw it on the floor and it shattered.' When asked about the pieces, Lady Thatcher's eyes 'blazed' as she responded, 'You couldn't pick up those pieces.'[12]

The immediate aftermath was particularly painful. There was a sense of bereavement and of grief. Alistair McAlpine wrote, 'At first she seemed dazed, unable to find enough work to fill a day that only a week before was not long enough for all the work in hand.' A doctor told him, 'It is like the death of a close relative for her.'[13] Others noted the similarity to death. In the *Sunday Correspondent* on 25 November 1990, 'National trauma: a doctor writes' was the headline of an article by Anthony Clare. It noted, 'Love her or hate her, the Prime Minister's resignation was like a national bereavement.'[14] On 22 November, Henry Kissinger, who was in 'a very emotional state', told Charles Powell, 'It was worse than a death in the family.'[15] The Thatcher Foundation speaks of 'the loss not only of power, but of occupation and home'.[16]

For all of this, even if not apparent at the time, by the end of 1990, the contours of Lady Thatcher's premier emeritus years were in fact already in place.

During Prime Minister's Questions on 22 November, Lady Thatcher responded to Jonathan Aitken by saying that it had 'secretly occurred' to her 'that one's voice might be listened to after.'[17] On the same day, on her typed letter to the Emir of Kuwait, she wrote in her own hand, 'I shall certainly continue to make my views known.'[18]

In a handwritten letter to Sir George Younger, dated 4 December,

Lady Thatcher thanked him for his help and advice. She went on, 'What has happened is now in the past and – in line with your advice – I am seeing how best I can continue to have some influence on politics at home and overseas.'[19] The same month she wrote to Robin Harris, 'It would perhaps be true to say that we have just come to the end of the *first phase* of our work. So short a time, but even now the fires need re-kindling, and that will be my main task.'[20]

Lady Thatcher expanded on this in a *House Magazine* profile in December 1990: 'I shall go on fighting for everything I believe in – the success of Britain at home and her high reputation overseas.' She concluded, 'Principles remain the same; they have a message for present and future generations. To distil that message, to persuade others of its validity and relevance – that will be my continuing purpose.'[21]

The main – but not sole – area of Lady Thatcher's continuing political work had also been identified. Receiving the Freedom of the City of Westminster on 12 December, she commented, 'Let us renew our resolve: that the sovereignty of the Westminster parliament will never be lightly relinquished.'[22]

Given the extent to which this area of Lady Thatcher's life is contested, it is necessary to examine the wider context in which she operated after 1990. This includes the impact of her loss of office and the extent to which it influenced her (continuing) work.

Reflecting on Lady Thatcher's resignation, Sir Bernard Ingham said, 'it was like somebody coming off heroin.'[23] In March 1991, Thatcher herself highlighted the effect of going 'cold turkey' as it were: 'I remember hearing when the tanks had gone into Vilnius. I kind of leapt up and dialled the telephone. Then I realised it was no longer me any more.'[24] Her driver started avoiding Whitehall 'because, as their car passed Downing Street, she would look up wondering why they hadn't turned in. Then she would remember.'[25]

Charles Powell famously commented that he did not believe that Lady Thatcher had had 'a happy day since she ceased being prime minister'.[26] This idea has become one of the fixed perceptions of Lady Thatcher's life after Downing Street. But is it correct? Did Lady Thatcher really never have a happy day after 1990? Or is this another area where nuance is needed? Moore wrote that while the statement 'captured how absolutely she thrived on being prime minister', it 'was not literally true'.[27] Someone close to Lady Thatcher went further, describing the suggestion as 'complete bullshit'.[28] As ever, the reality probably lies somewhere between the two positions. It should be noted too that, as will be seen, aspects of her life as a former Prime Minister gave Lady Thatcher a great deal of pleasure and in some of the photographs taken of her after Downing Street, including from 2002 onwards, she looks happy.

As for Lady Thatcher herself, when asked if she missed being in office, she usually replied by speaking of not living 'an if-only life' and talking about what she was doing now. That said, sometimes she did speak both privately and publicly about it. Early in December 1990, Lady Thatcher told Woodrow Wyatt, 'I have spent eleven and a half years making decisions. I have enjoyed it. Now I miss the decisions and I am not even able to say whether they are doing things right or wrong because I don't know how the problems are being presented.'[29] Asked in 1995 if she missed Prime Minister's Questions, she replied, 'Yes I do. It's a strange thing to say, isn't it? I miss it because it is part of being in a position to make decisions.'[30]

On occasion, Lady Thatcher also dangled the possibility of a return, even if she was only teasing.

In 1995, in response to David Frost's query about whether she would ever think of going back to Downing Street, she said, somewhat cryptically, 'If there is a terrible crisis of such enormous magnitude that we'd have to think about it, the answer would show itself.'[31]

In 2003, the *Daily Telegraph* wrote about Lady Thatcher's autumn drinks party in an article headlined 'The lady's all for returning'. At the gathering, she had reportedly asked a group of parliamentarians, 'Are you ready for government? Do you feel like a government in waiting?' When she received no reply, she commented, 'Well, I'm ready for government. Anytime.'[32]

After Lady Thatcher's death it was reported that Charles Powell would joke with her that the political world was waiting for her return. Powell would say, 'You see? They're waiting for us.' Lady Thatcher would reply, 'Oh, yes. We must go back.'[33]

There was also a sense of work unfinished. On 23 November 1990, Keith Joseph wrote, 'she has been obliged to leave the premiership before completing the tasks that she is best fitted to fulfil'.[34] In 2003, Lady Thatcher said, 'When I left Downing Street there was still a lot that I would have liked to do,' highlighting the Gulf War and the construction of 'a new framework' for the UK's relationship with the European Union.[35]

Not all former prime ministers necessarily feel like this. Interviewed by Peter Hennessy in 2014, John Major observed, 'I think there's different sorts of Prime Ministers once they leave office: there are those for whom office never quite goes away; there are others to a greater extent, and I hope I'm one of them, who have been able to say, that was yesterday, and I now have other things that I must do with the rest of my life.'[36]

Lady Thatcher was not one of the prime ministers for whom office went away. As Henry Kissinger reflected, 'Some leaders adjust to their retirement from politics with relative ease and elegance. They may even grow in stature, successfully writing a new, compelling chapter in their life's story. Thatcher was not one of those leaders. She lived for her vision and, out of office, struggled to find anything as meaningful as the challenges she had encountered while in 10 Downing Street.'[37]

Lady Thatcher was an executive person. As Sir Mark Worthington said, 'The Almighty had shaped her to be prime minister, but not to do anything else. She was made to sit there and take decisions. If there were no decisions to take, she did not know what to do.'[38] Moore wrote, 'After she had left office against her will, Margaret Thatcher was never reconciled. "There's so much to do!" she would exclaim, and she longed to be back in there doing it.'[39]

After announcing her resignation, Lady Thatcher kept saying to Tim Bell, 'But I haven't finished. I haven't finished.' He reflected, 'I've always wanted to tell everybody that they were her last words before she died. Unfortunately they weren't – but if this were an epic novel, they would be.'[40]

Arguably, there would never have been a time when Lady Thatcher had finished. Writing in November 1990, John O'Sullivan, who had been one of her advisers and speech writers, commented, 'No combination of successes in policy would ever have been complete enough to persuade her that her task was done. There would always have been a crisis somewhere to detain her in office.'[41] Just as there seemingly was for Lady Thatcher's great hero, Winston Churchill.

As if to prove the point, sometimes, after 1990, Lady Thatcher gave the impression of carrying on regardless, acting towards ex-colleagues, both political and official, as she had when she was Prime Minister – behaving, in fact, as if she were *still* Prime Minister.

Speaking after her death, Douglas Hurd said, 'She used to ring me up every now and then, not very often but occasionally, and let me know what I was doing wrong – she never hesitated about that. The fact that, as it were, she was no longer in charge of me didn't really alter the situation very much. She carried on rather with the same tone of voice she had always used with me.'[42] In a diary entry on 8 May 1991, Sir Patrick Wright, Permanent Under Secretary at the Foreign and Commonwealth Office and Head of Her Majesty's Diplomatic Service, noted that Hurd 'now finds himself as virtually a runner between Mrs Thatcher and No. 10'.[43] In June 1991, Hurd told Wright that in a recent meeting with Lady Thatcher '"shafts" had been sent in all directions'.[44]

She acted in the same way with officials. On 8 April 1991, Wright recorded that Sir John Coles had visited Lady Thatcher the previous week. Coles was 'hoping for a friendly, nostalgic chat'. Instead, he found Lady Thatcher 'sitting angrily at her desk, exactly as if she were still Prime Minister'. She was 'flicking through the latest Security Council Resolution on Iraq'.[45] On 16 April, Wright noted Sir Percy Cradock, chair of the Joint Intelligence Committee and former British ambassador to China, telling him that Lady Thatcher 'still rings him up and summons him' to her home 'exactly as if she was still Prime Minister'.[46]

While her personality largely explains this type of behaviour, others have highlighted her reaction to the circumstances of her resignation. Indeed, throughout the rest of Lady Thatcher's active political life, even after it, the words 'bitter' and 'bitterness' appear in the commentary. Her actions, particularly when she was critical of John Major and the government he led, were imputed to her being bitter at losing office. Ken Clarke, for example, commented, 'Margaret's bitterness about her fall from office became ever more all-consuming and she spent most of John's term in office plotting against him and stirring up hostility amongst that faction of the party whom she could still influence.'[47]

Lady Thatcher's behaviour was compared to Edward Heath's as a former Prime Minister, specifically the critical way in which he had behaved to her as his successor. More than once, Sir Bernard Ingham wrote of 'Lady Heath'. Following her April 1992 *Newsweek* article, which was critical of Major, a *Sun* leader commented, 'This much is sure. One Ted Heath is enough in any half century!'[48] Lady Thatcher was conscious of this comparison, saying: 'I had faced sufficient difficulties from Ted Heath not to wish to inflict similar ones.'[49]

Lady Thatcher certainly felt bitter. Carol Thatcher wrote, 'It would be years before the gales of bitterness softened into breezes of reminiscences.'[50] In 2013, reflecting on a conversation he had had with Lady Thatcher not long after she resigned, Jonathan Aitken spoke of 'a painful, embarrassing and apparently recurring scene'. He concluded that almost a quarter of a century on, 'it is fairer to draw a veil over these depths of her agony'.[51]

What is less clear is the extent to which that bitterness caused Lady Thatcher to behave in the way that she did during her premier emeritus years, especially her siren era. We should be aware, too, that often the charge of bitterness can be levelled at someone as a way of avoiding engaging with the content of what they are saying. Alistair McAlpine commented that it was too easy 'to paint Margaret Thatcher as a bitter woman angry at loss of office and to shout this facile refrain every time that she has a word of criticism for the government'.[52] In its analysis of the files in the National Archives covering her contacts with John Major between 1990 and 1992, the Thatcher Foundation reflected that her actions were not motivated by small things.[53]

Another way of looking at this is to consider what, if anything, would have been different had Lady Thatcher left office at a time of her own choosing, or if the electorate had removed her.

As seen above, politics was all she wanted to talk about. In 2002, Bruce Anderson noted, 'As long as she is above ground, she will remain restless, defiant and dissatisfied.'[54] As an executive person, Lady Thatcher would have missed making decisions, however she left Downing Street. Her personality was such that it was very unlikely that she would not have spoken out on issues she felt were important.

On some issues, attempts were made to persuade Lady Thatcher not to speak out. On 12 June 1991, Sir Patrick Wright wrote in his diary 'some hope!' when he recorded that that day's press was 'full of stories of attempts to muzzle Margaret Thatcher'.[55] Lady Thatcher protested about these attempts, both privately and publicly, throughout her active political life after Downing Street. She variously complained that she did not have 'freedom of speech',[56] asked, 'Why should one be gagged?',[57] declared, 'I can't be quietened. I can't be stopped from saying what I believe in,'[58] and, perhaps most memorably, commented, at the 1999 Conservative conference, 'I am told I have to be careful about what I say, and I don't like it.'[59]

Analysing the National Archives' 1994 release, the Thatcher Foundation noted, 'Of course, it was never remotely possible MT would simply leave well alone. The issues were too important in themselves, and the history too fraught.'[60]

Looking at what Lady Thatcher's work involved – philosophy, party, policy and performance – it is impossible to imagine her not working on them. Given the policy issues on which she concentrated – the European Union, the former Yugoslavia, General Pinochet, and Hong Kong and China – it is equally impossible to imagine her not speaking out on them. This is irrespective of how she left Downing Street, even if that may have added an extra ingredient.

As we turn to examine Lady Thatcher's (continuing) work, it is important to note five themes which both underpin that work and are key to understanding her life after Downing Street.

First, Lady Thatcher's work was not carried out in isolation. She often did things concurrently. Second, it had symbolic and practical aspects. Third, her work and people's reactions to it had contemporary political significance. This could have both negative and positive consequences for her successors as Conservative Party leader. It also had longer-term political impacts, shaping perceptions of Lady Thatcher and her premiership, thereby contributing to her legacy. Fourth, for all the drama and danger that swirled around Lady Thatcher's work, there was also nuance in what she did and in what she did not do.

Finally, throughout her premier emeritus years, we see Lady Thatcher being herself and playing the character that was Margaret Thatcher. Indeed, in many ways, this was her most important work after Downing Street, and seemed to be a full-time job. Sometimes Lady Thatcher was 'a source of national entertainment', at others, she played 'battling Maggie'. On occasion, she was being both at the same time. Whichever role she was playing, however, Lady Thatcher was portraying Margaret Thatcher the persona while also being Margaret Thatcher the person, which not only revealed more about her character, but further fixed the character that was Margaret Thatcher in political consciousness. This became, and remains, key to her legacy, and also helps to explain her continued and continuing influence.

Chapter Four

Philosophy

Lady Thatcher's philosophy work involved her being a 'prophet and crusader' for Thatcherism, a 'torch of freedom' for the Soviet Union and Central and Eastern Europe, coming 'as close to an apotheosis as a mortal can' in the United States, and being 'a major asset to Britain' in other parts of the world.

'Prophet and crusader': Thatcherism

Presenting Lady Thatcher with the Presidential Medal of Freedom in March 1991, President Bush said, 'Prophet and crusader, idealist and realist, this heroic woman made history move her way.'[1]

After 1990, Lady Thatcher was a 'prophet and crusader' for her own 'ism'. This was 'the role almost inescapably hers, as the guardian of Thatcherism'. It also 'brought her frequently into conflict with the government'.[2] Throughout the remainder of her active political life, Lady Thatcher evangelised on Thatcherism's behalf. After that, she continued as its symbol in the UK and also around the world.

As part of that, Lady Thatcher frequently spoke about her 'ism' on her visits abroad, as well as in the UK. But what was Thatcherism?

Sometimes she seemed to suggest it was a leadership type or personal style. In April 1992, she described its essence as 'a sense of direction, momentum and firmness and we will continue to do things however difficult they might be.'[3]

Other times, Lady Thatcher spoke of it as if it were a philosophy, spelling out 'The Principles of Thatcherism'.[4] She did not need to use the word to emphasise its continuing significance. The thrust of many of her speeches, such as those on the 'Challenges of the Twenty-First Century' delivered in the mid-1990s, was the continuing relevance of her 'ism'. In *The Path to Power*, she wrote, 'the basic themes I had preached and sought to practise over the years were as relevant and potent as ever.'[5]

Lady Thatcher argued Thatcherism's continuing relevance to the political issues of the day, indeed seemingly to all days. In a *Newsweek* article in 1992, she wrote, 'Thatcherism will live. It will live long after Thatcher has died, because we had the courage to restore the great principles and put them into practice, in keeping with the character of the people and the place of this country in the world.' She went on, 'The lesson is, you don't soften fundamental principles. You positively push them forward into the future.'[6]

Lady Thatcher's call for 'permanent revolution', as highlighted in *Newsweek*, was also applied to her time in office, with her arguing that the government she had led had pursued Thatcherism. Without using the word, this was some of the message of her Keith Joseph Memorial Lecture in January 1996.[7] Simon Jenkins reflected that she had 'become the Arthur Scargill of the Right, peddling myths of the party's ideological history'.[8]

Others have also challenged how Thatcherite Lady Thatcher's governments were. Chris Patten said it was 'ridiculous' to regard Thatcherism as a coherent political philosophy and instead thought it was 'whatever Margaret Thatcher did, day to day, week to week'.[9] Douglas Hurd reflected, 'I think there was a fundamental set of ideas, which she wasn't wholly devoted to, and which she often diverged from in practice.'[10] In 2016, Ken Clarke commented, 'Over the past twenty years absurd myths have built up about the Thatcher

era on both sides of the political divide.' He said a particularly per-
vasive myth was that Lady Thatcher was 'an ideologue who based
her judgements on deeply held philosophical convictions'.[11]

While the extent to which the Thatcher governments were themselves Thatcherite is open to question, Lady Thatcher retained her
Thatcherite purity in one respect after 1990. Asked in 1991 where
she expected to be in five years' time, she replied, 'Still preaching
what I believe in and doing everything I can to practise it and battling on.'[12] She was true to her word for as Simon Heffer wrote in
2001, 'It is still politics, or rather the ideology to which she gave her
name, that is her life-blood.'[13]

'Torch of freedom': Soviet Union, and Central and Eastern Europe

Writing in March 2002, Nicholas Watt said, 'Lady Thatcher has
held aloft what her admirers dubbed the "torch of freedom".'[14] This
area of Lady Thatcher's work involved the Soviet Union, and Central and Eastern Europe.

In May 1991, Lady Thatcher paid what the Thatcher Foundation
has called a 'quasi-state visit' to the Soviet Union.[15] Telegrams from
the British Embassy in Moscow to the Foreign Office provide the
details of the events she attended and the people she met.[16]

These included a two-and-a-half-hour meeting with Mikhail
Gorbachev and other officials as well as an address to the Supreme
Soviet's Foreign Affairs Commission.[17] To them, Lady Thatcher
said, 'I propose to speak frankly because that is my habit and I
know no other way. Also I shall be dealing with fundamentals, with
principles and policies in which I believe deeply.' In what might
possibly have been a career first, she went on, 'It is not for me to tell
you what to do. That would be intrusive and interfering.'

Lady Thatcher spoke to staff and students at the Moscow State Institute for International Relations. The Embassy noted, 'There was a lively question and answer session after her brief address.'[18] Lady Thatcher 'arrived and left to applause and her 20-minute speech and question session was interrupted at least a dozen times by cheering'.[19] A *Times* leader, 'Missionary in Moscow', noted, 'The adulation for Mrs Thatcher in Moscow is a reminder of the enduring power of the idea of political and economic liberty.'[20] She later claimed, 'When I spoke to the young people in Moscow, in Leningrad, they are Thatcherites to a man, and woman.' She added, 'Isn't it marvellous!'[21] The Embassy concluded that the visit had gone well. Lady Thatcher had been 'warmly received' and 'was able usefully to emphasise the need for the Soviet Union to persevere with its reforms'.[22]

As for the visit's impact in Britain, Lady Thatcher's public call for the Soviets to be invited to the G7 meeting being held in London that July was 'unhelpful'[23] with John Major becoming 'increasingly irritated by her erratic behaviour'.[24]

Reflecting on the August 1991 coup attempt, Lady Thatcher wrote that she was 'dismayed' by some Western leaders' willingness to wait to see if the coup was successful rather than offer 'full moral support' to the resistance gathered around Boris Yeltsin. When she had checked what had happened, she held a press conference outside her office. She then gave a series of interviews.[25] Lady Thatcher spoke of 'an old-fashioned style attempt at a coup belonging to the Stalin and Brezhnev era'.[26]

In what Michael Forsyth described as 'a typically robust telephone conversation', Lady Thatcher also encouraged Yeltsin to oppose the coup.[27] Moore records her intervention 'greatly irritated' John Major and Douglas Hurd. Her confident appearance on the world stage annoyed them. Major would have preferred her to have consulted them. He thought 'she was wrong to encourage the public to take to the streets in protest. Wrong to ask people to put their lives at risk.'[28] Harris wrote that Lady Thatcher was 'the target of some venomous briefing from Downing Street, resentful at her intervention.'[29]

The coup failed and Yeltsin returned the favour. When he visited in London in January 1992, Lady Thatcher was invited to meet him at the Russian Embassy. She had thirty minutes with him. Neil Kinnock had fifteen.[30] A note from Stephen Wall, Major's private secretary, reveals that during Yeltsin's visit, none of Lady Thatcher's private criticism of the British and American governments for not doing enough for Russia emerged publicly. Wall recorded that in fact, on television, she had said that the British had taken the lead in support for Russia.[31]

On Christmas Day 1991, Lady Thatcher was interviewed outside her office about Gorbachev's resignation as Soviet leader. Referring to him, Reagan and herself, she declared, 'We were a threesome, and I hope that together we managed to do quite a lot for peace and democracy.'[32]

Lady Thatcher and Gorbachev continued to meet over the years. As seen above, they met the day before her Scott Inquiry appearance in 1993. They had also met that July when Lady Thatcher accepted an honorary degree from Mendeleyev Chemical University. Lady Thatcher was accompanied by her daughter, and *The Times* featured a photograph of her straightening Carol's hair.[33] Carol later said, 'When I met Gorbachev, which I had longed to do, the only picture was of Mum trying to smooth down my fringe. I was incandescent.'[34]

Lady Thatcher's interest in the former Soviet Union continued throughout her siren years. In the early 1990s, she regularly spoke of the need to provide the Soviet Union and then Russia with practical help. The National Archives holds a note from the British ambassador to Russia about a possible visit Lady Thatcher might make there in September 1999.[35] In September 2000, Lady Thatcher criticised Vladimir Putin's response to the *Kursk* submarine disaster.[36] Her comments went viral in early 2023. In July 2000, Lady Thatcher had said, 'With every day that passes, modern Russia behaves more and more like the old Soviet Union.' She noted, 'it is capable of creating sustained mischief in several regions.'[37]

As for Central and Eastern Europe, Lady Thatcher saw the Thatcher Foundation as a way of providing practical help to the former communist countries of Eastern Europe. She opened a branch in Warsaw during a visit in April 1993.

A telegram from the British Embassy provides details of that trip.[38] Throughout her visit, Lady Thatcher spoke about Bosnia and the need to help the democratic reform movement in Russia. She also undertook various engagements, meeting political figures, including the Prime Minister, opening the refurbished Hotel Bristol and addressing the British Chamber of Commerce and Polish businessmen. Perhaps most importantly, she met Marek Edelman, one of the survivors of the Warsaw Ghetto uprising and laid a wreath at the monument to the uprising. She had been 'keen to play a full role'.[39]

Politics and practicalities aside, Lady Thatcher's real importance in Central and Eastern Europe after 1990 was what she represented symbolically. Charles Powell said, 'Part of people's vision of her, particularly in Eastern Europe and Russia, was of the great heroine of the Cold War, who had together with Reagan brought about its end.'[40] In 1993, the British ambassador, Sir Michael Llewellyn-Smith said, 'Lady Thatcher commands enormous respect in Poland for her political achievements and especially her contribution to the turning back of Communism.'[41] In 1991, reporting on the re-action to a speech Lady Thatcher had made to the Polish Senate,[42] the ambassador wrote of 'the affection and admiration in which Mrs Thatcher is held for her role in bringing about the downfall of Communism'.[43] Marek Matraszek, the Thatcher Foundation's Warsaw branch director, described her as 'very much a beacon'.[44]

Lady Thatcher's symbolic work had started before her resignation. On 23 November 1990, Hugo Young wrote, 'When that ice age [the Cold War] broke up, moreover, it was to the Thatcher model that many of the newly free countries consciously turned for guidance on the modalities of the free market. All this was due to her personal charisma. Evangelism and showmanship captured the east, beginning in the Soviet Union shortly before the 1987 election.'[45] After Lady Thatcher's resignation, it continued and intensified.

It reached its apotheosis in the story Lady Thatcher shares at the end of *The Path to Power*. During a church service on her 1993 visit to Poland, the priest said that people had not really believed that communism had collapsed and been replaced by democracy until they had seen Lady Thatcher in their church. Lady Thatcher recounted, 'At the end of mass I was invited to stand in front of the altar. When I did so, lines of children presented me with little bouquets of flowers while their mothers and fathers applauded.'[46] For Sir Julian Seymour, this was 'the most electrifying moment of my two decades-plus involvement with her'.[47]

While, according to Harris, there may have been something different about the reception Lady Thatcher received in Poland,[48] throughout Central and Eastern Europe, she remained an important figure. She visited Prague in November 1999 and unveiled a statue of Winston Churchill.[49] Seven thousand people were reportedly in Churchill Square, while more were 'hanging out of overlooking windows to get a better view'. The reception to her speech was 'tremendous', with Lady Thatcher adding, 'Some applause has a special quality that you remember for a lifetime. This had it.'[50] She received the Order of the White Lion, the Czech Republic's highest order, saying she was 'pleased that a lioness is to be admitted to this highly select pride!'[51]

'As close to an apotheosis as a mortal can': the United States

In September 1991, Lady Thatcher spoke at the Clare Boothe Luce Award Dinner in Washington. George Urban, one of Lady Thatcher's foreign policy advisers, was present. He wrote about the event in his book, *Diplomacy and Disillusion at the Court of Margaret Thatcher*. In Chapter 11, 'Fit for a Queen', he commented that Lady Thatcher 'advanced as close to an apotheosis as a mortal can'.[52]

As in other areas of her life after 1990, Lady Thatcher had practical and symbolic effect in the United States during her premier emeritus years. Beyond that, she also had personal triumph, at least in Republican circles, up to and even beyond her death.

Lady Thatcher's post-Downing Street personal triumph in the United States began almost as soon as she left No. 10. On 4 December 1990, Charles Powell met General Colin Powell. The general asked Powell to pass on to Lady Thatcher 'his warmest regards, together with best wishes and respect of the American Armed Forces as a whole for whom she was a hero'.[53]

Reporting to the British Embassy in Washington on Lady Thatcher's visit to Southern California in February 1991, Reg Holloway, the British Consul General, said she had been 'enthusiastically received'. He noted, 'the only disappointment' was among those who wanted to receive her but were unable to secure a place in the programme. At President Reagan's eightieth birthday party, Lady Thatcher 'received two standing ovations'.[54] One of those was the longest of the night. Lady Thatcher was described as the party's 'superstar'.[55]

Urban said the Clare Boothe Luce Award dinner was Lady Thatcher's 'great royal homecoming' – 'a transatlantic version of trooping the colour'. Urban described himself as 'stunned' by 'the realisation that America was conferring on MT the sort of honorary imperial presidency she had vainly sought at home'. He concluded, 'This was a scene out of Hollywood, certainly flamboyant and overdone to European eyes, but a wonderful opportunity for the historian to see MT the way she would probably like to be remembered.'[56]

In its obituary of Lady Thatcher, the *Daily Telegraph* commented, 'Her standing remained extraordinarily high in the United States, where she was venerated as one of the greatest figures of the 20th century.'[57] To Charles Powell on 22 November 1990, Henry Kissinger had said Lady Thatcher was 'one of the great figures of modern times'.[58]

Lady Thatcher did not just have personal triumph in the United States after 1990. She also had practical effect. Sometimes this saw her highlighting the importance of American leadership; at others, involvement in US domestic political issues.

To President-Elect Clinton, she wrote in November 1992, 'I count myself as America's most devoted friend.'[59] After 1990, America's 'most devoted friend' extolled what she saw as its achievements. She also spoke vigorously of the need for continued American leadership. Reflecting on speeches from 1996, John Campbell wrote that they presented her vision 'of a dangerous world which could only be saved by American leadership and military vigilance.'[60]

Beyond this strategic championing of the US, Lady Thatcher also involved herself, or was involved by others, in specific policy areas.

As will be seen, she attempted to influence American policy on Bosnia from 1992 onwards. In addition to using the media to make her case, she also spoke to key individuals. One of these was Senator Robert Dole, who she met in Britain in November 1994. As Harris records, 'Pressure from Dole, as the leader of the Republican-dominated Senate, was important in persuading the Clinton Administration to act decisively the following year.'[61]

Lady Thatcher was also championed by members of the House of Representatives for various international roles. In 1995, seventy-five representatives urged President Clinton to propose her as the new NATO secretary-general.[62] The next year, eighteen suggested Clinton nominate her as UN secretary-general.[63] In turn, she supported American figures in a similar way, for example, writing a letter backing John Bolton's nomination as the US ambassador to the UN in 2005.[64]

In September 2006, she attended an event in Washington marking the fifth anniversary of the 9/11 terrorist attacks. In a statement issued through the White House, she commented, 'This heinous attack upon America was an attack upon us all. With America, Britain stands in the front line against Islamist fanatics who hate our beliefs, our liberties and our citizens. We must not falter. We must not fail.'[65] In the UK, this was reported as Lady Thatcher and David Cameron being at odds after Cameron made a speech criticising Britain's 'slavish' relationship with the United States.[66] After the 9/11 attacks, Lady Thatcher had offered 'Advice to a Superpower' in a *New York Times* article in February 2002.[67]

Again, as with the former Soviet Union and Central and Eastern Europe, perhaps Lady Thatcher's greatest importance in the US after 1990 was symbolic.

In 2006, Tom Baldwin wrote that any 'right-thinking Conservative … is still seeking to bask in her reflected glory'.[68] This desire of American politicians to bask in Lady Thatcher's reflected glory featured throughout her life after Downing Street. In 2007, Martin Ivens described her as 'the greatest symbol of conservative hope to the American Republican party.'[69] The same year, Sarah Baxter said that Republican candidates 'regard her as an earthly representative of the late President Ronald Reagan'.[70] In 2008, Andrew Roberts wrote of Republican presidential candidates making 'the pilgrimage over to see her, such is the continuing regard in which Americans hold her'.[71]

In August 1999, 'an unusual row' had broken out among Republican presidential contenders as they battled over 'one of the greatest campaign trophies: the approval of Baroness Thatcher'. George W. Bush was said to be appalled at the prospect of Lady Thatcher endorsing Steve Forbes.[72] In July 2007, Toby Harnden wrote of Republican presidential candidates 'flocking to see Britain's icon of conservatism … in the hope that her blessing could help to secure them the presidency'.[73] In September that year, Rudy Giuliani was said to be 'making a pilgrimage to London … just to get his picture taken with her'.[74]

The same month, Giuliani unfavourably compared Hillary Clinton to Lady Thatcher. This followed Clinton's own presidential campaign chairman, Terry McAuliffe, saying that Clinton would be as strong on national security as Lady Thatcher.[75] In October 2012, presidential candidate Mitt Romney tweeted, 'Happy birthday to the Iron Lady, Margaret Thatcher – a tower of strength in the cause of liberty.'[76]

Lady Thatcher has also featured in American politics since her death. In February 2023, Nikki Haley kicked off her campaign to become the Republican presidential nominee. Asked what inspiration Lady Thatcher had been, Haley replied, 'Oh, I adore her. I've written about her in books and speeches. She was the ultimate Iron Lady.'[77] In a debate in August 2023, Haley referenced Lady Thatcher, 'I think this is exactly why Margaret Thatcher said: "If you want something said, ask a man. If you want something done, ask a woman."'[78] Lady Thatcher also featured at the conclusion of Haley's campaign. Ending her bid to be the Republican candidate in March 2024, Haley commented, 'Margaret Thatcher provided some good advice when she said, "Never just follow the crowd. Always make up your own mind."'[79] President Bill Clinton later reflected that he thought the first female President would be a Republican. Interviewed in November 2024, as part of the promotion of *Citizen: My Life After the White House* – a book about his post-presidency – he commented, 'I think it would probably be easier for a conservative Republican woman to win. Because, I mean, that's what Maggie Thatcher did.'[80]

'A major asset to Britain': other parts of the world

When Reg Holloway wrote to the British Embassy in Washington about Lady Thatcher's February 1991 visit to Southern California, he suggested that the Embassy consider what support it would be appropriate for her to receive in future. An Embassy official replied,

'Although she is no longer a member of the government, Mrs Thatcher is clearly a major asset to Britain'.[81]

The extent to which Lady Thatcher was 'a major asset to Britain' in the years after Downing Street is detailed in Foreign Office (FCO) files released by the National Archives since her death. These cover some of her travels in the early to mid-1990s, including to the Far East, the Middle East and South America, and provide a unique source for understanding Lady Thatcher's life after 1990.

Additionally, given the observations the files contain are largely those of officials, rather than political actors or journalists, they give an altogether different, perhaps more detached, perspective of Lady Thatcher's post-premiership – to the extent that anyone could (and can) be detached about Margaret Thatcher, of course.

A variety of themes flow from the files which provide insight both into Lady Thatcher's international role after Downing Street, and her long-term continued and continuing influence in British politics. That is because the files are alive with Lady Thatcher's personality, her performance of the character that was Margaret Thatcher, and people's reactions to both Margaret Thatcher the person and Margaret Thatcher the persona.

Wherever Lady Thatcher went, she created work for others. This included ministers and officials across various departments. Copious amounts of briefing were prepared for her, often at her request. A telegram from the Ministry of Defence to the British Embassy in Abu Dhabi in June 1994, released by the National Archives in January 2024, revealed that Lady Thatcher's office was not 'usually backward about coming forward' in asking for briefing.[82]

It was not just UK government departments which provided Lady Thatcher with briefing; so did the sponsors of her tours. Sir

Julian Seymour reflected on the amount of briefing that Citibank prepared for Lady Thatcher when she visited places under their auspices, noting how she arrived in the countries armed with both diplomatic and business briefings.[83]

In addition to briefing, British officials in the countries she visited, from the ambassador or high commissioner down, also provided practical help. In April 1991, the FCO issued a circular[84] detailing the support that posts might give the then Mrs Thatcher when she travelled abroad. Subsequently, another was issued about Lady Thatcher's overseas travels.[85] As FCO files show, those travels could involve a great deal of work for officials. On a copy of a May 1993 letter to Julian Seymour from the High Commission in Kuala Lumpur, someone wrote, 'I am still uneasy that our posts are doing so much work for Lady T.'[86]

The work ranged from administrative to strategic. On the latter, it included offering advice on which British interest engagements to undertake, be they commercial or political. Lady Thatcher regularly asked for such advice, seeking officials' views on what it would be useful for her to raise in her meetings. Ambassadors and high commissioners would sometimes accompany her when she met political and other figures.

Lady Thatcher did not, however, always wish to be accompanied, often preferring to meet people alone with just an interpreter or note-taker. 'She quickly learned to maintain a certain distance from the official machine,' according to the Thatcher Foundation.[87] When Lady Thatcher visited the United Arab Emirates in June 1994, it was made clear 'in perfectly polite terms' to the British Embassy that she would meet Abu Dhabi's ruler, Sheikh Zayed, 'without Embassy attendance'. Reporting this to the FCO, an official noted,

'Perhaps as a consequence of the absence of officials the meeting went on for three hours.'[88]

Another example was Lady Thatcher's 1991 trip to China. She did not want the British ambassador, Sir Robin McLaren, to accompany her to her meetings with Chinese leaders. McLaren told the Foreign Office he thought the Chinese would find the arrangements 'pretty peculiar'. Perhaps betraying something of the reaction Lady Thatcher excited in others, McLaren added, 'But you have no doubt pointed all this out already.'[89] Replying to McLaren, the FCO commented, 'We have indeed pointed out to her office that the Chinese may find the proposed arrangements for her meetings odd.' The FCO added, 'They are, however, her preferred choice.'[90]

Whatever the work Lady Thatcher generated, her visits were welcomed by ministers, ambassadors and high commissioners alike. Her pursuit of Britain's commercial and political interests, and her ability positively to further them, was acknowledged and praised.

Before she visited the Gulf in 1991, Tim Sainsbury, then a trade minister, wrote to Lady Thatcher saying, 'Your visit offers an unparalleled opportunity to provide support and encouragement to British exports to Kuwait.'[91] After Lady Thatcher's visit to Japan in 1991, an official from the British Embassy noted that the visit had had 'a positive impact on the UK's image in Japan'. She had 'echoed points that we ourselves had been making'.[92] The British ambassador said her 1992 visit was 'helpful to us'.[93]

About Lady Thatcher's visit that year to South Korea, the British ambassador, Sir David Wright, wrote to Julian Seymour, 'I am personally pleased with this news. Her visit will make a great impact here.'[94] Wright told the FCO it would be 'a high profile event' which would excite Korean attention. He added, in perhaps that way so beloved of diplomats and so revelatory of Lady Thatcher and others' reactions to her, 'without any of the associated problems which can occur, for instance, over visits to European capitals'.[95] After the trip, Douglas Hurd wished to write to Lady Thatcher to congratulate her on 'the outstanding success' of her visits there and to Taiwan. He believed they will have done 'a power of good'.[96]

Even when Lady Thatcher was not prepared to promote Britain's political interests, she still pursued its commercial ones. As will be seen, she paid a controversial visit to Malaysia in 1993, during which she attacked the British government's stance on Bosnia publicly and privately. She had seemingly not taken advice from the British high commissioner, Duncan Slater, to not let differences between the two countries on Bosnia deflect from their overall good relations. Even then, however, she still 'batted for Britain' commercially, high-lighting how high taxation on alcohol was affecting a company's sales of beer and stout. In a subsequent telegram to the FCO, Slater reported that the Malaysian finance minister 'hinted that he would not raise the tax again in his next budget'.[97]

Lady Thatcher's visit to Malaysia also showed her ability to generate turbulence. This sometimes affected the UK government. Other times, it affected the country she was visiting. On occasion, it was neither her intention nor her fault. Highlighting the nuance which runs through her post-prime ministership, FCO files reveal Lady Thatcher's keenness to avoid controversy.

That said, she was not always able to escape it. After she left Malaysia, the British high commissioner sent a telegram to the FCO alerting them to 'one piece of turbulence left by Lady Thatcher's visit': her public praise for the finance minister, Dr Anwar Ibrahim, had caused controversy. The Deputy Prime Minister, and Anwar opponent, Ghafar Baba, 'complained publicly about foreigners interfering in Malaysia's internal affairs'. Slater said this had implications for John Major's upcoming visit and he would examine possible gestures to the Ghafar Baba camp.[98]

Naturally, Lady Thatcher was not averse to expressing her views to those she was meeting. The British ambassador to South Korea noted that during Lady Thatcher's visit, a 'recurring theme was criticism of the Korean Government's establishment of diplomatic relations with Peking'. He said, 'She was most forceful about this with the Vice Minister for Foreign Affairs, Mr Roe.'[99] She would also raise issues that were politically sensitive with those she met. In 1992, she spoke 'well and firmly' with Sheikh Zayed about ex-employees of the Bank of Credit and Commerce International who were detained in Abu Dhabi.[100] When she visited the UAE in June 1994, local news stories appeared headlined 'Thatcher warns Arabs not to follow EU style' and 'Thatcher tells Gulf states to strengthen defence'.[101]

Lady Thatcher's name alone could also generate turbulence. A file released by the National Archives in March 2023 about Lady Thatcher's proposed visit to Brazil, Chile and Mexico in 1994 reveals discussions around the choreographing of her first meeting with General Pinochet. The British Embassy in Santiago advised the Foreign Office that any call Lady Thatcher made to the general just after the new Chilean government had taken office was 'unlikely to be welcomed' by them. It risked 'such prominence' in the press, in Chile and the UK, that 'it would overshadow positive aspects of the visit'.[102]

In 1992, there had been discussion about which of two invitations Lady Thatcher should accept to visit South Korea. The first was from Dr Kim Sang-Man, the publisher of the newspaper, *Dong-A Ilbo*. The second was from Chung Ju-yung, founder of Hyundai.

The latter was also a 1992 presidential candidate, and his invitation to Lady Thatcher therefore proved politically tricky, there being 'awkwardness over her close relationship' with him.[103] At the end of May 1992, the British ambassador received a 'very pressing request' from Chung's son to play golf at the weekend. Despite it being 'very inconvenient personally', the ambassador accepted the invitation, thinking there must be something behind it. He reported to the FCO, 'That something did not appear until about the 14th tee,' at which point he was asked if Lady Thatcher might be accepting Dr Kim Sang-Man's invitation. On the telegram, an official handwrote, 'Delphic golf stories'.[104] When Lady Thatcher accepted Kim's invitation – the trip finessed to ensure Chung involvement – an official noted, 'Honour (and face) preserved all round.'[105]

The South Korea visit illustrated something else that flows through the FCO files: whatever the turbulence, for Lady Thatcher herself there was almost always triumph.

The ambassador reported that a dinner in her honour was described by those present as 'an unprecedented event'. The attendees included all three presidential candidates, the then Prime Minister, five former prime ministers, the chairman of two of Korea's leading conglomerates, and 'a clutch of other political, economic and social luminaries'. The ambassador said it was 'an astonishing tribute to Lady Thatcher's reputation, her drawing power and the wish for Koreans to be seen in her company'. Of the visit overall, the ambassador reported that many Koreans, including the Foreign Minister, had told him that it had been 'a triumph'.[106]

In comparison, Edward Heath had visited South Korea the year before, also at the invitation of Kim Sang-Man. The dinner he arranged for Heath did not have the same impact as the one for Lady

Thatcher. Responding to the British ambassador's note on Heath's visit, a Foreign Office official said they hoped that Heath was not 'too unhappy' about how the dinner turned out, commenting, 'it was perhaps a pity that he may have got little out of it'. They added, 'No doubt he was mollified by the thought of the fat fee on offer from Dr Kim!'[107]

Lady Thatcher had 'astonishing tribute to her reputation' elsewhere, too. During her visit to Japan in 1991, she was 'treated rather like a head of government'. Her meeting with the Prime Minister was 'exceptionally' held in the state guest house. She was also allowed to use an airport that was 'a privilege normally reserved for heads of state'.[108] Visiting the UAE in 1992, she was described as 'the greatest leader Britain had ever had' by the President, Sheikh Zayed.[109] Of her visit to Singapore in September 1993, the high commissioner wrote, 'I have never seen a lunchtime audience of the size and influence which she attracted for her major address.'[110]

Political actors across the globe seemed to want some of Lady Thatcher's triumph to brush off on them too. In November 1993, the British Consul General in São Paulo, Roger Brown, sent a letter to the British Embassy in Brasília about Lady Thatcher's March 1994 visit. Its subject line was 'Proposed visit by Lady Thatcher: Paulo Maluf's Secret Weapon'. The Consul General wrote that if Maluf, then the Mayor of São Paulo, were to declare a presidential candidacy in 1994, 'he may well have calculated that it will do him no harm whatever to be seen to be playing host to Lady Thatcher at around the same time'.[111] Of her 1991 visit to Japan, the British ambassador commented that the Japanese Prime Minister 'clearly wanted to make an event of the meeting'. 'A huge crowd of reporters was on hand to record the initial moments of their meeting.'[112]

In 1993, the British ambassador to Poland commented that Lady Thatcher's public endorsement of the Prime Minister, Hanna Suchocka, 'will have been helpful' to her.[113]

As in the UK, political leaders in the countries Lady Thatcher visited could find themselves wanting when compared to her. In 1991, John Field, a minister in the British Embassy in Japan, wrote that Lady Thatcher's 'strong leadership' resulted in 'comparisons which are most unflattering to Kaifu [the then Prime Minister] and other Japanese politicians'.[114] One newspaper presented Lady Thatcher's meeting with Kaifu as 'Mrs Thatcher lecturing the prime minister'.[115] In 1992, Lady Thatcher's 'grasp and understanding of world events' and 'her ability to go into considerable detail' resulted in 'unflattering comparisons with Japanese prime ministers'.[116] The ambassador spoke of 'a good cartoon' appearing in one newspaper which featured Lady Thatcher 'giving frank advice' to the Prime Minister, Kiichi Miyazawa.[117]

Lady Thatcher also had triumph among members of the public. In 1991, the British Embassy wrote of Lady Thatcher having 'almost pop star status' with Japanese women.[118] The Japanese had broken the 'gush barrier' for her.[119] After her 1992 visit, the British ambassador said she had made 'a strongly positive impression on all and sundry': 'the Japanese love Lady Thatcher'.[120] On a visit out of Tokyo, Lady Thatcher 'was hemmed in at times by a throng of people anxious to shake her hand'.[121] During a 1993 visit, she appeared 'to have lost none of her power to induce rapture'.[122]

Inducing rapture did not just happen in Japan. Before visiting the Gulf in 1991, the British Embassy in Kuwait noted, 'We are already being asked by Kuwaitis when they will have an opportunity to meet her.'[123] During her visit to Brunei that September, Lady Thatcher was 'virtually mobbed by the residents of Kampong Tanah

Jambu'.[124] Ahead of her 1992 visit to South Korea, the British ambassador told her, 'Wider public interest in your visit would also be considerable.'[125] Reporting on her 1993 visit to Singapore, the High Commission commented, 'She made quite an impact. She still has quite a reputation in this part of the world as an iron lady and her style goes down well.'[126]

Lady Thatcher's style also went down well with the British community in the countries she visited. During her 1992 visit to the Gulf, Britons were 'visibly thrilled at her presence'.[127] At a private, largely British, breakfast during her South Korea visit, Lady Thatcher 'spoke off the cuff in a forthright and unequivocal manner for about 25 minutes'. This was on her criticism of the European Union and Maastricht. Lady Thatcher's remarks reportedly began with 'Thank God for the Vikings', the ambassador noted, 'and proceeded accordingly'. For the British community, the breakfast 'provided a unique opportunity to witness Lady Thatcher in full flight which they enormously enjoyed'.[128]

While Lady Thatcher may have been in full flight when being Margaret Thatcher the persona, as ever, Margaret Thatcher the person could be more nuanced than often appreciated. This is clear from telegrams sent to the FCO. For example, in the same message that reported Lady Thatcher being in full flight in South Korea, the ambassador recorded that she was 'particularly scrupulous over rejecting in advance questions in her interviews about British politics'.[129] In 1991, Lady Thatcher was approached about allowing her name to go forward for the Atatürk International Peace Prize. She was reluctant to do so. Not wanting to offend Turkey, she sought advice from the Foreign Secretary about it.[130] When she met Lee Kuan Yew privately in Singapore in 1993, she told the high commissioner afterwards that she had 'studiously avoided the subject of

Hong Kong, given that Lee Kuan Yew's views are well-known and she does not agree with them'.[131]

Margaret Thatcher the person, and how best to handle her, including on potentially sensitive matters that might come up during her visits abroad, could generate work for ministers and officials. Ahead of her 1992 Gulf visit, there was discussion in government about the Sultan of Oman's request for Britain to vacate its Embassy. In Douglas Hurd's absence, David Gore-Booth, the Assistant Under Secretary/Director, Middle East and Africa in the Foreign Office, briefed Lady Thatcher in person. On the note recommending this to Hurd, Gore-Booth wrote, 'I suppose I deserve to be the fall guy…'[132] Hurd's 'particular concern' was that Gore-Booth should 'soften her up' on the Embassy. As it happened, Gore-Booth had nothing to worry about. After his meeting with Lady Thatcher, he noted, 'she came like a lamb, agreeing at once that it would have been foolish to oppose the Sultan'. Gore-Booth spoke of his 'euphoria'. On the note, someone wrote, 'Relief all round!'[133]

Lady Thatcher was, however, always her own person and her nuanced approach should not be overexaggerated. She did not always take advice and sometimes she was not even offered it, including for fear it might not be well-received, or it might backfire.

In November 1992, as part of a trip to Israel, she visited the Citadel Museum in the Occupied Territories in East Jerusalem. Officials were worried about how Palestinians might react. Under existing guidelines, British ministers and officials would avoid going to it. In a note in October to Douglas Hogg, then a FCO minister, an official said they did not propose raising the issue with Lady Thatcher's office at that stage 'in case unsolicited advice from this quarter proved counter-productive'. At the top of the note, Hogg wrote, 'She is likely to do as she pleases.'[134] Hogg eventually wrote to Lady Thatcher about the visit.[135] This had been recommended to 'at least prevent Lady Thatcher from being able to say that the FCO never warned her about the sensitivities'.[136] Officials were also concerned about potential 'Foreign Office snub Thatcher' headlines in the UK press.[137]

Both the nuanced and less nuanced way in which Lady Thatcher approached her work after Downing Street is captured in the correspondence and the meeting she had with Douglas Hurd after her visit to South East Asia in September 1993.

In a letter to Hurd of 29 September, Lady Thatcher makes no substantive mention of her controversial visit to Malaysia, even though it ran to two sides of A4. Nor is the visit mentioned in the notes of the meeting she had with Hurd on 13 October. The letter does, however, set out Lady Thatcher's views on the places she had visited and what she thought the government should do to further Britain's interests in them. For all her well-known, often expressed, criticism of the Foreign Office, she often had praise for individuals. In her letter, she said that the UK was 'outstandingly represented at Ambassadorial level in virtually every country in these regions', though went on to say that 'we may lack people of sufficient understanding in some cases at the lower levels'. She asked Hurd to pass on her thanks to FCO staff for the 'excellent briefing material' she had received before her trip.[138]

Ever practical, having identified a problem, Lady Thatcher also had a solution. The record of her meeting with Hurd notes that Lady Thatcher said that if money were needed to 'reinforce our efforts' in Asia, 'we could do this by cutting our subsidy to Europe or halving the number of European conferences'. She went on, 'We should not cut the defence equipment budget to pay for an increased diplomatic effort.' No response by Hurd is noted.[139]

Reflections

Lady Thatcher's philosophy work after 1990 – her being the person-ification of Thatcherism across the globe (however she and others chose to define it) – illustrated a point made by William Walde-grave: 'Nor was it possible to escape her, anywhere in the world,' he wrote in his memoirs.[140] This reinforced an observation made to this author by a member of Lady Thatcher's government in 2000: 'She never really lost her status as a world power, did she?'

This should not, however, be overexaggerated. As the Thatcher Foundation says of her meeting with United Nations secretary-general Pérez de Cuéllar on 8 April 1991, 'How far she had fallen, and how steeply.'[141] Cecil Parkinson echoed this, commenting the same year, 'There's no shortage of people who would love to enter-tain her, but that's not a career, is it?'[142]

From reading the FCO reports, some ambassadors had the im-pression that Lady Thatcher was undertaking valedictory tours of the places she visited, with some subsequent visits being reported as being less important than previous ones. Of Lady Thatcher's trip to Japan in 1992, the British ambassador wrote that her profile 'has somewhat diminished, inevitably, with the passage of time'. He said, 'It was harder than in former years to get top politicians to dinner.'[143] Of her visit to the United Arab Emirates in 1992, the British ambassador in Dubai noted, 'Mrs Thatcher's popularity here remains undiminished, though there was inevitably a feeling that this was a farewell visit.'[144]

That said, even if Lady Thatcher appeared to some to be making such trips, they were just part of what this author described to Gyles Brandreth in 2001 as 'a never-ending farewell tour'.[145] She was never not in demand during the 1990s.

In addition, Sir Julian Seymour noted Lady Thatcher's continuing ability to command meetings with significant figures, both political and economic. He recalled Sir Leonard Appleyard, the British ambassador to China, commenting that only American Presidents could see three members of the Politburo Standing Committee on the same day. On one of her post-prime ministerial visits to China, Lady Thatcher did the same thing. Of one engagement on her 1994 trip to Brazil, Seymour recalled a business figure commenting, 'Sixty per cent of Brazil's GDP is in this room.'[146]

Beyond that, as was the case in the UK, Lady Thatcher's engagement with today's 'non-top politicians' – those who typically become tomorrow's 'top politicians' – also helped to ensure her continuing influence in the medium to longer term.

The practical difference that Lady Thatcher made should also not be underestimated. FCO files detail numerous occasions on which ministers, FCO officials, ambassadors and high commissioners make suggestions about issues she could raise, both commercial and non-commercial, with the people she was meeting. Courtesy alone surely did not dictate this. Ministers and officials must have thought that Lady Thatcher could make a positive difference. Otherwise, why would they ask her to do something, with all the attendant work and risk it involved? Indeed, in the British Embassy note cited above, which described Lady Thatcher as 'a major asset to Britain ... to whom it is in our interest to give help', they added, 'As a former Prime Minister of 11 1/2 years standing, she is entitled to it.'[147]

It should be noted, too, that it was not just figures in the UK who wished Lady Thatcher to intervene on issues. A file in the National Archives reveals that Nelson Mandela hoped to meet Lady Thatcher during her 1991 visit to South Africa. Sir Robin Renwick, the British ambassador, recorded Mandela asking if Lady Thatcher was going to see Dr Andries Treurnicht, the Leader of the Opposition. 'Pressure needed to be put on the right wing parties to join in negotiations.'[148] As it happened, Mandela was not able to meet Lady Thatcher when she visited. He was 'very embarrassed' about this, not having felt able to overrule the ANC's youth wing, which opposed the meeting. 'Fully aware' of the 'considerable personal debt' he owed Lady Thatcher, Mandela asked Renwick to arrange 'a long telephone conversation' for him with Lady Thatcher.[149] In 1994, a merchant in Abu Dhabi told an official from the British Embassy 'it was good that her meeting with Zayed had lasted for three hours, since few of Zayed's advisers could be relied upon to speak frankly to him.'[150]

In addition, whatever difference Lady Thatcher did or did not make politically, commercially she certainly did. Naturally, the latter was always easier to achieve, and to acknowledge, than the former. It did not carry political risk, open Lady Thatcher to the charge of being a 'back-seat driver' or threaten the government with being overshadowed by her on an issue of policy.

Sir Julian Seymour commented that outside of America, one third of the time Lady Thatcher spent in each place was devoted to British interest engagements. He also revealed that she would support British commercial companies provided they were not competing with other British companies.[151]

In 1992, Lady Thatcher helped BP secure a contract in Azerbaijan. Asked by the UK government and BP to do so, she stopped over in the country to fulfil President Abulfaz Elchibey's request that she witness the deal's signing.[152] Moore wrote of her being 'smuggled in … much to the dismay of BP's rivals'.[153] FCO files also reveal that following Lady Thatcher's use of Jaguars during a visit to Taiwan in 1992, there was a consequent dramatic rise in sales.[154]

The FCO suggested to posts in the places Lady Thatcher visited in South East Asia in September 1993, 'Your local distributors might think of following suit.'[155] In thanking Lady Thatcher for what she had said about the attractiveness of Britain for Korean investment in late 1991, the British ambassador told her he was 'particularly grateful': 'We will now be trying to use your comments more widely,' he added.[156]

There was also the 'publicity for UK PLC'[157] that Lady Thatcher generated. In 1991, the Governor of Hong Kong noted her visit to 'Japan, China and Hong Kong generated considerable media interest.'[158] Her 1992 visit to Fukui, a Japanese prefecture, 'achieved considerable publicity for the UK'.[159] In 1992, the British ambassador to Abu Dhabi recorded that 'her famous presence certainly gave us a lot of publicity'.[160] Of her visit to South Korea, the British ambassador said it had 'undoubtedly redounded to Britain's credit. It gave the UK a good deal of high-level and high-quality exposure.'[161]

Lady Thatcher's visits could add to other countries' standing too, not just the UK's. Of an invitation for her to visit Panama, the British ambassador, Thomas Malcomson, said it would 'help to boost Panama's own standing both regionally and internationally'.[162]

There was also the impact of these visits on Lady Thatcher herself. Not only did they enable her to make a living, but Sir Julian Seymour noted the pleasure her travels to America and Asia gave her. He noted particularly how she enjoyed meeting businesspeople on the ground on the tours sponsored by Citibank because 'they told her straight what was going on'. Seymour reflected on how Lady Thatcher both 'loved the applause' and was 'fascinated' by the places she visited and the people she met. As for the latter, Seymour reflected that 'curiosity and respect' got some of them to the events, and meeting her gave them both 'prestige' and 'huge face'.[163]

The continuing symbolic difference that Lady Thatcher made after 1990, both in her siren years up to 2002, then in her symbol years up to 2013, should also be noted. Lady Thatcher alluded to this in *The Path to Power*. Reflecting on her speeches abroad, she wrote, 'What I really enjoyed and found intellectually bracing was when I was received not just for the office I had held – or even what others considered I had achieved – but for what in some more general sense I "represented".'[164]

What the FCO files reveal perhaps most clearly is Lady Thatcher never being without honour in the countries she visited, however much she was without honour in the UK in the early to mid-1990s. Sometimes Lady Thatcher was multiply honoured in the places she visited. Reporting on her 1994 UAE visit, the British Embassy noted a 'slight hitch' when she visited Abu Dhabi. Plans to present Lady Thatcher with an honorary medal were 'swiftly scrapped when it was realised that she had received the same award on her last visit!'[165]

More seriously, it is also arguable that what emerged as Lady Thatcher's legacy after 1990 – the Margaret Thatcher persona against which those who followed her have all been, and continue to be, measured – was divined abroad before it was at home. What is clear from her philosophy work is that all over the globe Margaret Thatcher shone bright, both as a person and a persona. Arguably, the latter shone brighter and earlier than it did in Britain. First exported to the rest of the world after 1990, when this version of Margaret Thatcher was eventually imported back into the UK, it came with Lady Thatcher's mythical status largely accepted.

There is a wider point, too, about Lady Thatcher's nuanced approach to her role as a former Prime Minister. Throughout almost the entire period that the FCO files cover, 1991 to 1994, Lady

Thatcher was critical of government policy, increasingly so on both the European Union and the former Yugoslavia. That never seemed to stop her 'batting for Britain' commercially. It did not always stop her promoting Britain's political interests either, even if on occasion it did, such as will be seen in Malaysia in September 1993.

Files in the National Archives also tell us more about Margaret Thatcher the person. When a contribution from Hyundai to the Thatcher Foundation came up during her South Korea visit, the British ambassador reported that its founder, Chung Ju-yung, simply asked Lady Thatcher 'to name a figure'. The ambassador recorded, 'For once, I think she was nonplussed and short of an answer.'[166] Illustrating her workaholic nature, when Lady Thatcher headed to South Korea, she had a less than two-hour stopover in Tokyo. Still, she wanted to speak to someone about developments in Japan. The FCO therefore telegrammed the British Embassy saying, 'We appreciate that it may not be convenient on a Sunday morning, but would you, or a senior member of the Embassy, be able to be at the airport to do this?'[167] Another FCO telegram revealed that Lady Thatcher preferred to avoid red meat, enjoyed chicken and fish, and liked 'anything to do with chocolate'.[168]

Telegrams, memos and letters include vivid examples of Lady Thatcher's personality in action and its effect on other people. Giving a nod to the regal way in which Lady Thatcher sometimes acted, and was often perceived and treated after 1990, when referring to Lady Thatcher's assistant, Cynthia Crawford, one FCO telegram includes the line 'quote lady in waiting unquote'.[169] There are also examples of officials anticipating how Lady Thatcher might react to issues. The letter to Julian Seymour of May 1993 from the High Commission in Kuala Lumpur advises him that the likely venue for a dinner with the Malaysian Prime Minister was the 'Carcosa

Sri Negara (the former residence of British High Commissioners: now a luxury government-run hotel).' On the letter, someone has underlined 'the <u>former residence of British High Commissioners</u>' and written in the margin, 'I hope they don't tell Lady T that!'[170]

As in all areas of her work after Downing Street, Lady Thatcher being 'a major asset to Britain' also saw her playing the character that was Margaret Thatcher. During an event in South Korea, there was an 'uncontrolled invasion of the stage by photographers'. Perfectly capturing both Margaret Thatcher the person and Margaret Thatcher the persona, the ambassador revealed what happened next: 'In this particular instance, she characteristically interrupted the proceedings, ignored ineffectual university officials and police, and herself marshalled the press into appropriate positions before resuming.'[171]

Chapter Five

Party

The second area of Lady Thatcher's work is party, which involved her roles as a 'missile with a handbag' (in Conservative Party leadership elections), a 'genie, in gorgeous, opalescent peacock blue' (at party conferences) and a 'warrior queen' (during general election campaigns), as well as her relationships with Sir Edward Heath and Sir John Major.

'Missile with a handbag': leadership elections

In 2003, William Hague wrote a review of John Campbell's *Margaret Thatcher, Volume Two: The Iron Lady*. Headlined 'Missile with a handbag', it opened with Hague's perspective on Lady Thatcher's support for him in the 1997 Conservative leadership election.[1]

After leaving Downing Street, Lady Thatcher played a key role in the 1995, 1997 and 2001 leadership elections, and a symbolic role in the 2005 leadership election.

Lady Thatcher was in America when news broke that John Redwood was challenging John Major in the 1995 leadership election. Asked for her response, Lady Thatcher commented, in character as Margaret Thatcher, 'Both candidates are sound Conservatives.' This was met with laughter. 'Next question,' she continued – cue more laughter.[2]

As Charles Moore argues, while the obvious question was whether Lady Thatcher would back Redwood, the almost equally obvious answer was that she could not. Julian Seymour strongly advised her that to do so would cross a Rubicon.[3] Harris recalls Major's campaign manager 'plaintively pleading for Lady Thatcher's public endorsement'.[4] This she did, issuing a statement saying she supported John Major and would vote for him if she were still an MP. She concluded, 'I hope that the matter will be resolved by a ringing endorsement of the Prime Minister as soon as possible.'[5] Despite this, years later Major had no memory of Lady Thatcher's support, saying, 'On no occasion when I was in difficulties can I recall her coming out to help … I don't think I ever knew that she supported me against Redwood.'[6]

After John Major's resignation in 1997, the *Sunday Telegraph* reported the seeking of Lady Thatcher's support as being the 'second cut-throat contest' in the leadership election. It noted that none of the leadership camps were trying to claim Major's backing.[7]

While initially favouring Michael Howard, Lady Thatcher had no intention of becoming involved and was reluctant to do so.[8] The pact between Ken Clarke and John Redwood was sufficient to have 'the Iron Lady firing up her handbag', in the words of Jo-Anne Nadler.[9] Lady Thatcher said they had formed an 'incredible alliance of opposites that can only lead to further grief'.[10]

It was not only the Iron Lady's handbag that was fired up. So was Lady Thatcher herself. She deployed her handbag and herself to dramatic effect. First, in what Charles Moore described as 'a cameo' outside the Commons with William Hague.[11] In reality, Lady Thatcher was not a cameo person. As Robin Harris said, 'The performance dominated the headlines.'[12] For John Campbell, the photocall was 'excruciating',[13] with Robert Shrimsley writing of her intoning Hague's name.[14] Matthew Parris noted that Lady Thatcher was 'the only non-royal woman in Britain whom it is unnecessary to name: it is sufficient to mention the blue suit, the coiffure and the handbag'.[15]

Hague then took the 'Ultimate Weapon'[16] to the Commons' tea room. Demonstrating Lady Thatcher's ability to generate a strong, almost exaggerated and sometimes theatrical, reaction in others, Hague recalled that he felt as though he was 'taking a cruise missile to a clay pigeon shoot'. He noted that while Lady Thatcher stood in the queue so she could talk to the staff, longer-serving Conservative MPs 'straightened up' in their seats or 'scrambled for the exit'. Newer Labour MPs 'looked on with awe', never having seen her before. Surveying the scene, Ken Livingstone told Teresa Gorman that 'a great presence' had arrived.[17] 'The handbag is back,' commented one Labour MP, while a Conservative stated, 'They have unleashed the V1.'[18] Hague later reflected, 'No one else would have been greeted that day in the tea room with the reverence due to the Queen and the Duke of Wellington put together.'[19]

As in 1997, Lady Thatcher hoped to stay out of the 2001 contest even though she privately favoured Iain Duncan Smith.[20] She was effectively forced to intervene.

On 15 July, two days before the third ballot, the *Sunday Telegraph* reported that Lady Thatcher supported Michael Portillo.[21] Her office had denied the story before it was published.[22] Andrew Pierce wrote that its publication was 'the fatal blow', leading to an 'explosion from the Thatcher headquarters'.[23] Lady Thatcher issued a statement saying the story was wrong, and that she was not backing Portillo against Duncan Smith.

Before the final ballot, on 21 August Lady Thatcher wrote to the *Daily Telegraph* expressing support for Duncan Smith. She said he was 'a fitting spokesman for a new generation of Tories'. She also commented, 'Oscar Wilde once wrote that "experience is the name everyone gives to their mistakes". It would have been reassuring to hear from Ken Clarke about some of the mistakes which in 1997 led the Conservative Party to the greatest defeat in its history. After all, he – not Iain Duncan Smith – was one of those who made them.'[24]

The *Daily Mail*, supporting Clarke, criticised Lady Thatcher. It said her intervention was ill-advised and arguably counter-productive: 'We have, after all, been here before. Let it not be forgotten that she intimated that Mr Major was her favoured successor. Look what happened. The Lady anointed William Hague. The result speaks for itself.'[25]

Moore writes that when David Cameron was elected leader in 2005, Lady Thatcher 'played no part'.[26] In reality, she did play a part symbolically. At the time, Nick Assinder wrote that it was often claimed that 'no Tory candidate will get a look in with the grassroots party unless they pay due respect to her political memory'. He argued this explained why the candidates mentioned her name or invoked her memory during their campaigns.[27] Cameron later reflected that the other candidates 'had been very closely linked to her and her ideology'.[28]

Reflections

In his interview with Lord Carrington for *Maggie: Her Fatal Legacy*, John Sergeant asked him how much influence Lady Thatcher had had on the leadership elections after 1990. Lord Carrington replied, 'She intervened in all of them, and always with disastrous results.'[29]

While Lady Thatcher may have favoured ABC (anyone but Clarke) in both 1997 and 2001, her candidates won, even if the Conservatives went on to lose the next election. It is also important to recognise that the composition of the parliamentary party had been changing since 1992, becoming ever more Eurosceptic. In those circumstances, it is worth reflecting on whether a Ken Clarke victory in 1997 or 2001 would have restored party unity and enhanced the prospects of the Conservatives winning the 2001 and 2005 general elections.

Beyond the leadership elections in Lady Thatcher's lifetime, she has also featured in ones after her death, as will be seen. This included in the 2024 leadership election. As the editor of ConservativeHome, Giles Dilnot, observed in September 2024 when reflecting on Sir Keir Starmer moving Lady Thatcher's portrait in No. 10, 'Her presence beyond portraiture, both politically and historically, can always be felt when the Conservative party enters the lists of another leadership contest.'[30]

At an early stage of that year's leadership election, both Priti Patel and Robert Jenrick named Lady Thatcher as one of their political heroes,[31] and Mel Stride said she was one of the people in politics he most admired.[32] Jenrick later revealed that his daughter's middle name is 'Thatcher'.[33] In one campaign speech, Tom Tugendhat commented, 'We need a new conservative revolution. That's what Margaret Thatcher did, that's what we need to do again and we can do it.'[34] In his speech to the Conservative Party conference, James Cleverly referenced Lady Thatcher three times.[35] As for the eventual winner, Kemi Badenoch, Andrew Roberts wrote that he could 'spot echoes and cadences' of Lady Thatcher in her.[36] Michael Forsyth said that in Badenoch he saw 'some of the qualities' that had enabled Lady Thatcher to change both the Conservative Party and the UK.[37] In her first message to party members, Badenoch said she promised 'to follow the lead of the two leaders who got us back into power: Margaret Thatcher and David Cameron'.[38]

'A genie, in gorgeous, opalescent peacock blue': party conferences

Writing about the 1999 Conservative Party conference, Boris Johnson said Lady Thatcher 'seemed to hover above the scene ... like a genie, in gorgeous, opalescent peacock blue'.[39]

Between 1991 and 2000, Lady Thatcher was a staple feature of party conferences, often overshadowing – or upstaging – them. Her appearances generated extensive coverage, and she seemed never to be far from the centre of controversy. Sometimes this had negative political consequences for the Conservative leadership. Indeed, in October 1999, a former Labour Cabinet minister, Lord Shore of Stepney, commented to the present author, 'In terms of your study, the behaviour of ex-prime ministers at the recent Conservative Party conference provides, or should provide, you with rich material.'

Such material was also produced in 1991, Lady Thatcher's first attendance at conference since resigning. In *Breaking the Code*, Gyles Brandreth wrote of the response to her appearance: 'Moment of the week: on Wednesday, when Mrs T. arrived on the platform and pandemonium broke out. She didn't say anything: she just *was* and for five minutes we stood and clapped and stamped our feet and roared. Even Michèle was cheering. There were tears in the eyes. You couldn't not be moved. It was wonderful.'[40]

Not everyone felt the same. Edwina Currie was 'appalled at the long queues waiting to get into Conference ... for Mrs T'.[41]

Moore wrote that the ovation only stopped when the session chairman announced that Lady Thatcher had asked everyone to sit down. Moore stated that this may not in fact have been the case. He also noted that the conference's response to Lady Thatcher was 'annoying for Major and his team'.[42] Earlier, Moore had written that according to eyewitnesses, the party chairman, Chris Patten, had been seen 'interposing his foot so that Mrs Thatcher could not push her chair back to stand up and start talking'.[43]

Her appearance in 1992 also caused annoyance. On 8 October, Lord Whitelaw wrote an article in the *Daily Mail* under the headline, 'Don't wreck our party, Margaret'.[44] This conference might be deemed 'the battle of the articles', for Lady Thatcher also had one published during it.

Presciently, given what was to come, John Major wrote to Chris Patten, then Governor of Hong Kong, on 7 October congratulating him on a speech he had made that day. During the speech, Patten announced electoral reforms which, as will be seen, Lady Thatcher strongly supported. In his letter, Major commented to Patten, 'I am not sure which is worse – the Party Conference here or the one in Peking. Either way, I suspect we are in for a rough ride over the next few weeks, but I am sure we will ride the storm.'[45]

Lady Thatcher contributed to that rough ride. She had agreed with the party chairman, Norman Fowler, that she would appear but not say anything. Having arrived at the conference, Lady Thatcher twice turned down the chance to speak, saying to Fowler, 'It would be quite inappropriate.' As part of 'the Thatcher manoeuvre',[46] she appeared on stage. Andrew Rawnsley noted, 'The brief encounter on the platform between the Prime Minister and the Leader of the Disloyal Opposition was the most touching display of genuine affection since Judas planted one on Jesus.'[47]

Lady Thatcher also did more. Anthony Seldon commented, 'Thatcher was a prima donna not susceptible to *sotto voce* stage management. Silent in speech, yes, but not in print.'[48] Lady Thatcher had written an article for *The European* criticising Maastricht. Its publication was timed for her arrival at the conference on 8 October. The article featured a photograph, taken very shortly before, of

King Juan Carlos of Spain kissing Lady Thatcher's hand. He seems to be bowing to her as he does so.

Someone close to Lady Thatcher said, 'We knew it was dynamite.' The conference organisers had not been consulted and were 'furious at her obedience to the letter, but breach of the spirit, of the deal'. The Major camp regarded it as 'a declaration of war'.[49] Major later wrote that the article, which was published on the eve of his speech, was 'perfectly timed to inflame opinion and play to the Euro-sceptic gallery'.[50]

The media lapped it up. The *Daily Mail* said Lady Thatcher was 'the most shameless of show-stealers'.[51] Martin Kettle spoke of a 'week of remorseless melodrama', noting Lady Thatcher's 'disproportionate ability to call attention to herself'.[52] *Private Eye*'s 9 October cover, 'Tory conference show of unity', featured a photograph of John Major shaking Lady Thatcher's hand. Major says, 'Hello Margaret'; Lady Thatcher replies, 'Goodbye John'.[53]

Melodramatic might also be how best to describe Lady Thatcher's visit to the 1993 conference. Robert Hardman wrote that she 'swept into Blackpool … for 24 hours of mayhem among the faithful'.[54] Hardman reported on a reception she attended. During it, she declared, 'The battle is never over. Socialism can return by many routes.' Someone interjected, 'Ted Heath!' Lady Thatcher responded, 'Point taken.'

Just before the conference, extracts from Lady Thatcher's forthcoming memoirs were leaked to the *Daily Mirror*. The memoirs were critical of Lady Thatcher's former colleagues, including Major, and so caused considerable controversy, overshadowing the conference.

As if to limit the potential damage, Lady Thatcher issued a statement supporting Major. She said she had voted for him in 1990, would do the same today, and that she continued to support him.[55]

Lady Thatcher was equally supportive in private. Philip Webster reported her as being 'fulsomely loyal to Mr Major at her private lunch and was clearly anxious that the word should go out to her supporters in the conference'.[56] Seldon concluded that the potential damage to Major was 'largely neutralised by Thatcher's unusually pro-Major comments in Blackpool'.[57] On 8 October, *Private Eye*'s cover was headed, 'Conference unity special'. It featured Lady Thatcher on the telephone. From it, a speech bubble reads, 'It's time to make things up'. From Lady Thatcher's mouth, the speech bubble reads, 'All right, John, I'll say I support you'.[58]

Asked later that month if Thatcherism was alive and well in No. 10, Lady Thatcher replied, 'I believe Thatcherism is alive and well and I believe that that was confirmed very much by the Prime Minister's speech at the party conference. We're back to the same fundamental principles that influenced my policies.'[59]

Lady Thatcher also featured prominently at the 1994 conference, not for the happiest of reasons. Of her arrival, Matthew Parris wrote, 'Up she came, like Aphrodite from the sea, or a monster from the deep, depending on your viewpoint.' His article was entitled 'Majestic vision from the deep sails serenely through media storm'.[60]

Lady Thatcher's attendance, and indeed the conference itself, was overshadowed by two things. First, claims that Mark Thatcher had made £12 million from a British-Saudi arms deal. Lady Thatcher was said to be 'heartbroken'.[61] Second, her appearance. On 12 October, Gyles Brandreth recorded in his diary, 'I saw Margaret Thatcher. She looks quite terrible: gaunt, pale, shrunken. She's lost at least a stone, and the mad glint in her eye had gone. She just looked sad.'[62] Dr Thomas Stuttaford wrote an article, 'A weight on Tory minds', about her health.[63]

Highlighting her continuing presence in the cultural life of the

UK, some years later, the National Portrait Gallery published a post-card of Lady Thatcher sitting alongside members of the Cabinet at the conference. It was part of a series, 'Iconic women (captured by Reuters photographers) in the press'. She looks almost ghostly.

In 1995, her seventieth birthday year, her attendance seemed to be a happier experience. Matthew Parris said that Lady Thatcher's arrival was 'moving and no longer divisive'. In wishing her a happy birthday, Parris continued, 'Oh, and we really do miss you. Sketch-writing isn't half difficult since you went.'[64]

John Sergeant wrote that Lady Thatcher's 'brief visit was better managed than usual'. Brian Mawhinney, the party chairman, carried out 'elaborate negotiations'. He would accompany Lady Thatcher onto the platform, at which point the audience would applaud her. Mawhinney would then go to collect the Prime Minister. When he appeared on stage, both he and Mawhinney would kiss Lady Thatcher on the cheek once. The trio would then receive a standing ovation. Everything seemed to go to plan, but, as Sergeant noted, it was 'somewhat marred' by footage he used of Michael Heseltine's and Leon Brittan's 'very slow handclapping'.[65]

Kissing also featured at the 1996 conference, both physically and seemingly symbolically, there being a sense of 'kiss and make up' about it, at least in terms of Lady Thatcher's relationship with John Major. Before the conference, Lady Thatcher agreed to put out a statement supporting him. Seldon wrote this was 'rendered all the more necessary' as *The Times* was serialising the diary of one of Lady Thatcher's former foreign policy advisers, George Urban,[66] which revealed her very early disillusion with Major.

Upon arrival, Lady Thatcher made clear her determination to be Major's 'new Stealth bomber'.[67] Sergeant says that Lady Thatcher 'beamed' at Major when he appeared the platform. She gestured to him to sit next to her, 'patting the seat beside her to make the point'. Major did so with 'as much grace as he could muster'.[68] Her appearance on the platform, greeted by Major with a kiss, led to 'wild cheers from delegates'.[69]

As she toured the conference stands, someone called out to Lady Thatcher, 'I've always wanted to meet your handbag.' She replied, 'Well, don't worry, I'm still swinging it.'[70] Lady Thatcher and Major appeared together at a reception and, according to Seldon, 'She had taken great trouble over her speech, and had accepted that it should be unequivocally emollient.'[71] Lady Thatcher commented, 'It has never been more important to see the Conservatives returned to office – and you to Downing Street.'[72] *The Times* reported, 'Back Major, Thatcher tells Tories';[73] *The Daily Telegraph* ran with 'Get cracking, says Thatcher'.[74]

At the 1997 conference, Lady Thatcher was in full Margaret Thatcher character, with her attendance perhaps being best remembered for her performance at the British Airways stand.

Seeing the design of the company's new tail fins, in full view of the cameras, Lady Thatcher declared, 'absolutely terrible': 'We fly the British flag, not these awful things,' she went on.[75] Retrieving a handkerchief from her handbag, she covered the tail fin with it. She then left the stall, but not before giving the British Airways staff what Elizabeth Buchanan has described as 'The Thatcherite Stare'[76] along with one final instruction: 'Tape it up!'

Judgements of this incident vary, although they may all in fact be true. For Moore, it was 'a late example of her subversive flair for a visual message'.[77] For Harris, it was 'characteristic play-acting, with a large element of self-mockery'.[78] Campbell put it in a wider context: 'Altogether she was increasingly seen as a batty old eccentric, a caricature of her former self, who won most headlines when she played up to her image – as when she descended on the British Airways stand'. He concluded it was 'an elaborate pantomime'.[79]

There were showbusiness overtones to her visit to the 1998 conference too, not least because it saw a headline-grabbing appearance on stage with Edward Heath. Both were seated in IKEA chairs, 'within spitting range' of each other.[80] Michael Brown's story on this was headlined 'Buddha and the grandmother face it out at the funeral'.[81] Lady Thatcher and Heath were captured both looking at their watches at the same moment. *Private Eye*'s cover on 16 October used this photograph with the headline, 'Hague speech lifts Tories'. A joint speech bubble coming out of the former prime ministers' mouths reads, 'He's even worse than you'.[82]

Prior to appearing on the platform together, Lady Thatcher and Heath had spoken to each other backstage. Writing in *The Guardian*, Ewen MacAskill noted that this 'did not exactly amount to detente, but at least words were exchanged'.[83] Michael McManus, Heath's former political secretary, gives the background. Before arriving at the conference centre, Heath was in 'a most dyspeptic and disagreeable mood', speaking of 'those silly, bloody, damned-fool chairs'. When Lady Thatcher greeted Heath, she asked him, 'What ever do you think of those *ghastly* chairs?' Heath 'paused for a moment and, with an entirely straight face, shrugged his shoulders and answered, "Oh, I rather like them."' McManus noted Lady Thatcher being 'deflated' and 'a twinkle' in Heath's eye.[84] That said, in November 1998, Heath was asked what he thought of Lady Thatcher now. He replied, 'our only recent exchange was about the IKEA chairs on the platform at the party conference. We were in broad agreement about them!'[85]

Agreement was hardly a word that could be used about her attendance at the 1999 conference, with the *Daily Telegraph* reporting that from the moment of Lady Thatcher's arrival at the conference, she had been 'setting the agenda'.[86] William Hague was said to have told the shadow Cabinet to write Wednesday off as 'Thatcher's day'.[87] Perhaps in what turned out to be a doomed attempt to keep Thatcher's day to just one day, at one event the 'salsa band was told to continue playing throughout so that none of her remarks could be recorded by the microphones'.[88]

On the Monday, a *Daily Telegraph* article by Lady Thatcher attacked Tony Blair, saying his speech to the Labour conference was 'a hymn of hate against conservatism'. She said she was 'distrustful' of Blair's stewardship and described his comments that he accepted the reforms of the 1980s as 'one of the most shameless confidence tricks in British political history'.[89] Lady Thatcher was said to have 'grown disenchanted' with Blair's policies on Europe and Northern Ireland.[90] On the Tuesday, she launched an 'impromptu attack on continental Europe'.[91] On the Wednesday, she delivered a speech about General Pinochet.

Following the conference, the *Sunday Times* reported Lady Thatcher having 'emerged from her triumphant visit to Blackpool as the party's president-emeritus in all but name'.[92]

If Lady Thatcher had been on the attack at the conference, she was under it afterwards. So was the party leadership. The criticism came from John Major. In an interview to promote his memoirs, Major described Lady Thatcher's comment that only problems came out of mainland Europe as 'a crazy concept'. He also expressed surprise that the shadow Chancellor, Francis Maude, had credited the 'golden [economic] legacy' to Lady Thatcher, making no mention of the 1990–97 government. Noting the 'divided inheritance – the poll tax and a recession' he had received, Major said, 'If the Conservative party wish to say they left a golden economic legacy, which they do, they have got to acknowledge where that golden economic legacy came from – and it came from 1990–1997.'[93]

Fittingly, perhaps, given it was the last time she attended a party conference, Matthew Parris' sketch of Lady Thatcher's arrival was on the front page of *The Times* in October 2000 and it perfectly captured the reaction Lady Thatcher could generate in others almost ten years after leaving Downing Street. 'The world had been told to expect her at 09.15,' Parris recorded. 'By half past eight the crash-barriers were in place and world-class commentators, TV presenters, serious political analysts – grown men who have written books – were clinging to stairs and parapets in hopes of a better view. And this was just to see her arrive!' Parris noted Hague tried to shepherd Lady Thatcher inside the venue before she could open her mouth, knowing that, as Lord St John of Fawsley said, 'the danger when Margaret speaks without thinking is that she says what she thinks'.[94]

In a story headlined 'Two pensioners try to rewrite history', *The Times* detailed a clash over pensions policy between Lady Thatcher and Baroness Castle. The baronesses were described as 'the two *grandes dames* of British politics'.[95] Lady Castle accused Lady Thatcher of having a 'damn nerve' when the latter declared government changes to pensions policy to be 'outright fraud'. When William Hague described Lady Thatcher as one of the greatest prime ministers of all time, 'the audience erupted in loud cheers and applause.' Her ninety-second standing ovation was reportedly twenty seconds longer than John Major's.

Reflections
This drew Lady Thatcher's conference appearances, if not to say

performances, to a close. In September 2001, it was reported she would not be attending that year's conference.[96]

Whatever else may be said of them, they had been a boon for sketch writers. They had also demonstrated Lady Thatcher's continuing ability to command headlines, and to make the political weather, even if only to cause a storm. Sometimes they had political implications for her successors. Throughout, the character that was Margaret Thatcher had been performed.

'Warrior queen': general elections

In April 1997, Dominic Kennedy wrote an article about Lady Thatcher's role in that year's general election. It was headlined 'Warrior queen raises ancient battle standard'.[97]

In the 1992, 1997 and 2001 general elections, Lady Thatcher campaigned vigorously on behalf of the Conservative Party. She did so in typical style and full Margaret Thatcher persona. As Sir Denis Thatcher said in 2001, 'She loves it. Brings it all back.'[98]

Certain themes run through her campaigning in these three elections. First, Lady Thatcher's tendency to stretch, if not go completely off, the Conservatives' policy messages, although she probably thought it was more the case that the Conservatives had gone off *her* message. Second, her stretching of the conduct of the campaign, with unfavourable comparisons being made between her and other political actors. Third, perhaps above all, there was her performance of the character that was Margaret Thatcher, people's reaction to that, and how the press reported it.

Initially, John Major had not been inclined for Lady Thatcher to have a role in the 1992 election.[99] In the end, however, it was decided she would. How she might get involved was the subject of a letter from the then Conservative Party chairman, Chris Patten, to John Major's private secretary, Judith Chaplin, on 5 February 1992. This was ahead of the Prime Minister's meeting with his predecessor the next day. The letter sets out Conservative Central Office's suggestions for what Lady Thatcher might do during the election.[100]

Central Office was very keen to have Lady Thatcher speak at the Candidates' Conference. This she did.[101] She gave 'a passionate and emotional address', 'repeatedly interrupted by cheers, deafening applause and laughter'.[102] When Major went up to speak after her, 'the unspoken murmur in every mind was "Follow that"'.[103]

Patten's note also said Central Office would be happy to provide any support Lady Thatcher would like for her election tour. This involved twenty-nine constituencies in eight days.[104] It excited significant media attention, Craig Brown writing of '50 or so press and cameramen following Margaret Thatcher's every move'. He reflected, 'This might be half the number that followed her at the last election, but it is still 10 times the number the average cabinet minister would ever hope to attract.' When Brown asked the press why they were there, the response that came up most often was 'just in case'.[105] Valerie Elliott wrote of 'an air of expectation at every venue – will it be here that she rubbishes the Major campaign? Will she now criticise the policy U-turns?'[106]

While Lady Thatcher did not go seriously 'off message', she did stretch it in terms of content. Asked if the manifesto preserved her legacy, she replied, 'Yes. The main thrust of my policy is in it, even if I don't agree with all of the details.'[107] Stories headlined 'Save my legacy says Thatcher',[108] 'Thatcher hints Major gutless on tax gap'[109] and 'Thatcher hints at a new Tory fight over Europe'[110] appeared.

Lady Thatcher also stretched the campaign's conduct. The *Sunday Times* quoted her saying privately that the campaign 'did not have enough oomph, enough whizz, enough steam'.[111] Lady Thatcher provided these in almost industrial quantities herself. Bernard Jenkin recalled her campaigning for John Whittingdale when 'a junior reporter from the *Essex County Standard* breathlessly caught up with her hectic pace and asked, in front of 200 other journalists, "Do you agree that the Conservative campaign is lacking in oomph?" Mrs T retorted, with heavy irony, "That's what I'm here for, dear."' Whittingdale noted, 'The pavements had crowds four or five deep of people who had turned out to see her.' He went on, 'Not all were supporters of hers or of mine, but they wanted to be there because they recognised that she played such a hugely important role in their lives and the life of their country.'[112]

Coverage played to the character that was Margaret Thatcher and its ability to generate (generally exaggerated) reactions in others. *The Sun* spoke of 'Maggie Mania', noting the 'Fan-tastic welcome takes her 20 minutes to walk 100 yards'. Asked if she would take part in a live TV debate with Neil Kinnock, Lady Thatcher replied, 'I would prefer to have a cross-examination by an interviewer for four hours on my own so I could really get the message across.'[113] The *Daily Star* reported four people being knocked over 'by a stampeding mob when Mrs Thatcher went on an election walkabout', adding, 'She was almost crushed by the 1,000-strong crowd.'[114]

Such was the reaction Lady Thatcher generated, *The Sun* published a leader, 'Street wise'. Reflecting on the hundreds of shoppers who had mobbed Lady Thatcher on the streets, *The Sun* asked if it was 'Princess Diana on tour' or 'Madonna going walkabout'. Responding 'no' to each question, *The Sun* described Lady Thatcher as 'the centre of attraction'. It concluded, 'You haven't lost the magic, Maggie.'[115]

Naturally, the reaction was not all adulation. One woman hit

Lady Thatcher with some daffodils. The *Daily Mirror* headlined the story, 'Daffed!'[116] After one visit, 'a man ran after her car making a V-sign'.[117] Under the headline, 'Lady T proves she can still get your goat', Simon Hoggart recorded Socialist Workers at the Hampstead Conservative rooms yelling, 'Maggie, Maggie, Maggie! Out, out, out!' Perhaps presciently, Hoggart commented, 'There seems no reason why the anti-Thatcher demonstration should not remain part of our lives, long after she has departed public life or even died.'[118] Alastair Campbell reported a Conservative official saying, 'She means well. But sometimes she can be the best campaigner the Labour party has got.' The article was headlined 'Now what's that interfering old battleaxe up to?'[119]

To end with that note from Central Office. In what could have been one of the great missed opportunities of British political history, Central Office did not propose inviting Lady Thatcher to any of its press conferences.

As could be seen in the 1997 election, Lady Thatcher did not need to attend any official press conferences to generate coverage. She managed that on her own, including through being interviewed by Charles Powell.[120] 'Normandy Landings and Falklands War rolled into one' was how he described her, adding, 'She is plainly longing to be first on to the beaches.' Lady Thatcher spoke on the European Union, pension reform, inheritance tax and defence spending. Powell wrote, 'When it comes to passionate intensity and conviction … she still leaves the rest of the political establishment dead in the water.'

As in 1992, Lady Thatcher's election tour was a gift to sketch writers. Of a supermarket appearance, Matthew Parris wrote, 'Senior staff stood in line, as if for inspection. Several Tory women

swooned, one so excited that her knees gave way.' One person revealed, 'I named my Dobermann Margaret, after her.'[121]

Dealing with journalists, Lady Thatcher remained in character.
In Christchurch, she was asked if John Major should rule out a
single currency: 'I have said what I am going to say about that, I
hope you listened' was her response. In Aldershot, it was put to her
that Major had signed the Maastricht Agreement: 'Well, I voted
against the Maastricht Treaty,' she replied. 'Will you please now,
if you are able to, concentrate on the big issues. Why are you not
doing so?'[122]

Magnus Linklater, in an article headlined 'Irn Bru Lady drinks
in admiration of Scottish voters', noted Lady Thatcher's impact in
Scotland when campaigning for Michael Forsyth: 'To see a posse of
political reporters straining to detect what the former Prime Minister had to say about kitchen surfaces, whether she approved of
the Spice Girls, or understood the significance of Irn Bru, is to see
politics reduced to surrealism.' When asked about being called the
first Spice Girl, Lady Thatcher replied, 'I rather agree.' She added,
'Michael and I put as much spice into politics as the Spice Girls put
into singing.' Linklater reflected, 'Baroness Thatcher's processions
these days are more royal than political, except that you can get
closer to royalty.' He wrote of her being 'accorded something close
to respect, if not admiration', concluding, 'It's amazing what the
absence of power will do.'[123]

Lady Thatcher also campaigned with John Major in Stockton. It
was not a happy experience. Due to recording a new party election
broadcast on Europe, Major was delayed. Harris wrote that Lady
Thatcher saw this as 'unprofessional behaviour', describing it as 'an
insult to the people of the North'. Major was distracted when he

arrived, not looking out of the windows of the campaign bus. He ignored 'his predecessor's stern injunctions: "Voters to the left – wave! Voters to the right – wave!"'[124] Seldon reports Lady Thatcher saying, 'I do want to be helpful, John.' The atmosphere 'tangibly lightened' when she left.[125]

As for content, in his diary on 27 March, Gyles Brandreth wrote, 'Yesterday Mawhinney wheeled out Margaret Thatcher to bash Blair for toadying to the unions. She's clearly barking, but she's undeniably a superstar, and it was a *coup*, and it should have, and would have, led the news, and dominated the front pages, but for Tim Smith.'[126]

During this election, Lady Thatcher did go off message. Sergeant notes, 'For the last time while Mr Major was prime minister, Lady Thatcher publicly disagreed with party policy.'[127] Asked if Britain should join a single currency, she replied, 'Good heavens. No!' She went on, 'I was the one who invented the answer: "No. No. NO!"'[128] John Prescott, Deputy Leader of the Labour Party, responded, 'No sooner has John Major recruited Baroness Thatcher to his campaign than she adds to the deep-seated divisions in the Tory Party. She made it clear that, whatever he says, she says something different.'[129]

There was also a telling incident when she was being interviewed during a campaign stop in Dorset. Speaking to camera, Lady Thatcher commented, 'What is a matter of concern for the future is the major issues…' She interrupted her own flow with, 'I used the word major!' She momentarily turns to her left, seemingly having fluffed her lines. She's then straight back in character, continuing with the seemingly correct line: '…is the main issues'.[130]

Much that had happened in 1992 and 1997 was repeated in 2001, in what turned out to be the last election in which Lady Thatcher campaigned in any significant way, with Charles Moore writing,

'From Conservative Central Office's nervous point of view, if there was one thing worse than Margaret Thatcher intervening in the campaign, it was Margaret Thatcher not intervening.'[131] '[T]he Conservatives were desperate for Margaret Thatcher to play a significant part in the campaign,' Harris noted. 'But they were also wary. So were her staff, who understood that her capacity to contribute had diminished.'[132]

Nevertheless, campaign Lady Thatcher did. She did so in the usual style, in full Margaret Thatcher character, generating the usual response, anti- and pro-. Describing her as 'the old witch', Will Self said Socialist Alliance protesters had told him it was Lady Thatcher, not William Hague, they had come to shout at.[133] Brian Reade wrote of 'her maniacal face, now a cross between Barbara Cartland and Ace Ventura'.[134] In an article headlined 'A noise like Omaha Beach. "Out, out, out." But she is out', Simon Hoggart noted that 'an offending remark makes the eyes blaze like a panther with a coke habit'.[135] When Lady Thatcher visited a market in Northampton, one of the stallholders said, 'I'd have preferred a visit from Cliff Richard.'[136]

Simon Sebag Montefiore described Lady Thatcher as 'an undying political force', commenting that 'Gloriana Thatcher *is* Britain', and noting 'one strange and wonderful thing about all those who meet her: they bow, instinctively, out of respect'. 'What's it like to be a titan surrounded by political pygmies?', he asked her. 'I'm not a titan and they're not pygmies,' she replied. When questioned about Tony Blair, she responded, 'Let's not get personal.'[137] Matthew Parris also shared details of his conversation with Lady Thatcher: 'You seem to be attracting a lot of attention.' Lady Thatcher 'glared'. 'Are you surprised, Matthew?' Parris 'blushed'. 'You should be ashamed of yourself.' Someone said, 'And you should be Prime Minister.' Lady Thatcher leant over to Parris, 'Did you hear that, Michael [*sic*]?'[138]

An *Independent* leader, 'Out of tune', was thinking of the new generation. It opened with, 'She's back!' and spoke of 'a fresh generation of voters' being able to 'witness the Thatcher phenomenon at first hand'. *The Independent* concluded, 'Play it again Maggie.'[139]

Maggie certainly played it again on 22 May, when what was described as the 'Thatcher Intervention Moment' occurred.[140] The *Daily Mail* published an interview Lady Thatcher had given Simon Heffer. Headlined 'Blair is destroying my legacy by stealth', it proved controversial. Asked whether Blair had been a good Prime Minister, she replied, 'Well, he hasn't wholly carried on the Thatcher tradition.' Lady Thatcher's comments about a multi-cultural society caused the controversy: 'I want a society of opportunity for all, irrespective of colour or ethnic background. But I don't wish to have what they call a multi-cultural society.'[141] Michael Portillo reportedly told William Hague he must denounce her.[142]

Later that day, Lady Thatcher appeared with Hague at a rally in Plymouth. At the event, she made her famous 'The Mummy Returns' remark. Ben Macintyre spoke of 'a magnificent old battleship, no longer in service but still the pride of the Tory fleet' which had 'sailed into Plymouth last night to give aid to a small, beleaguered vessel in some danger of being swamped'.[143] Lady Thatcher was said to have 'elbowed her way into the centre of the general election' and to have gone 'on stage and off message'.[144]

In her speech, Lady Thatcher said, 'Mr Blair says he wants to "lead in Europe", but the price of that is that he's expected to lead Britain by the nose into the single currency. And he's prepared to do it! I would never be prepared to give up our own currency.'[145] This went beyond party policy, which was 'not in the next parliament'. A Garland cartoon in the *Daily Telegraph* on 24 May headlined

'Pearls Harbour' had Lady Thatcher in an aeroplane releasing a bomb called 'Never'.

Blair responded, 'It is time to draw a line under the era of Thatcher,' adding, 'Whatever the rights and wrongs of the 1980s, that era is over and done with, let's move on.'[146] Labour, however, did not move on from Lady Thatcher, publishing a set of posters depicting Hague as Lady Thatcher in a wig. This inspired a Peter Brookes cartoon in *The Times* on 31 May. Featuring Blair as Lady Thatcher, the speech bubble read, 'It takes one to know one'.

June opened with Lady Thatcher writing an article for the *Daily Telegraph* headlined 'Tony Blair is committed to the extinction of Britain'.[147] She also dismissed his comments about the 1980s. 'Most people have already moved beyond the Eighties, so they don't need telling, particularly as the Nineties have gone by too.'[148]

Having gone off message on policy, Lady Thatcher also went off message about the party leadership. Visiting Romford, she said she had no idea who would be leading the party at the next election. Reporting this, Damian Whitworth added, 'She certainly pulls a crowd, the size of which Blair and Hague might fantasise about in their most excited dreams.'[149]

Lady Thatcher did not just pull voters. Noting the volume of press following her, Simon Carr commented, 'The whole Shadow Cabinet would have to get into a truck and try to jump the Grand Canyon to get this sort of attention.'[150]

Reflections

Even though Lady Thatcher had retired from active political life by the time of the 2005 and 2010 elections, she played a role in them. In 2005, the *Evening Standard* reported that Conservative

Central Office had turned down her offer to put out a joint press release challenging Gordon Brown's claims she would be appalled by the Conservatives' economic plans.[151] She wrote a letter to the Stirling Conservative candidate, Stephen Kerr, arguing in favour of saving Scotland's regiments[152] and supported Andrew Rosindell in Romford, being photographed at the greyhound stadium with a dog called Tom's Euro. The *Daily Telegraph* wrote this up under the headline, 'Lady Thatcher declares her support for Euro'. As for policy, Lady Thatcher commented, 'I'm not going to start talking about the Budget, or I'll be here all day.'[153] In addition, she campaigned for Conor Burns in Eastleigh. She also supported various candidates in the 2010 election.

On occasion, Lady Thatcher actively chose not to take part in elections. She refused to campaign in the European Parliament elections in 1994. Describing her as a 'non-combatant', Norman Fowler recorded Lady Thatcher saying, 'I see your problems, Norman, and I don't envy you your job'.[154] Lady Thatcher then added, 'comfortingly' according to Fowler, 'I shall be voting, dear, and so will Denis.' Fowler found her refusal 'most difficult to take'.[155]

The wider impact of Lady Thatcher's post-prime ministerial electioneering is that, as with her attendances at party conferences, it highlighted her seemingly undiminished capacity to generate headlines, with political consequences for her successors as Conservative Party leader. Most of all, Lady Thatcher's appearances also provided a platform on which she could – and did – perform the character that was Margaret Thatcher at her most show-stopping and scene-stealing. Indeed, it is probably in the 1992, 1997 and 2001 elections that we see Lady Thatcher's peak performance of Margaret Thatcher in the UK – and the public's reaction to her and it.

'That would be difficult':
relationship with Sir Edward Heath

When Lady Thatcher resigned, Sir Edward Heath was said to have responded to the news with 'rejoice, rejoice'. Heath denied it, explaining, 'I didn't say "rejoice, rejoice", I said "rejoice, rejoice, rejoice"!'[156]

Throughout her premier emeritus years, the relationship between Lady Thatcher and Sir Edward continued to generate headlines. Sometimes this had political implications for John Major and his government; other times it provided 'national entertainment'. Occasionally, it did both.

Following speeches Lady Thatcher made in Chicago and New York in June 1991 criticising the European Union, Heath accused her of having a 'minute mind'. Speaking on Channel 4, Heath rejected comments she had made about the European Commission, describing them as 'blatant falsehoods, in ordinary English: lies'. He went on, 'She is also so ignorant.' He spoke of the inheritance she had bequeathed Major. 'She shows no appreciation of the ghastly legacy she has left her successor … She does not realise the situation which John Major is having to deal with. She does not realise she was the cause of it.'[157] A member of Lady Thatcher's entourage said Heath was an 'occupational hazard'.[158]

Following the Channel 4 interview, Heath wrote an article in the *Daily Mail* on 20 June. In another of the great 'what might have been' moments of British political history, Heath said, 'I will offer her a challenge. I propose a televised debate between us which would provide a context in which the question of Europe could be fully aired as she has demanded.'[159]

A *Times* leader on 19 June opened with, 'Poor John Major': Just when he hoped to have calmed down his party's argument over Europe,' it went on, 'his two predecessors lock horns in one of the most vituperative, and ideologically fundamental, arguments imaginable.' Saying that no one could claim the former prime ministers were 'fudging', it said that 'these great giants of Euro-debate' had left Major 'twiddling his thumbs'.[160] Alan Travis noted the impact on the Conservative Party: 'The spectacle of two former prime ministers ... engaged in what one former cabinet minister yesterday described as "an artillery duel conducted at long range" and others an "alley cat fight" shocked the Conservative Party to the core.'[161] The ex-premiers reminded Jonathan Hill, a member of Major's policy unit, 'of the two grannies in Laurie Lee's *Cider with Rosie*, kept alive by their loathing of each other.'[162]

This all played out in Parliament too. Lady Thatcher spoke in a House of Commons debate on the European Community on 26 June 1991. So did Heath. During his opening speech, the Foreign Secretary, Douglas Hurd, commented, 'There has been something unreal about some parts of the recent public debate.' He said he had 'felt sometimes like a soldier in one of those wars recounted by Homer or Virgil'. Hurd spoke of 'interventions from on high' and attention passing 'to the clash of fabled gods, or even goddesses, in the heavens above his head'. He added, 'Naturally and rightly, their thunder holds all our attention.'[163]

Gerald Kaufman, the shadow Foreign Secretary, reflected on the impact for John Major. Noting the ex-premiers disagreed with each other, but both said they agreed with the Prime Minister, Kaufman commented, 'The Prime Minister must decide which of the two who agree with him he agrees with ... If he repudiates one or the other, he splits part of his party away from him. That is why the government's position is so equivocal that even his most sycophantic admirers in the press condemn it.'

Heath's criticisms of Lady Thatcher also featured during the 1992 election. Describing Heath as 'devastatingly frank', Sergeant recorded Heath telling reporters that the Tories had an 'awful legacy' to live down. 'It is established that Thatcherism was an aberration,' he said.[164]

Matthew Engel wrote up his experiences of following Heath during the campaign under the headline, 'Thatcher still a factor as Heath goes on and on'.[165] 'Our main task in this election is to grab back the people who've left because of the Thatcher policies,' Heath pronounced. When asked about Thatcherism's most valuable achievement, he replied, 'She's gone.' 'She's living in a dream world, a world of fantasy,' Heath remarked when asked about Lady Thatcher's view that Britain now had enhanced status in the world. 'Does that give you enough for a gossip paragraph?' he later asked Engel.

The Heath–Thatcher relationship returned to Parliament after the election. 'I have been absolutely disgusted by the bigoted, xenophobic, rabid statements made about Germany,' Heath said in a House of Commons debate after a speech Lady Thatcher made in The Hague in May 1992, adding, 'I do not wish to enter into personalities.'[166]

Party conferences were also not free of the two former prime ministers' differences. In October 1992, Heath reflected, 'I have been booed for years at party conferences. What does make me sad is that these younger people, which we must recognise are the product of the Thatcher years, behave like a lot of soccer hooligans.'[167] Writing in 1993 about Lady Thatcher's arrival on the platform, Matthew

Parris noted, 'Ted Heath managed a hand-clap so slow, so intermittent and so limp that his hands seemed to move like the wings of a dying butterfly.'[168]

As suggested by their joint appearance at the 1998 party conference, by the end of the century things had changed. Commenting on that appearance, McManus concluded, 'The rapprochement had some way to run, but it had begun.'[169]

In April 1999, Heath attended a dinner marking the twentieth anniversary of Lady Thatcher becoming Prime Minister. McManus described this as a 'more overt sign of a thaw'.[170] In her speech, Lady Thatcher gave a nod to how Heath might have thought of her. 'Denis was always direct. When I first told him I intended to seek the party leadership he said: "Good Lord! You must be mad, but I'll support you all the way." I suspect that Ted Heath, who's done us the great honour of being here tonight, would agree with at least half that statement.' Heath was 'taken aback' by the reference to him.[171]

Lady Thatcher then paid a headline-grabbing tribute to Heath: 'I would like to take this opportunity publicly to pay tribute to Ted as one of Britain's most forceful and effective Prime Ministers. Go back and read his 1970 manifesto: it's one of the boldest and best the Conservative Party ever produced – a document not for burning.'[172]

This generated significant media coverage. Michael White summed it up by writing that Lady Thatcher had 'laid to rest one of the most sulphurous feuds in modern British politics'.[173] At the event, Lady Thatcher, Heath and William Hague were photographed together. Before the photograph was taken, Lady Thatcher said to Heath, 'You should be on my right.' He replied, 'That would be difficult.'[174]

The rapprochement went on. At a dinner to mark the thirtieth anniversary of the Heath government in 2000, Lady Thatcher made 'generous remarks'.[175] She spoke of 'a record of matchless service' and thanked Heath for all had done 'for our party and for our country'. She said she had 'only one more thing to say, Ted. Keep going: Britain still needs you.'[176]

The same year, Lady Thatcher attended a party given by Speaker Boothroyd to mark Heath's fifty years in the Commons. Tony Benn commented how nice it was that she was there. Lady Thatcher replied, 'Oh well, you know, as you get older you get mellow.'[177]

This may not have been the case with Heath. Speaking after Lady Thatcher's death, Conor Burns recalled he had hosted visits from both her and Heath in the same month in Eastleigh, something the MP described as a 'unique privilege'. Ahead of Heath's visit, Burns warned people in his association not to put out the Thatcher–Tebbit flyers. They did anyway. Seeing them, Heath asked Burns, 'What on earth are you doing with those two?' When Burns said they had agreed to visit, Heath replied in what Burns described as 'a grudging compliment': 'I suppose that is something of a coup.'[178] This highlighted a comment McManus made: 'Heath–Thatcher was show business; it was box office; and it was good knockabout material by this stage, with any genuine malice faded and gone.'[179]

Reflections

Whatever the nature of Lady Thatcher's relationship with her predecessor, and their views of each other, when Heath died, Lady Thatcher issued an eighty-word statement in which she described him as 'a political giant'. Making no mention of Europe, she referenced the 1970 manifesto and concluded, 'We are all in his debt.'[180] She attended both his funeral and his memorial service.

'Entirely clement': relationship with Sir John Major

Speaking in 2018, Sir John Major said that while he was Prime Minister his relationship with Lady Thatcher was 'entirely clement'.[181] This could be an example of what Lord Home of the Hirsel described as 'old men forget'.[182] Home used this phrase in 1989 when, during one of his final speeches in the House of Lords, he opposed the War Crimes Bill.

Lady Thatcher's relationship with and behaviour towards her immediate successor is one of the most contested aspects of her premier emeritus years and something for which she was heavily criticised. Ken Clarke wrote of Lady Thatcher's 'appalling behaviour', concluding: 'It was a desperately sad end to Margaret Thatcher's remarkable and brilliant career.'[183] Chris Patten said he did not think she was 'fair to her successor',[184] while Norman Fowler wrote of her doing 'everything in her power to undermine [Major's] authority'.[185]

Sometimes such criticism also came from her supporters. 'Her denigration of John Major was a bad blot on her record,' Aitken wrote, believing that in comparison to Heath's behaviour towards her, Lady Thatcher's towards John Major was 'infinitely worse and far more destructive'.[186] In April 1992, after the publication of Lady Thatcher's *Newsweek* article, Sir Bernard Ingham wrote of 'the need to stay silent',[187] and when her memoirs were published in 1993, he advised Lady Thatcher to 'take the money and run'. If she did not, she would 'rightly be called Lady Heath – the one with the handbag – to the desecration of her memory and considerable achievements'. He said John Major 'deserves her support – and, from now on, her reticence'.[188] Robin Harris, no fan of Major, wrote, 'It was natural that Major should feel hurt and betrayed by her behaviour.'[189]

Long-term colleagues of Lady Thatcher's spoke to her about it. In his diary on 27 April 1991, Kenneth Rose noted, 'Peter Thorneycroft has written to Mrs Thatcher telling her that she is placing her niche in history at risk by waging a vendetta against John Major and his Government.' On 8 December 1992, Rose noted, 'The other day Peter Carrington asked Margaret Thatcher: "Why are you so nasty to John Major when you made him?" She afterwards complained that Peter had been rude to her.'[190] Douglas Hurd once asked Lady Thatcher why she had pressed people to vote for Major in 1990. She replied, 'I'll tell you something I wouldn't tell to everybody. He was the best of a very poor bunch.'[191] Whether Lady Thatcher recalled Hurd's candidature is unclear. In 1995, Lady Thatcher said Major was 'the best of the three who were available at the time'. Her comments were likened to someone having had 'a disappointing response to an advert in Exchange and Mart'.[192]

Lady Thatcher was also criticised in the press. In his memoirs, Max Hastings, one-time editor of the *Daily Telegraph*, wrote that the paper was 'bitterly critical' of her 'incessant political interventions' and that her 'almost deranged intemperance exceeded the bounds of political decorum'.[193] Hastings noted a change from 1994 when the paper became critical of John Major: 'After her years in office, when I never received any communications at all from a chronically angry Prime Minister, suddenly in my new guise as a critic of John Major, I was astonished to receive a seasonal greeting signed by "Margaret and Denis".'[194]

All of this caused John Major huge irritation. Seldon noted that when Major was very irritated, he would call Lady Thatcher's behaviour 'emotional' and her views 'loopy'.[195] Judith Chaplin, a member of Major's policy unit, noted in her diary, 'PM often makes foul remarks about her ... very unattractive considering what he owes her. One night he says, "I want her destroyed."'[196] Andrew Turnbull commented, 'For the most part Major kept his anger under control, but occasionally the mask slipped.'[197] In 1999, Major acknowledged, 'I was very frustrated, and I think there's no doubt at times, in the privacy of someone I thought I could trust I let off steam, quite a different matter from the considered view later.'[198] In 2018, Major was asked if he thought Lady Thatcher's illness had influenced her during the early days of his premiership. He replied, 'Well, I do actually.'[199] Despite it being denied by Lady Thatcher's aides,[200] Major has repeated the claim.[201] Ken Clarke has said something similar.[202]

The relationship between Lady Thatcher and John Major, as past and current party leaders and prime ministers, had started to go wrong even before Lady Thatcher had ceased to be Prime Minister. In the television series accompanying his memoirs, Major reflected on his predecessor saying she would be a 'back-seat driver'. Major said, 'I was very alarmed.' He saw 'immediately' that it would cause damage and 'would cast a very long shadow indeed'. He said it was 'the first part of the wedge that was to become between us'.[203] In his diary on 27 November 1990, Woodrow Wyatt wrote, 'I was very alarmed. I rang her and said, "This is going to cause some trouble."' Lady Thatcher replied, 'But it was only a chance remark.'[204]

Whatever the nature of their relationship, up to his resignation in 1997, Lady Thatcher publicly supported Major's leadership. This was the case even when she was being critical of him directly or of government policy. She also on occasion publicly praised him.

During a June 1992 *Frost on Sunday* interview, Lady Thatcher backed John Major's leadership, even while she attacked the Maastricht Treaty and encouraged MPs to vote against it. She commented, 'Vote on what you believe. You are answerable to your constituents. I don't believe it would bring down John Major.' She went on, 'John I want to stay on … I chose John. I worked for him. I made the right choice. We disagree on certain things and those are things which are central to our constitution. He disagrees with me. He is fully entitled to. Equally, I am entitled to disagree with him.'[205]

The next year, she was equally publicly supportive of Major's leadership, telling the party in June 1993 to 'get behind John'.[206] 'There can be no question of a leadership challenge at the moment,' she said to ITN. 'Any such challenge would be ill judged and ill timed.'[207] Seldon noted, 'The great lady ringmaster qualified her views by saying she did not favour a leadership challenge "at the moment".'[208] He also acknowledged that Lady Thatcher's call was 'undoubtedly influential in persuading the right-wing 92 Group to offer Major almost unanimous backing'. On 17 June, Gyles Brandreth recorded in his diary, 'Mrs T. has emerged from the undergrowth to endorse her successor. She'll stand by her man.'[209]

In October 1993, Lady Thatcher called for a change in the Conservative leadership rules and expressed her support for Major. On *Breakfast with Frost*, she said there should be 'no threat of leadership elections'. She could not, however, bring herself to say Major was the great Prime Minister she had predicted he would be when she left Downing Street on 28 November 1990.[210] As seen above, Lady Thatcher (eventually) publicly supported Major in the 1995 leadership election. She also put out a statement supporting him in October 1996.

Nevertheless, Lady Thatcher was also publicly critical of her successor, and recognised this herself. In her 1996 Keith Joseph Memorial Lecture, she commented, 'It is no secret that between John Major and me there have been differences ... on occasion. But these have always been differences about *how* to achieve objectives, rather than *what* those objectives should be.'[211]

It may not always have felt like that to John Major, certainly not after her *Newsweek* article was published in 1992 in which she said, 'I don't accept the idea that all of a sudden Major is his own man,' adding: 'There isn't such a thing as Majorism. There couldn't be, at the moment.'[212] The article caused considerable controversy, generating extensive coverage. Lady Thatcher was heavily criticised, including by some of her supporters. Moore described it as 'incendiary',[213] Campbell as 'devastating'.[214] When it was published, Harris noted, 'there was a brutal confrontation with her staff'.[215] It caused Major 'much personal offence'.[216] For Norman Fowler it was 'faintly potty', 'irritating but frankly irrelevant'.[217]

According to Seldon, 'Over the next three years there were to be many low points, never worse than when the second volume of her memoirs was published in 1995.'[218] *The Path to Power* was only partly the story of Lady Thatcher's life to her becoming Prime Minister. There was also a second part, devoted to her life after 1990. It offered reflections on the European Union, foreign policy and defence, social policy and the economy. She also offered 'some thoughts about putting these things right'. In words echoing Geoffrey Howe's resignation speech, she added, 'It is now, however, for others to take the action required.'[219]

That specific phrase is discussed in a file in the National Archives, as is the book more generally.[220] On 24 May, Tina Stowell, then a member of the No. 10 press office, sent a two-page note to Christopher Meyer, Major's press secretary, headed 'Sunday Times – Mrs Thatcher's Memoirs'. It detailed Stowell's lunch with journalists Michael Jones and Andrew Grice. Meyer requested the note be copied to the Prime Minister. Stowell recorded that Jones had interviewed Lady Thatcher but had been told he could not ask her about the second part of the book. The 'not' is underlined in Stowell's note. She also records Jones saying Lady Thatcher 'rambles all over the place: "sticking the knife in, taking it out, sticking it in again" and so on'.

Meyer had asked Stowell to find out as much as she could about Lady Thatcher's book. But why was Downing Street seeking information from journalists about the immediate former occupant's book at all? Why did officials not speak to Lady Thatcher's office directly about it? They had been in touch about the *Sunday Times* publishing the 'It is now, however, for others to take the action required' phrase on 21 May. The *Sunday Times* had also reported Lady Thatcher's aides emphasising that her criticism of Major's handling of affairs was neither a personal attack nor a threat to his leadership.[221]

On 22 May, Julian Seymour faxed Alex Allan a statement Lady Thatcher's office would be issuing. The statement said the phrase had been seriously distorted because its full context had not been given. That context was that the phrase related to the West as a whole and not just Britain. This demonstrated 'that Lady Thatcher is ruling herself out of the long-term task of taking the action needed to deal with the problems she outlines'. Stowell recorded Jones saying Lady Thatcher's claim of 'distortion' was wrong. Jones had said it was perfectly obvious what she meant when she said, 'it was now for others to deal with'.

As for Major, at the top of some notes on 22 May, he wrote, 'If I responded to every hyped story in the press I'd do little else.' On the same day, Wyatt noted in his diary Major saying, 'I'm bloody angry and I'm going to give her a hell of an attack and go for her.'[222]

In his memoirs, Major wrote that the second part of *The Path to Power* 'could only be interpreted as an attack on my own policies', noting 'it was a good deal more publicity-worthy than the rest of the volume.' 'Such blows from my predecessor were impossible to disregard,' he went on, 'since every interviewer raised them with me at every opportunity, as she must have known they would.'[223]

Things were no better by 1996. On 4 January, Julian Seymour faxed Alex Allan comments Lady Thatcher would be making in a television programme on the Gulf War. Forwarding these to other officials, Allan wrote on the front page, 'Oh dear – I smell trouble'.[224]

On 11 January, Lady Thatcher delivered the Keith Joseph Memorial Lecture. On 9 January, Alex Allan sent a note to John Major. It advised the Prime Minister that Lady Thatcher had denied a story due to be published by *The Times* the next day that she thought it was inevitable the Conservatives would lose the next election. Allan attached Lady Thatcher's full statement. Allan then moved on to the lecture. 'This is described as a big set-piece,' he noted, going on to say that the lecture would restate Lady Thatcher's views on Europe and admit that there were areas where she and Major had differed. 'But – according to her office – it will be very supportive of you and of your position,' he added. 'It also contains a long and detailed criticism of Tony Blair's recent speeches and non-policies.' He ended by saying that the following Saturday Lady Thatcher was leaving for a trip to the Far East.[225]

Given the speech's content, and the reaction to it, Major might have wished Lady Thatcher had gone on her trip a week earlier and never delivered the speech. Billed as her first speech on domestic policy since her resignation, it proved intensely controversial. Lady Thatcher talked of 'No Nation Conservatism' and said the middle classes and the aspirant middle class no longer had the incentives and opportunities they expected from a Conservative government.

Naturally, the speech generated considerable media coverage. Equally naturally, that coverage did not focus on the 'long and detailed criticism of Tony Blair's recent speeches and non-policies'.

Peter Riddell wrote of Lady Thatcher opening 'the post-mortem on the Conservative election defeat of 1996–97'.[226] *The Times* reported it as a 'punishing blow' to Major's attempts at party unity.[227]

'Deep anger greeted the speech on the centre and left of the Party, as well as in Number Ten,' Seldon commented. Major was 'riled' by the speech, and by how 'it ignited talk of leadership challenges, dormant for the previous six months'.[228] On 12 January, Gyles Brandreth noted in his diary, 'Mrs T. is on the rampage – and the front page – big time.' He went on, 'The crafty little garden gnome [Robin Cook] is already exploiting the situation: "John Major has to decide whether he sees himself in the tradition of Thatcher and Keith Joseph or the One Nation tradition of Disraeli and Iain Macleod." The potential for grief is considerable.'[229]

There were further difficulties later in the year when, in June, Lady Thatcher made a donation to the European Foundation. At the time, the Conservative establishment was pressuring its donors not to do so.[230] In his diary on 13 June, Gyles Brandreth recorded, 'PM is white with anger.'[231] Seldon reports Major uttered three words: 'This is treachery.' Overruling advice, Major publicly stated, 'Everyone must choose what to do with their own money. Lady Thatcher must answer for her own actions. Personally, I would have given the money to the Conservative Party.' Seldon concludes, 'It was the most severe public exchange in their long-running six-year difference.'[232]

Whatever their public differences, the real damage to the relationship, and to Lady Thatcher's reputation, was when what she said in private often became public. In 1999, blaming Lady Thatcher's aides, Major argued that 'every whisper, every mention, every tiny bit of frustration she uttered in private [was carried] out into public'. Noting this spread into the public and Conservative Party,

Major reflected that 'almost daily' there seemed to be reports of what Lady Thatcher had said. 'Whether she had said them or not,' he went on, 'I don't know', but the reports caused 'great difficulty' in the Conservative Party.'[233] Seldon wrote of 'the pot being stirred by Thatcher friends'. Describing them as 'like mediums in a seance', he said, 'Fleet Street became awash with rumours of Thatcher's inner thoughts.'[234]

People close to Lady Thatcher recognised this too. 'What she can be blamed for is her indiscretion,' Robin Harris reflected. 'She was too free with her opinions about Major's failings, and her observations were mischievously but predictably passed on to the press, often in an exaggerated form.'[235] Charles Moore shares an indiscretion that did not leak. At a private dinner in New York in the summer of 1991, someone asked Lady Thatcher if she was trying to show contempt for her successor. 'On the contrary,' Lady Thatcher replied, 'I was trying to conceal it.'[236] On 2 June 1991, the *Sunday Telegraph* published an article entitled '"I'm disappointed in Major", says bitter Thatcher'.[237] *Private Eye*'s cover on 7 June 1991 had a speech bubble coming out of Lady Thatcher's mouth with the words, 'It would be very wrong for me to comment on Mr Major's abysmal performance…'.[238]

On the other side, Lady Thatcher was also the subject of counter-briefing. On 23 June 1991, Wyatt recorded Lady Thatcher telling him she that felt 'very battered'. Speaking of being 'misrepresented in America', Wyatt noted her saying that she 'had never known such a barrage of untruthfulness and falsehood being leaked out from Number 10 and everywhere else.'[239] In January 1995, she told Wyatt, in 'a testy voice', 'I won't speak to [Major] on the telephone because there are always leaks if I do.'[240] In 1999, Robin Harris wrote that 'a stream of unpleasant little press briefings sought to play down any initiative that Lady Thatcher took ... as ill-judged and ridiculous'.[241]

Lady Thatcher and John Major were in an almost impossible situation. Two such different personalities are difficult to imagine. As are two people to be this predecessor and this successor. As James Prior concluded in November 1990, 'Not an easy act to follow.'[242] Lady Thatcher never would have been, whoever was her successor.

Yet, the Thatcher–Major relationship faced specific challenges. They had different characters. They disagreed on policy, some of it of first-order importance. They never seemed to find a way of making their relationship as current and former Prime Minister work.

In October 1993, Peter Riddell wrote of Lady Thatcher's 'curiously ambivalent approach'. She had wanted 'to appear publicly loyal' to Major, but she also 'asserted her right to speak her mind'.[243] After her death, Michael Forsyth reflected, 'John Major never worked out a way to contain her and relations did get strained'.[244] It is unlikely that anyone could have found a way to contain Lady Thatcher. She was not a containable type of person. Others, however, might have cared less about, or been less impacted by, her activity than Major. It is hard to imagine either a Prime Minister Heseltine or a Prime Minister Hurd reacting as Major did.

John Major was a sensitive man. Not for him William Hague's detachment when, not long after his election as party leader, Edward Heath described Hague's victory as 'a tragedy for the party'. Hague had, Heath said, 'no grounding at all on policies'. 'He's got no ideas, no experience and no hope,' he went on.[245] 'You know you have become established as the Leader of the Party when Ted delivers his traditional compliment,' Hague said in response.[246]

In June 1991, under the headline 'Thatcher remains the unexploded bomb in her party's heart', Robin Oakley wrote that Lady
Thatcher created problems for the Conservatives, 'simply by being'.
Major, 'conscious of the comparisons with a charismatic predecessor', did not yet have 'the confidence to relax and do his own
thing'.[247] Noting how much Major cared about what Lady Thatcher thought, Sergeant argued, 'this was one of the reasons why she
became so influential in the years that followed'.[248] Across the top
of the speech Lady Thatcher delivered to the Boyden Forum in
Frankfurt in November 1992, Alex Allan wrote, 'Prime Minister
what we have come to expect'.[249] With all the economic and political instability surrounding the government in late 1992, it seems
incredible that John Major might have been reading the speeches
of his predecessor, if he was.

To Sergeant, Christopher Meyer commented, 'He would have
been a happier man had she not existed.' 'It wasn't as if she was
always attacking him,' he went on. 'These things came and went,
but he was always aware that there was this brooding presence out
there.'[250] That brooding presence, and its impact on Major and the
officials working for him, is also present in the National Archives.
Reading the PREM files covering the period 1990–97, there is a
sense of the Prime Minister and civil servants being under siege, or
of them feeling themselves to be.

Some of this was put to Major publicly. In 1993, he was asked if
Lady Thatcher treated him like Heath had treated her. 'We both
face a problem,' he replied. 'Every time Lady Thatcher says anything, colleagues of yours in the media crawl over it to see if some
interpretation can be placed upon it that causes difficulty for the
government. Every action I take, people crawl over it to see if Lady
Thatcher might have done it the same way.'[251]

In June 2023, Major reflected, 'When we were together, the relationship was entirely amiable.'[252] Yet they were not always comfortable in each other's company. Major himself acknowledged this, writing in his memoirs, 'It was evident in her body language when we met: she was uncertain how to react to someone who now held what she regarded as *her* job.'[253] Moore notes 'on the rare occasions when their conversations were one to one, they were not productive. Neither was frank with the other. He was temperamentally averse to direct confrontation and so, to a surprising extent, was she, except when in the heat of argument.'[254]

The Thatcher Foundation writes of a 'stilted dialogue'.[255] Referring to the lengthy, handwritten letter dated 26 December 1990 that Major sent Lady Thatcher,[256] the Thatcher Foundation comments, 'But that it was written at all surely suggests something uneasy between the two of them. Why had he not rung her up – a friendly confidential call from Chequers?' In his memoirs and elsewhere, Major has highlighted occasions when Lady Thatcher said things publicly that were counter-productive because similar discussions were being had behind the scenes. Knowing Lady Thatcher as he did, he might have spoken to her or ensured she was briefed before she made her comments. He could, for instance, have spoken to her before the November 1991 debate in which, as will be seen, she called for a referendum on the single currency, or alerted her to his thinking. Douglas Hurd had met her before the debate. Was a referendum idea discussed? If not, why not? It seems a missed opportunity.

Then there was the fact that, on some policy issues, Lady Thatcher and John Major disagreed. This was not just on Europe. For instance, when they met in January 1991, Lady Thatcher warned Major that, in her opinion, the government risked a 'historic error'

on the economy. She went on to highlight the difficulty of criticising the principle of the community charge.[257] Given the economic
and political inheritance Major had been bequeathed, this cannot
have been an easy meeting to sit through. In November 1994 and
January 1995, Wyatt asked Lady Thatcher if she had been talking to
John Major. She said no both times – because 'we'd only disagree'
and because she 'would only have a row with him' respectively.[258]

In addition, there was also Lady Thatcher's increasing disillusion
with John Major and the government he headed. This had started
very early. George Urban noted that at a Centre for Policy Studies lunch on 19 December 1990, 'MT immediately launched into
expressing her doubts about John Major's administration.'[259] It continued and grew as time passed. As Sir Mark Worthington said,
Lady Thatcher was 'starting to disbelieve in him'.[260]

As Lady Thatcher's disbelief grew, so did the disillusion, and the
criticism, both public and private. Throughout Wyatt's diaries are
entries recording Lady Thatcher's criticisms of both Major and the
government. Michael Spicer's diaries also contain similar entries.[261]
One of Lady Thatcher's closest friends concluded, 'She behaved
very badly at every level: she gossiped, she put out messages, she
withheld support. She used all her political cunning to knife him
and stab him and demoralise him and weaken him.'[262]

As a premier emeritus himself, Major has revisited his relationship with his predecessor. He did so in his memoirs, both written
and televised, in 1999. Describing Lady Thatcher's move to the Eurosceptic camp as 'pivotal', he judged that the subsequent 'dispute
and conflict' reached its 'inevitable conclusion' in the 1997 election.[263]

By the mid-2010s, Major offered another perspective on that
election result. 'I was never in any doubt that winning the 1997 election would be very difficult,' he said to Peter Hennessy in 2014. He

spoke of sitting with Chris Patten in No. 10 the day after the 1992 election, agreeing that 'in winning a fourth successive term, we had stretched the democratic elastic as far as it would go'. Major went on: 'Unless Labour collapsed, we would have little chance of winning the next election. I was reinforced in that view by the impact of Black Wednesday. I thought it overwhelmingly likely that we would lose.'[264]

Major revisited his relationship with Lady Thatcher when endorsing Ken Clarke in the 2001 leadership election. 'When he intervened during the last leadership contest to endorse Ken Clarke, he spent the entire interview attacking Lady Thatcher,' Steve Richards remarked in 2002.[265] Noting Lady Thatcher's ongoing political significance, Richards went on: 'There was, it seemed, no escaping from her even in a leadership contest held more than a decade after she left office.' Speaking to the *Today* programme, Major put Lady Thatcher's work on the European Union in a wider context. 'And the problem that caused has gone far beyond the European issue. Because of the dominance of the European issue, all other issues we were trying to deal with, particularly the economy, became much more difficult.'[266] Major has continued to speak about the relationship into the 2010s and the 2020s.

Reflections

For all the differing views on how Lady Thatcher and John Major behaved – and misbehaved – towards one another, perhaps the last word should be left to Anthony Seldon. Writing in 1997, he concluded that Lady Thatcher and Major were 'both at fault for their poisoned relationship. She was perhaps the more guilty.'[267] Reflecting on their joint visit to Teesside in 1997, he went on, 'It was an extraordinary meeting of two powerful figures who, between them, had held the premiership for nearly a fifth of the century, yet had never enjoyed each other's company, nor indeed valued each other's gifts.'[268]

For all the difficulties Lady Thatcher caused Major, she could also be both helpful and encouraging to him and his government. Sometimes she could be seen to be so by others.

In September 1994, Lady Thatcher wrote to Major following a visit to India: 'I write to say how impressed I was by the standing of Britain and the British government in that country.' She also said she was pleased Major's trip to South Africa had been successful. She expressed herself 'delighted that we managed jointly to control the malicious attempt by the media to cause difficulties'. Responding, Major thanked her for her 'rapid help when I was in South Africa', saying it was 'transparently obvious' that some journalists were attempting 'to stir up trouble through selective and distorted quotation'.[269]

The reporting of comments Lady Thatcher had made about investment in South Africa while in India had threatened to undermine John Major's visit to the former. *The Times* had headlined its story on this, 'Thatcher casts shadow over Major's visit'.[270] Asked about Lady Thatcher in Pretoria, Major defended her, commenting, 'I think the statement she issued to correct some misunderstanding last night answers the point thoroughly.'[271] *The Times* reported this as 'Major heals rift with Thatcher over visit'.[272] To Lady Thatcher, Major wrote, 'I am sorry that the press tried to put you in a false position, but your statement successfully knocked the story on the head as soon as it started running.'

As this shows, whatever the press reported, whatever was written in memoirs, and whatever the principals and those around them said, while Lady Thatcher's and John Major's relationship may not have been 'entirely clement', neither was it (on occasion) totally the opposite.

Of course, Lady Thatcher being helpful might also have added to the irritation that she seemed uniquely able to generate. At times, she might have thought, as indeed might others, that she was a person, if not *the* person, that others could not do without – however much people might have wished otherwise.

Beyond that, during Lady Thatcher's later years, Major displayed public kindness towards her, including supporting her at various public events. After her death, he paid tribute to her and issued a statement.[273] To the BBC, he said she was 'a remarkable Prime Minister and she did some extraordinary things'.[274] He spoke to ITV, describing her as 'a very great Prime Minister' and 'a very big measure to be measured against'.[275] In May 2013, he also became patron of the Margaret Thatcher Scholarship Trust.[276]

Chapter Six

Policy

The third area of Lady Thatcher's continuing work is policy. In this, she was an 'incendiary force' (on the European Union), a 'voice of conscience' (on the former Yugoslavia), a 'tower of support' (on General Pinochet), a 'better and stouter friend' (on Hong Kong and China), and 'tempted to talk' (on other issues).

In three of these areas – the European Union, the former Yugoslavia and General Pinochet – Lady Thatcher was involved in what Harris has described as 'often bitter conflict with respectable opinion'.[1] They 'formed a turbulent conclusion to Margaret Thatcher's active political life'[2] and, in them, we see Lady Thatcher as 'stateswoman – and subversive'.[3]

The importance of these issues to Lady Thatcher herself is demonstrated by her interventions in Parliament, since they took up all but two of her fifteen interventions, the others being on the Gulf, and, as we have seen, on the Scott Inquiry.

In analysing Lady Thatcher's policy work, we will focus on four questions:

1. What was her objective?
2. What did she do?
3. What reaction did she generate?
4. What did she achieve?

'Incendiary force': the European Union

In August 1999, in an article headlined 'Thatcher puts a bomb under Europe policy', Roland Watson and Tom Baldwin described Lady Thatcher as 'an incendiary force'.[4]

One of the most dominant areas of Lady Thatcher's work after 1990 was the relationship between the UK and the European Union (EU). While criticising how the EU was developing, Lady Thatcher also pursued a 'campaign for an alternative Europe'.[5] She also sought to influence what became the Maastricht Treaty both before and during its passage.

Journey to Maastricht 1991–92

On 3 January 1991, John Major met Lady Thatcher. Charles Powell briefed Major that the press had tried to make a great deal of a change in style, but the substance of the policy on Europe was 'very much that which was endorsed by Cabinet during her time as Prime Minister'.[6] The write-up of the meeting contains no observations from Lady Thatcher on Europe. It specifically states that on the economy, 'she did not mention the ERM explicitly'. It includes comments on the community charge, the economy and health reform.[7]

On 6 January, Lady Thatcher's role as president of the Bruges Group was announced. A *Times* leader the next day noted that this might 'prove tricky' for Major. It argued that if the Bruges Group welcomed his European policy, Major would be open to the charge of Lady Thatcher back-seat driving. On the other hand, if the Bruges Group was angry about policy, Major would find the group headed by 'a most formidable opponent'.[8]

Major recognised this. In his memoirs, he wrote that this and her decision to accept a post with the No Turning Back Group 'provided a focus for battle lines to be drawn'. 'She insisted that this had been far from her intention,' he went on. 'Not for the first or last time, it was hard to know whether she was a great deal more, or somewhat less, naïve than she seemed.'[9] In any event, it 'sent out a powerful early signal that Mrs Thatcher would remain a political presence'.[10] Lady Thatcher was reported to be 'deeply embarrassed by the furore'.[11]

In March 1991, Major spoke of his desire for the UK to be 'at the very heart of Europe'. Major later reflected that from then on, the European problem never left him. Moore wrote that criticism from Eurosceptics would have happened without Lady Thatcher, but 'with her mostly tacit but intermittingly noisy backing Major's critics were emboldened'.[12]

Lady Thatcher's first really 'noisy' intervention was in June 1991. Keen to influence the debate before the intergovernmental conference later that year, she delivered speeches in Chicago and New York.[13] These 'put the EC in the dock'.[14] Shared with the government, they caused controversy back in the UK.

Ministers were reported to have mounted 'a "don't panic" operation' in an article headlined 'Tories calm Thatcher speech tremors'.[15] Michael White's story, 'Sunset star casts a shadow', noted the wider context: 'Watching her it is hard not to feel that it is all going to end in tears, like Gloria Swanson coming down the staircase in *Sunset Boulevard*.'[16] A *Guardian* leader on 20 June said Lady Thatcher was 'a leader emeritus, who can still reflect with authority, even sometimes with wisdom', but she 'no longer calls the shots'.[17] In light of what was to come, ministers might have felt the opposite about that last part.

Lady Thatcher followed up the speeches by taking part in a House of Commons debate on the European Community on 26 June.[18]

Edward Heath also spoke. As a measure of the reaction her speech excited, including in comparison to Heath, 'Member for Finchley' (her constituency) was mentioned forty-three times; 'Member for Old Bexley and Sidcup' (Heath's), twenty.

'I fully support the firm stand that my right hon. Friends have taken', she declared at one point. '[Interruption]' is noted in Hansard. After the Speaker, Bernard Weatherill, called 'Order', Lady Thatcher repeated, 'I fully support the firm stand that my right hon. Friend the Foreign Secretary and my right hon. Friend the Prime Minister have taken against any commitment to a federal Europe.' Having set out five points she hoped the government would consider, she ended, 'In my right hon. Friend the Prime Minister we have a leader with the vision and sense of purpose to do just that.' She repeated, 'I give them my full support.'

As for the possible effect on John Major, 'I watched the [Prime Minister's] face as his predecessor spoke this afternoon and I have never seen such inspissated gloom etched on a human visage in my life,' Denis Healey commented. 'When the right hon. Member for Finchley (Mrs Thatcher) said that she planned to support him in the next election, he must have been reminded of Lenin's promise to support the social democrats as the rope supports the hanged man.'

The next day, a *Guardian* leader, 'The blast that came out of the handbag', described Lady Thatcher as 'triumphant in adrenalin pink'. She had turned 'a quietish, balanced debate into Westminster theatre'. 'The growing question, though, is how much she and the familiar diatribe continue to matter.'[19] As events were to prove, the answer was quite a bit.

That was seen on 20 November 1991, when Lady Thatcher

intervened again in Parliament, on the first day of a two-day debate ahead of the meetings at Maastricht.[20] Mirroring the impact she had had on MPs in June, 'Member for Finchley' was referenced forty-seven times; 'Member for Old Bexley and Sidcup', by contrast, just three.

A note to John Major revealed that she had rejected a draft speech prepared by Charles Powell.[21] The Thatcher Foundation says this was 'something she rarely if ever did in their days together at No. 10'.[22] The draft she did have was 'not too bad', Powell concluded, but he cautioned it might be toughened up before delivery. Douglas Hurd called on Lady Thatcher on the first morning of the debate. This was ostensibly so he could brief her ahead of her visit to Kuwait and Bahrain starting later that week.[23] That said, as Hurd's private secretary, Richard Gozney, noted after the meeting, 'Most of the Secretary of State's discussion with Mrs Thatcher was about EC matters.'[24] In his diary, Hurd recorded, 'She will vote for the Govt tomorrow, but mobilise huge forces against us after Maastricht if we sin.'[25]

In the debate, Lady Thatcher urged John Major to remove those proposals which he himself had said were 'quite unacceptable'. In full Margaret Thatcher character, she went on, 'In my day, that would have required the occasional use of the handbag. Now it will doubtless be the cricket bat, but that is a good thing because it will be harder.'

At one point, Lady Thatcher spoke of Hurd as 'my Foreign Secretary'. '[Laughter]' is noted in Hansard. Hurd intervened saying Lady Thatcher had had a number of Foreign Secretaries. He added, 'I accept the tribute on behalf of them all.' Lady Thatcher replied, 'I am not quite sure whether he should.' To Frank Haynes' question on what she would be negotiating if still Prime Minister, Lady Thatcher responded, 'I am making a pretty good fist of just that.'

Lady Thatcher also called for a referendum if the main parties supported a single currency. This was 'extremely awkward' for John Major.[26] Lady Thatcher did not know, but Major had been considering offering a referendum. He later wrote, 'Her advocacy proved counter-productive.'[27] 'The fact that *she* had called for the policy killed the policy,' he told Moore. 'I couldn't get it through the Cabinet.'[28] This is clear from the minutes of the Cabinet held on 21 November. John MacGregor, the Lord President of the Council and Leader of the House of Commons, reported that a referendum was the key issue to have emerged from the previous day's debate. This was 'largely as a result of Mrs Thatcher's speech'. The Cabinet identified 'dangers in explicitly acknowledging the possibility of a future referendum, exemplified by criticisms from the Opposition and in the media that the Government had altered their position in response to Mrs Thatcher's speech'. Summing up, John Major said that 'it was the clear view of the Cabinet that the Government should place on record its firm opposition to the use of referendums'.[29]

Immediately following Lady Thatcher, Paddy Ashdown commented, 'We love to hear her expressing her views in the House, although judging by the faces of those on her own Front Bench, I am not sure that the same applies to them.'

In his diary, Woodrow Wyatt wrote of Lady Thatcher being 'in high form, sparkling away, commanding the attention of the whole house'. He noted she made 'a lot of jokes', showed 'great sense of humour', and engaged with 'the deep seriousness of the problem'.[30] In her diary, Edwina Currie said Lady Thatcher 'stole the show (and the headlines and front pages)'. Currie said the speech was a '*tour de force*: strong on body language and sentiment'.[31] 'MPs on both sides of the Commons treated her affectionately,' Sergeant wrote. 'It was like the return of a well-loved actor. She gave no impression of being reduced in her new position.'[32]

Michael White's story was headlined 'Thatcher hijacks Major's line'.[33] Andrew Rawnsley put it in a wider context. Under the headline, 'Ghost of Bruges applies her handbag to wobbly ministers', he noted it was the first anniversary of the Cabinet putting 'a stake through Margaret Thatcher's heart'. Describing her as 'the Finchley Phantom', Rawnsley recorded that as Lady Thatcher resumed her seat at the end of her speech, a Labour MP called out, 'Will there be a collection?' Rawnsley concluded, 'Of course there will. The Cabinet is already organising a whip-round to buy a silver bullet to do the job properly.'[34]

The next day, 21 November, Edward Heath spoke.[35] He was referenced seventeen times, his successor thirty-eight.

'I have here a quote from my right hon. Friend the Member for Finchley,' Heath said during his speech, 'who said in the debate on the referendum [in 1975]: "It would bind and fetter parliamentary sovereignty in practice." I agree with her entirely. It would, and I see no reason to change my view, or her view, at this moment or in the future. I do not believe in referendums as a means of government.'

'I know that I inherited that position from my right hon. Friend, and I loyally upheld it,' Lady Thatcher intervened. 'Now, it looks to me as if three parties will be for a single currency and for sacrificing a great deal of the work that it has previously been the right of Parliament to do. How are the people to make their views known in this absence of choice? That was the particular point. My right hon.

Friend will remember that our right hon. Friend the noble Lord Hailsham made an interesting speech on elective dictatorship.'

Hansard records 'Oh' and Madam Deputy Speaker [Betty Boothroyd] calling for order.

In her final words in the House of Commons, Lady Thatcher continued, 'Therefore, as he has been in the House longer than I have, will my right hon. Friend tell us how people can make their views known when all parties take the same view but each is divided?'

Heath replied, 'This is an occasion which constantly occurs in parliamentary history.'

As per the conclusions of the Cabinet meeting earlier that day, Lady Thatcher's referendum call was rejected. Two days after the debate, she appeared on *News at Ten*. She said the rejection of a referendum was 'arrogant', though this was 'a choice of word for which she quickly apologized'.[36] A *Daily Telegraph* leader, 'Act of disloyalty', asked, 'Is it really her wish to see her place in history stained by pettiness, by bitterness, by what the world is liable to perceive as belated barracking from the stalls?'[37] Sergeant reports that Major was particularly annoyed because Lady Thatcher 'turned on him personally' for rejecting a referendum.[38]

Major met Lady Thatcher on 6 February 1992. The suggested foreign policy topics put together for him did not include the European Union, and instead they focused on the former Soviet Union, a special meeting of the UN Security Council, Iraq, and the GATT.[39]

Passage of Maastricht 1992–93

Analysing Lady Thatcher's appearances in official files from 1992, the Thatcher Foundation notes, 'Following the election, in April 1992, MT swiftly moved into a position much more critical of

Major and his government as the ERM crisis, the ratification of the Maastricht Treaty and the war in Bosnia provided combustible material on quite a scale.'[40]

After the Maastricht Treaty's signature, Lady Thatcher continued her 'campaign for an alternative Europe'. Speaking to a South Korean journalist in April 1992, she commented, 'I have to go and do a tour of Europe, because quite a number of them are becoming very questioning about Maastricht.'[41]

One stop on that tour – perhaps the most important – was in The Hague, where Lady Thatcher delivered a speech on 15 May.[42] The speech had been planned for a while. On 18 February, Lady Thatcher's office advised the British Embassy in the Netherlands that she 'would be making a "major European speech"' in a couple of months' time.[43] On 28 April, the British ambassador, Sir Michael Jenkins, advised the Foreign Office, 'I am not sure how controversial the speech may prove to be – although I can hazard a guess!'[44]

Entitled 'Europe's Political Architecture', Lady Thatcher later wrote that 'I deliberately intended it as Bruges Mark II'. 'Of course,' she went on, 'I could not expect that it would have the same impact; after all, I was no longer a head of government. But for that very reason I hoped that the ideas could be developed more provocatively and would help to alert the more open-minded members of Europe's political élite to new possibilities.'[45]

Seldon noted that the speech set out 'a vision for the future of Europe radically different from the government's planned Maastricht Bill'.[46] Nevertheless, Lady Thatcher praised the Prime Minister: 'John Major deserves high praise for ensuring at Maastricht that we would not have either a single currency or the absurd provisions of the social chapter forced upon us.' The speech was followed a few days later by an article in *The European* entitled 'No substitute for the nation state'.[47] In it, Lady Thatcher set out her doubts about the Maastricht Treaty.

Published just before the House of Commons Second Reading of the bill that would implement the provisions of Maastricht, both speech and article generated extensive media coverage.

Lady Thatcher delivered the Hague speech in full Margaret Thatcher character. George Brock wrote of 'an outnumbered Margaret Thatcher humiliating important men in suits', describing her as 'glowing like a fluorescent bulb'.[48] The article was headlined 'Gleeful gladiator puts "Euro-snobs" to the sword'. Reflecting on the speech, and on a dinner that he had given for Lady Thatcher the evening before, the British ambassador reported to the Foreign Office, 'I was struck – no doubt naively – by the degree of emotion which surrounded all Mrs Thatcher's pronouncements.' He added: 'and by the colourful language, usually counter-productive, with which she advanced her arguments in private'.[49]

The ambassador also posed a question: 'What effect does an intervention of this kind have on the Prime Minister's and Secretary of State's policy of building on the Maastricht Treaty and its pillared structure?'[50] It was a question debated in leader columns in the British press. *The Independent* stated, 'In the transformed post-election landscape of British politics, what Margaret Thatcher says about the European Community simply does not matter.' It said that on the future of Europe and on government policy, 'the impact is likely to be near zero'.[51] *The Times*, in 'Thatcher's Europe', commented, 'She speaks sense',[52] while the *Daily Telegraph* concluded that 'what she says is heard attentively; but she is no longer any part of the decision-making process'.[53] Its leader was headlined 'Entitled to her views'. Given the reaction Lady Thatcher's views excited, ministers might have felt like adding, 'provided she does not express them'.

As for Downing Street, the *Daily Telegraph* reported a muted response to the speech. Officials described it as 'interesting'.[54] A minister, perceptively in light of what was to come, was reported as saying, 'Those who are ridiculing her as the harridan in never-never land misunderstand that she articulates the views of an embarrassing number of Tory MPs – and what she says will encourage them to go on saying it.'[55]

The encouragement, and whether it was proactive or reactive, that Lady Thatcher gave to MPs, including during the Maastricht Bill's passage, is one of the most contested aspects of her premier emeritus years, and one for which she was most criticised.

In his memoirs, John Major wrote that after the Danish referendum in June 1992 Lady Thatcher started urging Conservative MPs 'to oppose the government and defeat the treaty'. He wrote of Gerald Howarth telephoning new MPs, inviting them to meet Lady Thatcher so 'she could persuade them to vote against Maastricht'. It was 'a unique occurrence', Major said, in Conservative Party history, an ex-Prime Minister 'openly encouraging' backbenchers to defeat their successor's policy, a policy that had been a manifesto commitment in a general election only months before. Major noted that many of the MPs 'revered' Lady Thatcher and claimed that her support for the defeat of the Maastricht Bill 'helped to turn a difficult task for our whips into an almost impossible one'.[56] He repeated some of this when interviewed on Radio 4's *Today* programme in 2001. He said that young backbenchers being encouraged to rebel by a former Prime Minister whom they revered caused 'immense damage' and twice described it as 'unprecedented'.[57]

Ken Clarke wrote of Lady Thatcher 'Holding court behind the lines', 'injecting the poison and stiffening wobbly rebels to become more and more impossible'.[58] In March 1993, Edward

Heath described MPs being taken to Lady Thatcher's room, where 'she tries to influence them against Maastricht and against the Government'.[59]

One person Lady Thatcher saw was John Whittingdale. He recorded it as a very painful meeting.[60] John Major said Whittingdale was 'deeply upset at being made to feel so divided from the ex-Prime Minister he had served faithfully'.[61] Of the meetings with MPs, Whittingdale said Lady Thatcher 'was responding, not organizing. They saw her as their de facto leader.'[62]

Responding not organising is also the line advanced by Michael Forsyth.[63] He recalled Lady Thatcher 'seeing large numbers of Tory backbenchers – at their request, I should add'. 'Many of them left these meetings unsettled or determined to vote against,' he noted. Major was becoming 'increasingly irritated' about these meetings and asked Forsyth to speak to Lady Thatcher about them. Reflecting after her death, Forsyth commented, 'I obliged, and it proved to be a deservedly unpleasant experience for me.' When he went to see Lady Thatcher, Forsyth found her 'clutching a heavily annotated copy of the impenetrable document'. She asked him which part he wished to discuss. He said he did not wish to discuss the Treaty, but to talk about the potential impact these meetings might have on Lady Thatcher. 'I am concerned that you are getting yourself into a position where the government machine will start attacking you, and this will harm you,' he said to her. 'It was a stupid mistake and I should have known better. There followed an almost thermonuclear explosion.' Forsyth concluded: 'I crawled under the door, thoroughly ashamed of myself.'

Richard Ryder, the Chief Whip, regarded the Maastricht rebels as 'self-starters'. Ryder knew from having worked for Lady Thatcher that organisation was not her forte.[64]

Whether organising or not, the differences over Maastricht were certainly, as John Major said, 'magnified by her',[65] and this took place in and out of Parliament.

Introduced to the House of Lords at the end of June 1992, Lady Thatcher made her maiden speech on 2 July in a debate on the UK's presidency of the European Community.[66]

Before she spoke, Lord Jenkins of Hillhead noted that there was 'a certain breathless hush in the close ... as we await the non-controversial remarks of the noble Baroness, Lady Thatcher'.

'I have never knowingly made an uncontroversial speech in my life,' she said at one point in her speech. 'Nevertheless, I hope to be more controversial when we get down to discussing the details.' Her words seemed to generate immediate impact in the House. In the debate, she was referenced by name thirty-six times. In comparison, another former Prime Minister, Lord Callaghan, who immediately followed her, was referred to thirteen times.

Callaghan opened his speech with, 'My Lords, it is a very great pleasure for me to welcome the noble Baroness to this House and also congratulate her on her maiden speech, especially on getting it over so quickly. She said that she had served for many years before the mast. I thought that this afternoon she was perhaps hoisting the Jolly Roger when I heard some of her comments.'

Earl Ferrers, a minister at the time of Lady Thatcher's maiden speech, later commented to this author: 'A maiden speech mustn't be too long, and it mustn't be controversial. Margaret Thatcher spoke for twenty-five minutes. Callaghan got up and said: "What a wonderful thing it is to have the noble Baroness here and she made a remarkable speech. She gave us so much of her time too" – or words to that effect. He did it like that and, of course, the House roared.'

Naturally, the media covered Lady Thatcher's speech. Andrew Rawnsley wrote of Lady Thatcher having 'difficulty being non-controversial about the time of day', describing her as 'an ageing Hollywood starlet declaiming the lines from forgotten parts long ago'. Perceptively, he added, 'The Blue Baroness has lots of head-lines left in her.'[67] Matthew Parris noted that Lady Thatcher's 'lieutenants, crowded at the door to watch, understood'.[68] In *The Independent*, it was reported as 'a meticulously executed rehearsal for the suspected dramas to come'.[69]

While attending many of the debates on the Maastricht Bill, Lady Thatcher only spoke on it twice. A former Conservative Cab-inet minister reflected to this author, 'She came for all the Maas-tricht debates. She was very unhappy about our agreement to the Maastricht Treaty, certainly wanted a referendum on it. She was here for days on end for that.'

On 16 September 1992, the UK left the Exchange Rate Mecha-nism. For Lady Thatcher, this was a form of vindication. It was seen to be at the time, including by Lady Thatcher herself. In its obituary of her, the *Daily Telegraph* commented, 'Only with the collapse of the ERM and of the Major government's reputation for economic competence in September 1992 did her political standing recover, as her warnings were proved correct. From now on she was again a major force within the Conservative Party.'[70]

At the time, Norman Fowler predicted that Lady Thatch-er would 'find it very difficult to suppress her glee' when Major rang to tell her about the UK's departure.[71] As if to prove Fowler's point, on 20 September 1992, the *Sunday Telegraph* reported that when the news broke, Lady Thatcher started telephoning friends in London from Washington, where she was due to speak at a CNN financial conference, to point out that she had been 'right all along'. 'Her telephone bill must have been enormous,' one of her friends commented.[72]

Lady Thatcher described being in Washington as 'a nice coincidence'. She was staying at the British Embassy. So was Norman Lamont who was attending an International Monetary Fund conference. His room was down the corridor from Lady Thatcher's. She later wrote, 'At least I heard no singing from the bath.'[73]

On 18 September, Lady Thatcher visited Vice-President Quayle, and was accompanied by the British ambassador, Sir Robin Renwick. They also briefly met President Bush. Bush asked about the currency crisis in Europe, to which Lady Thatcher said that it had not been possible for the UK to stay in the ERM. She thought Maastricht was dead and hoped it was. In his write-up of the meeting, Renwick noted, 'The President gave me a large wink, apparently unnoticed by his visitor, but otherwise did not comment.'[74]

Lady Thatcher duly delivered her speech to the CNN World Economic Development Conference on 19 September.[75] Bearing out Fowler's prediction, Moore said she was 'indecently happy' to say the markets could not be bucked.[76] The speech was followed by the article in *The European* which overshadowed the Conservative Party conference.[77] In it, she wrote, 'The ERM and Maastricht are inextricably linked.' 'The government must recognise that Maastricht, like the ERM, is part of the vision of yesterday. It is time to set out the vision for tomorrow,' she concluded.

As the Maastricht Bill's parliamentary passage went on, so did Lady Thatcher's tour of Europe. On 15 January 1993, Julian Seymour spoke to Christopher Prentice, an FCO official, about Lady Thatcher's travel plans that year. She was due to speak in Copenhagen and Stockholm the following week, and Prentice's write-up of the call noted that she would be 'making speeches in both capitals, on familiar themes.' 'Both Ambassadors were in the picture,' Prentice added. 'For obvious reasons they were not looking to us for anything further on these.'[78]

Indeed, Lady Thatcher's office acknowledged that 'trips to Europe pose particular difficulties'.[79] Of the visit to Stockholm, the British ambassador to Sweden, Robert Cormack, subsequently reported that Lady Thatcher had 'left a pretty wide circle of influential Swedes with her powerfully expressed view that Maastricht is a bad thing, that Europe lacks leadership and will become increasingly undemocratic, and, by implication, that her successor is weak and HMG's policy on Europe is wrong'. Guests at a dinner attended by Lady Thatcher were described as 'greatly enjoying the performance' but 'pretty shocked by the virulence of her anti-German stance'.[80]

The ambassador's report to the Foreign Office also revealed something else. Lady Thatcher could generate the same kind of reaction in foreign leaders that she could – and often did – in British ministers. This was particularly the case in European countries where 'the tendentious nature of the comments likely to be made'[81] when she was speaking on 'familiar themes' seemed to cause more turbulence than triumph for Lady Thatcher. 'She had no contact with Ministers,' the ambassador reported, noting that her not seeing the Prime Minister, Carl Bildt, 'was rubbed in by his Foreign Policy Adviser when I spoke to him on other matters during her visit'. Given this, Lady Thatcher might have been interested – if not amused – to learn that her comments at the dinner 'had already got to the Prime Minister by the time [the ambassador] spoke to his office the following morning'.[82]

Cormack also asked the Foreign Office how closely diplomats

should be involved in Lady Thatcher's overseas visits. He hoped 'any steer which emerges' would be circulated to those 'at risk of a visit'.[83] The FCO reply said that he had spelt out 'very clearly' the 'particular difficulties' that trips to Europe posed. 'In addition,' it went on, 'there tend to be fewer commercial opportunities in Europe which might benefit from Lady Thatcher's presence or political intervention. But it is still right for Ambassadors to help Lady Thatcher, as a former Prime Minister, with practical arrangements.'[84]

Lady Thatcher returned to 'familiar themes' on 7 June 1993, during the Maastricht Bill's Second Reading.[85] Her 'widely-trailed speech',[86] delivered on the first day of the debate, resulted in her being referred to by name fifty-six times, and on the second day fifty-eight times. In comparison, Lord Callaghan, who spoke on the latter day, was referenced fourteen times.

Years later, while acknowledging his possible bias due to Lady Thatcher sacking him, Lord Carr of Hadley, a former Conservative Home Secretary, said to this author, 'She made life very uncomfortable on Maastricht, but she encouraged a determination amongst many of us to see the thing through.' About the Single European Act and ERM entry, he went on, 'there were enough of us who thought that you cannot say this to us now when you've done what you've done. She cannot dodge her responsibility.'

Lord Rawlinson, a former Conservative Solicitor General and Attorney General, told this author, 'I did feel a resentment to the public posture being adopted by Margaret Thatcher, who had, after all, signed the Single European Act, from which Maastricht inevitably flowed. It would have been much more dignified, and I would have thought effective, if she'd done it privately and kept silent publicly rather than to have done it in the way she did.' Rawlinson added, 'But she was not that kind of person.'

'But she was not that kind of person' – a sentence that captures so much of Lady Thatcher's character, others' reactions to her, and explains so much about her post-prime ministership and, indeed, her career and life.

Such was Lord Rawlinson's anger at the approach Lady Thatcher took that he devoted a speech to it. Without mentioning her by name, he commended the behaviour of Lord Home of the Hirsel.[87] To this author, he commented, 'It was very tiresome at the time to have this constant bickering between leaders of the same party.'

Anticipating the Single European Act being quoted against her, Lady Thatcher defended her previous conduct and current position. First, by stressing what she said were the very limited circumstances in which she had approved an extension of qualified majority voting. Second, by saying that having got our fingers burnt, we should not return them to the fire. 'I could never have signed this treaty,' she added. 'I hope that that is clear to all who have heard me.' She had earlier said Maastricht was a 'treaty too far' and that she would vote against it.[88]

As ever, Lady Thatcher's speech generated press coverage. Andrew Rawnsley said most of it was 'sub-nuclear', adding: 'The act does not work on this stage.'[89] 'It wasn't one of her better speeches, but who cared?' judged Matthew Parris. 'It was herself. That's all people need to know these days … In the gallery her Commons disciples took notes, or gazed, dumbstruck in wonderment. Who cared *how* she said it? The point was that *she* had said it. It was herself who had spoken. They had seen her. They had been there.'[90]

This wider effect of the speech was noted by others, too. Anthony Bevins wrote of Lady Thatcher having 'stiffened the resolve' of the Conservative rebels.[91] A *Daily Telegraph* leader, 'Forceful but flawed', reflected that the speech would make 'predictable headlines' and 'bring comfort' to Eurosceptic MPs, but would be 'unlikely to do much more than that'.[92]

Lady Thatcher intervened again at Report Stage, on 14 July, supporting an amendment on a referendum tabled by Lord Blake.[93] As with her previous interventions, one measure of the effect she had on other peers was demonstrated by the number times she was referenced by name – on this occasion thirty-one times. She did not just speak, she also voted – against the government.[94]

Lady Thatcher was concerned her support for the amendment might be seen as an attack on John Major or as an attempt to damage him. 'It will not be an attack on the Prime Minister,' she stated before the debate. 'It will be a furtherance of what I have believed in for a very long time.' Noting her speeches were interpreted as attacks on Major, she said, 'That is why I speak very rarely.'[95]

Perhaps having read the reviews of her last performance, this time Lady Thatcher gave what Andrew Rawnsley described as 'a powerful finger-wagging, spectacle-stabbing, eye-blazing performance'.[96] *The Times* reported it as being 'delivered with the same passion as her bravura resignation speech'.[97] Some said it was her best speech since that one.[98]

Woodrow Wyatt took a different view, deeming the speech 'very poor, illogical, [and] contradictory'. It was also 'evasive' about why she had not had a referendum on the Single European Act. He described Lady Thatcher as talking 'absolute piffle'. 'It is very sad,' he went on. 'She demeans herself by entering the arena in so carping a fashion.'[99]

However powerful her contribution may or may not have been, the referendum amendment was defeated overwhelmingly. During discussion at the Cabinet the next day, it was noted that the amendment 'had been defeated by a substantial majority in the highest vote recorded in the Lords'. Interestingly, another former Prime Minister featured in that day's Cabinet. The second item on the agenda was the Prime Minister telling his colleagues that he had 'received a warm letter of thanks' from Lord Home for the ninetieth birthday present the Cabinet had given him.[100]

Fittingly, *The Guardian*'s article on the debate was headlined 'Thatcher's last stand'.[101] For this speech was to be the last ever speech Lady Thatcher made in Parliament on the EU. She did not speak in the Lords again for almost two years.

Beyond Maastricht: 1993 onwards

The EU continued to be one of Lady Thatcher's most important areas of work after Maastricht. 'Lady Thatcher now concentrated increasingly on the referendum question,' Charles Moore noted.[102] In addition, from the mid-1990s, news stories appeared saying Lady Thatcher favoured leaving the EU.

In 1995, Lady Thatcher devoted a chapter of *The Path to Power* to the subject: 'Bruges or Brussels?' Its final section was entitled 'A New Beginning',[103] which 'concluded that it was necessary to renegotiate the treaties that underpinned Britain's membership', Harris writes.[104] As if this were not bad enough for the government, according to John Major things were made worse by a television interview in which Lady Thatcher talked of a single currency wrecking a thousand years of history.[105]

In late 1996, it was reported that Lady Thatcher believed Britain might have to 'review its position' in the EU without changes to the common agricultural and fishery policies, and the powers of the European Court of Justice. 'This is last thing we need,' a minister responded.[106]

In April 1999, Edward Heathcote-Amory recorded one of Lady

Thatcher's friends as saying that privately, 'After a few glasses of whisky, she's always talking about pulling out of the EU.' Heathcote-Amory wrote that Lady Thatcher was planning 'a major speech' on Europe in which she would probably call for the UK to leave the EU unless the Treaty of Rome could be renegotiated. Describing this as an 'explosive intervention', Heathcote-Amory said that it was to have been delivered in March 1999, but the threat of her private office resigning en masse if she went ahead had forced a change of plan.[107]

In August 1999, Rachel Sylvester wrote of Lady Thatcher telling friends that she now believed the UK should 'sever its links because the EU is turning into a federal superstate'. Sylvester noted the impact: 'Her private intervention has strengthened the resolve of Tory Eurosceptic MPs.'[108] Labour and the Liberal Democrats issued a joint statement calling on the Conservatives to 'slap down' Lady Thatcher.[109] As for Lady Thatcher herself, she was described as 'quite happy' with Conservative Party policy. This was an attempt 'to calm the furore over her recently revealed support for Britain's withdrawal from Europe'.[110]

2002's *Statecraft* went the furthest Lady Thatcher had yet gone – and ever went – publicly in suggesting that 'leaving was a thinkable possibility'.[111] Robin Harris, who worked on the book, said it 'called more starkly for Britain to leave'.[112]

Front-page coverage of the book in *The Times* on 18 March was under the headline, 'Thatcher: Britain must start to quit EU'.[113] In the same paper, Michael Gove commented, 'The Conservatives should have said that it was just plain wrong to assert that EEC membership had been an error.'[114] The article was headlined 'It is time for the Tories to turn away from Thatcher'. A front-page article in *The Times* on 22 March, 'Thatcher wrong on Europe say

Tories', reported that 71 per cent of constituency chairmen rejected Lady Thatcher's call for withdrawal from key parts of the EU.[115]

On 18 March 2002, Tony Blair delivered a Commons statement on the European Council in Barcelona. He mentioned Lady Thatcher's position on Europe twice. Referring to Iain Duncan Smith's response to his statement, Blair commented, 'There was one name that he did not mention in his response – one little thing that he did not get round to talking about: the position of Margaret Thatcher on Europe.' Blair further commented, 'We did not get a single word of dissociation from the remarks of Margaret Thatcher.' '[Interruption]' is noted in Hansard. Equating Conservative policy with Lady Thatcher's, Blair said it was 'to talk about withdrawal and end up ruling out a single currency for ever, whatever the economic circumstances'. He went on, 'I say in response that his policy on Europe is not an act of patriotism: it is an act of folly.'[116]

'She was convinced that Britain should leave the European Union,' Harris argued in his biography of Lady Thatcher. 'She also sensed she had little time left. She wanted her conviction to be on the record before she died. And so it was and is.'[117] Speaking to Charles Moore, Christopher Collins, who had worked with Lady Thatcher on her memoirs, commented, 'We were alone and she said in a kind of stage whisper, "I think we would be better off outside." I took the whisper to mean "Don't tell anyone I think that."' Collins remembers Harris 'expressing frustration that she would not go that far in Statecraft – almost, but not quite'.[118]

After Lady Thatcher's death, Andrew Roberts revealed that he once asked Lady Thatcher why she did not publicly say she favoured withdrawal. Replying, in Roberts' words 'somewhat disingenuously', Lady Thatcher said, 'No one's ever asked me the question.' 'Far from being the outspoken back-seat driver she was accused of being,' Roberts continued, 'Lady Thatcher never came out publicly for Britain's withdrawal from the European Union, for all her passionate belief that it was the right course to take.'[119] '[T]he story of Mrs Thatcher and Europe does reveal something interesting,' Moore wrote in 2016, noting that when in office she never said that the UK should leave, but out of office said she privately, both to him and others, that she thought it should.[120] In 2013, he had written that Lady Thatcher's advisers had persuaded her not to say publicly that she favoured withdrawal 'since it would have allowed her opponents to drive her to the fringes of public life'.[121]

While we will never know what Lady Thatcher might have said publicly after 2002 had illness not brought an end to her active political life, it seems somehow fitting that she was silenced after one last intervention on this particular issue. It also seems fitting that she was silenced just at the moment where she had gone further than ever before in publicly advocating withdrawal. That said, to paraphrase Lady Thatcher herself, 'Brothers, I believe in "almost, but not quite"' is hardly the line of the prophet and crusader she would have claimed herself to be. But it does suggest nuance, something so long overlooked in the commentary on Lady Thatcher's premier emeritus years.

Reflections

The Maastricht Bill, or the European Communities (Amendment) Bill to give it its proper title, received Royal Assent on 20 July 1993. Thus, the treaty that Lady Thatcher had claimed she could never have signed passed into law. It did so without the referendum she had sought. On that measure, Lady Thatcher had failed to achieve her objective. It is worth emphasising given all that has been written about Lady Thatcher's work after 1990 in this area. No matter how close the government had been brought to the brink of disaster, it did not go over the cliff. No matter how much some people thought Lady Thatcher was responsible for the situation the government found itself in, and however much some blamed her for it, the government got its Act. Lady Thatcher did not prevent it reaching the statute book. So, in the final analysis, on Maastricht, John Major won. Lady Thatcher lost.

The same could be said for Lady Thatcher's campaign for an alternative Europe, described by Harris as 'abortive'.[122] Members of the European political élite did not seemingly pay much attention to the 'new possibilities' that Lady Thatcher advanced. Even if her comments made an impression on people, they did not necessarily make people act differently, or at least not in the way that Lady Thatcher might have wanted them to do. Lady Thatcher recognised this herself. Having delivered her Hague speech in May 1992, the British ambassador reported her saying to him that 'she was most dismayed by the negative response of my dinner guests and of her audience the next day to her attempts to open their eyes to what was going on'.[123] In January 1993, the British ambassador to Sweden reported, 'While I doubt if many Swedes will have changed their minds about EC entry as a result of her visit, some of those I have spoken to were not unaffected by her portrayal of an indecisive and progressively less democratic Europe.'[124] It was the same in those countries where Lady Thatcher was seen as 'a beacon'. In a telegram to the Foreign Office about Lady Thatcher's visit to Warsaw in April 1993, the British ambassador, Sir Michael Llewellyn-Smith, noted that Lady Thatcher's 'strictures on Maastricht were listened to politely but without effect on Polish desire to join the Community (in whatever form it takes)'.[125]

Beyond that, her comments on the EU were largely priced in or effectively discounted in other places she visited outside Europe. Reporting on Lady Thatcher's visit to South Korea in 1992, the British ambassador said, 'the intra-European debate about Maastricht simply went right over Koreans' heads'.[126] Also in 1992, Britain's ambassador to Japan, Sir John Boyd, reported to the Foreign Office, 'Her views on Europe, not remotely concealed here, are accepted as part of the landscape.' Boyd went on, 'I do not think that in Japanese government circles they undercut a detached appraisal of the current facts in Europe or Japanese interests – which remain strongly axed on coherence and stability in the Community.'[127]

That said, as is widely documented, Lady Thatcher caused the Major government significant difficulties during the Maastricht Bill's passage. She was to continue causing difficulties for the Conservative Party leadership, in and out of power, on the EU issue for the rest of her siren years. In her symbol years, and even beyond her death, she continued to play a role in the debates on the EU. There are several reasons for this.

First, as the former Conservative MP Sir Michael Marshall wrote to this author in June 1998, 'one cannot escape the numbers game'. Given the size of the government's majority after 1992 and given the number of people who shared her views on the EU, Lady Thatcher was in a more powerful position to influence the debate than she would otherwise have been. 'There were opportunities for her to exert some influence during the Major administration because of the narrow parliamentary majority,' says Marshall. 'Thus, much of the drive by the European sceptics was sustained through linkage at least in name with her.'

Allied to this is the change in the make-up of the parliamentary party, starting in 1992. That election brought in Iain Duncan Smith, John Whittingdale and Bernard Jenkin, to name just three who went on to have leading roles on Lady Thatcher's side of the debate. As John Major recognised, some of the young backbenchers revered Lady Thatcher.

That continued in 1997. In correspondence with this author in May 1998, former Conservative MP Sir David Knox said the 1992 and 1997 Conservative intakes 'were strongly anti-E.E.C'. Interviewed in July 1998, Sir David elaborated: 'We're now talking about eight years after it happened. Now I think her influence is declining in terms of what she says about things today but it's not declining in respect of her children. They are in Parliament.' Speaking of the 1997 intake in his memoirs, Ken Clarke reflected that it was 'much more Eurosceptic than previous cohorts, altering the balance of the party considerably'.[128] Clarke noted they were called 'Thatcher's Children'. This helped to cement Lady Thatcher's continuing ability to influence the debate, which went beyond even the 1997 intake. Some of the tributes paid to Lady Thatcher in the House of Commons after her death were from even newer MPs who talked about how she had inspired them to get involved in politics.[129]

The extent of Lady Thatcher's influence in this area is further illustrated when we consider that during her siren years, and indeed beyond, there was another Conservative former Prime Minister who was as passionate about the EU, even if from the other side of the argument to Lady Thatcher.

Edward Heath was almost always at odds with party policy, but whereas Lady Thatcher tended to think that party policy was too accommodating to the EU, for Heath it seemed it was never sufficiently accommodating. Each thought party policy did not go far enough, just in the opposite sense, and both were clear in their views wherever in the world they stated them. Reporting on responses Heath had given Chinese leaders at the end of September and beginning of October 1992, when they asked about Maastricht and the ERM, the British ambassador to China, Sir Robin McLaren, reported, 'It will surprise no one that the views which Sir E. Heath gave in response to their questions were very much his own.'[130] In 1991, the British ambassador to South Korea had told the Foreign Office that Heath had said to the South Korean Foreign Minister, 'Europe was bound to develop to some form of "constitutional unit".' The ambassador added, 'I disassociated myself from this comment.' In the margin of the telegram, someone wrote '!'[131] Yet, for all of this, it was Lady Thatcher who seemed to generate the greater and more intense response.

It is also important to note Lady Thatcher's role in Brexit, over which her spirit seemed to hover. This was taken to surreal levels at the beginning of June 2016, when a man in Portsmouth photographed a cloud formation that he jokingly said looked like Lady Thatcher and suggested it was a sign that she was 'watching over' the EU referendum.[132]

More seriously, as Moore argues, the final volume of his biography shows how much Lady Thatcher did to lay the groundwork for the 2016 referendum. 'Of all past political leaders, Margaret Thatcher is the single biggest influence in Britain's struggle over Europe,' he concluded.[133]

In March 2015, in his penultimate Commons' speech, Gordon Brown said Lady Thatcher's Bruges speech was 'seminal' and quoted from it in support of 'three maxims that sum up what I believe is the patriotic view of Britain's future'. Having done so, he noted, 'I know that many Conservative Members may find some of those statements challenging or difficult.'[134] Two months later, Jonathan

Freedland wrote, 'The coming referendum on Europe will, for many Tories, carry a spectral echo of [Lady Thatcher's] famous battle cry: "No. No. No."'[135]

Marking the thirtieth anniversary of Lady Thatcher's resignation in 2020, Jon Craig commented, 'Mrs Thatcher's demise unleashed a ferocious Tory psychodrama over Europe which reached its climax with the EU referendum in 2016.'[136]

Speaking in the Lords in July 2016, Nigel Lawson said the referendum result would enable the completion of Lady Thatcher's work. He said the next government and the next Prime Minister would have 'a historic opportunity to make the United Kingdom the most dynamic and freest country in the whole of Europe – in a word, to finish the job that Margaret Thatcher started'.[137] He repeated the point in a *Daily Telegraph* article in September 2016. It was headlined 'Brexit will complete Margaret Thatcher's economic revolution'.[138]

Before the referendum, debates were had about how Lady Thatcher would have voted. Charles Powell argued she would have backed David Cameron's renegotiation deal, while Norman Tebbit disagreed, commenting, 'I think it more likely that were she alive, then she would be saying: "No, no, no."'.[139] In February 2016, Charles Moore said that as Lady Thatcher's official biographer, whenever he made a speech, people asked, 'What would Maggie do?' He noted he was being asked the question in relation to the referendum and said he always gave the same answer, 'I do not know (and nor does anyone else).'[140]

After the referendum, debates were had about how Lady Thatcher would have handled the negotiations. In September 2018, Kathy Gyngell, editor of The Conservative Woman, wrote an article entitled 'Theresa May and Margaret Thatcher – compare and despair'.

In it, she recalled Lady Thatcher's Second Reading speech on the Maastricht Bill in June 1993, writing that Theresa May was 'in the process of caving in to almost every principle that Mrs T so excellently conveyed were vital for a nation state'.[141]

On 6 December 2020, *The Sun* ran an article headlined 'BOJO'S NOT FOR TURNING: Boris Johnson channels Margaret Thatcher as he vows to stand firm against France's 11th-hour Brexit demands'. The accompanying photograph was half Boris Johnson, half Lady Thatcher. 'EU turn if you want to but we're not for turning. That's what Boris is saying, so it's time for him to follow in Mrs Thatcher's footsteps and stand firm,' said Theresa Villiers.[142]

Lady Thatcher's role in Brexit, as a dead former Prime Minister, is worthy of a study on its own. So is the role of the living premiers emeritus, from John Major to Liz Truss, all of whom, as ex-premiers, have intervened on the issue. To illustrate the point, the front cover of the 16–29 October 2015 edition of *Private Eye* declared: 'Pro-EU campaign launched'. It featured a photo of John Major, Tony Blair and Gordon Brown chatting. A speech bubble coming out of their mouths says, 'We only ever meet at funerals and referendums'. From the bottom right, another speech bubble asks, 'Which is this?'[143]

'Voice of conscience': the former Yugoslavia

When they were released, the Thatcher Foundation analysed UK government files for 1994. Among the roles it noted Lady Thatcher playing at that point, it listed 'the familiar and powerful voice of conscience, a latter-day Gladstone flaying Western policy over Bosnia'.[144]

From 1991 until 1999, the former Yugoslavia was another policy area on which Lady Thatcher concentrated. About Bosnia especially,

Lady Thatcher felt deeply and personally. Feelings of shame and of disgust pervade her comments on the issue. 'I never again in my lifetime expected to see Britain appease an aggressor and leave him to attack innocent victims,' she said in October 1993. 'Britain! The bastion of liberty! I feel guilty about it.'[145]

Lady Thatcher's objective on Bosnia was the arming of the Bosnian Muslims and supporting them through air strikes on Serbian military targets.

By September 1991, Lady Thatcher was 'deeply concerned about the West's failure to see what was at stake in the former Yugoslavia, where Slovenia's and Croatia's bids for freedom from the oppressive impoverishment of communism were being challenged by armed force'.[146] John Campbell said she took 'an early, clear and courageous view' on the issue.[147]

Just before Christmas, Lady Thatcher recorded an interview for HRT (Croatian Radiotelevision)[148] in which she urged international recognition of Croatia and Slovenia. Herself holding the microphone, Lady Thatcher concluded by stating, 'And I shall continue myself to put their case and to put it as forcibly as I can.'[149] A month earlier, she had called publicly for Britain to recognise and arm Croatia.[150] 'She was the first figure of any stature to call for international recognition of Croatian independence,' the Thatcher Foundation notes.[151]

Lady Thatcher's views were recorded in the Cabinet meeting held on 28 November 1991.[152] So, in the space of two weeks, Lady Thatcher had been discussed in two separate Cabinet meetings (the first being her call for a referendum on a single currency).

Before going public, Lady Thatcher had raised concerns privately. 'I said early to people over whom I would have *hoped* to have had some influence that I thought, as the hostilities got worse and worse and more and more Croatians were being killed and massacred, that it would have been right to recognise Croatia and Slovenia as independent,' she told HRT.[153]

In his diary on 8 May 1991, Sir Patrick Wright recorded Douglas Hurd telling him that 'he had had a blast from Margaret Thatcher, at the party he had held for Charles Powell, about our policy towards Yugoslavia': 'She seems to have got the idea that Croatia is the heartland of Thatcherite democracy!' he added.[154]

On 27 June, Slovenia and Croatia declared their independence. Douglas Hurd was at a European summit in Luxembourg when it happened and noted in his diary: 'MT telephones me and issues instructions,' before reflecting that it was seven months since she had ceased to have that right.[155] Hurd spoke of Lady Thatcher sending him letters, making telephone calls and having meetings with him throughout the four years of war in Croatia and Bosnia.

On the briefing prepared for John Major on the announcement in June 1991 that Lady Thatcher would be standing down as an MP, Stephen Wall wrote in his own hand, 'Mrs T. will give interviews. We know of no firm intention to talk about Slovenia. Andrew [Turnbull] was simply worried that she might say something.'[156]

Robin Harris records that, in August 1991, as Yugoslav army tanks headed for the Croatian capital, Zagreb, pressure was placed on Lady Thatcher to remain silent in public. 'She was, though, allowed the opportunity to shout and protest with indignation to the Foreign Secretary, Douglas Hurd, over the telephone,' he went on. Hurd, apparently, 'took no notice'.[157]

In February 1992, Lady Thatcher was due to meet John Major. In a note for him ahead of the meeting, Stephen Wall wrote, 'I doubt if you will want to raise Yugoslavia. Mrs Thatcher might, though we have done what she wanted in recognising Croatia.'[158] This may not have really satisfied Lady Thatcher. Reporting on his dinner for her the evening before her Hague speech in May 1992, the British ambassador to the Netherlands, Sir Michael Jenkins, commented, 'Mrs Thatcher spoke at length and with remarkable passion about Yugoslavia, asserting that the Twelve should have recognised – and indeed armed – Croatia far earlier, and that when they did recognise it, it was for the wrong reasons, as a result of German pressure.'[159]

Lady Thatcher's work on Bosnia began in earnest in 1992. On 30 July, she sent two handwritten 'angry, agitated' letters[160] – one to the Prime Minister, the other to the Foreign Secretary.[161] To the latter she enclosed a fuller, formal letter. The Thatcher Foundation describes these letters as 'among the angriest she ever wrote' and notes that in the letter to Hurd, 'she was barely even polite'.[162]

'I am appalled that the countries of the west have taken no effective action to deal with the massacres taking place in the midst of Europe. It isn't that we can't, it's that we won't,' she wrote in her covering letter to Hurd. 'No-one with a conscience can let this go on.' 'Please do not give me a brush-off letter,' she added.[163] In the fuller letter, Lady Thatcher set out how she thought the situation could and should be dealt with.

Lady Thatcher's letter to Major states, 'As the Foreign Office knows I have been distraught about the situation in Bosnia and Croatia for months.' Ever practical, she added, 'As far as I personally am concerned I am trying to help relieve the suffering a little by assisting Lady Nott in her efforts to have a British camp to look after some of the refugees.'[164]

The Thatcher Foundation noted that the letters 'must have been acutely uncomfortable to receive'.[165] Major and Hurd discussed them. Major said Lady Thatcher needed a more or less point-by-point reply, including with input from the Ministry of Defence,[166] meaning her private intervention created work for not just Downing Street, but two other government departments. Commenting on a draft response, Major wrote that the ending was 'abrupt'. He suggested Lady Thatcher was offered a meeting or that Hurd would welcome her views at any time.[167] Hurd's reply to Lady Thatcher – running to seven sides of A4 – was dated 6 August. He wrote, 'Our analysis is not exactly the same as yours, but there are many common points.' He also rejected military action.[168]

By then, Lady Thatcher had gone global. Having decided it was her 'moral duty to act', she took 'the highest-profile initiative' she could.[169] Despairing of a hearing in Britain, she wrote an article for the *New York Times* on 6 August hoping to influence the American government and American public opinion.[170] The article was headlined 'Stop the Excuses. Help Bosnia Now'.

'I sought to awaken the conscience of the West by arguing that by doing nothing we were acting as accomplices,' she said of the article, stressing the moral and practical aspects of her call. 'But I also covered the strict practicalities.'[171] The article was accompanied by a television appearance. In 1995, when being interviewed by Larry King, she commented, in a possibly Freudian slip, 'It was in 1992 that I was so disgusted that I did a television performance'.[172]

Moore describes the *New York Times* article as 'a watershed moment'.[173] In a telegram to the Foreign Office on 11 August, the British Embassy in Washington noted, 'Lady Thatcher's views continue to attract prominent and sympathetic coverage.'[174] As for the impact back in the UK, Major and Hurd were 'incensed' by Lady Thatcher's intervention.[175]

They had cause to be further incensed the following April. On 12 April 1993, the Bosnian Serb army attacked Srebrenica killing over fifty people, including children.

The next day, Lady Thatcher 'solicited interviews to make her views plain'.[176] On the BBC *Six O'Clock News*, she described Douglas Hurd's comment that lifting the arms embargo on the Bosnian Muslims would create a 'level killing field' as 'a terrible and disgraceful phrase'. She accused the West of being 'a little like an accomplice to massacre' and called for the Bosnian Muslims to be armed and for a Western ultimatum to be given to the Serbs with the threat of force.[177]

On *Channel 4 News* that evening, Malcolm Rifkind, the then Defence Secretary, described Lady Thatcher's phrase 'a little like an accomplice to massacre' as 'emotional nonsense'.[178] A *Times* leader described Rifkind's comment as a 'cheap rejoinder',[179] though he stood by it in his memoirs.[180] In comparison, Hurd later reflected that 'level killing field' 'shocked rather than educated'.[181]

Whether 'emotional nonsense' or not, the Bosnian Serbs agreed with Rifkind's assessment. In a letter dated 14 April, Radovan Karadžić, the Bosnian Serbs' leader, told Rifkind he had accurately described the response.[182] The then Senator Joe Biden took a different view, arguing, 'Mrs. Thatcher's call to arms reflects not emotionalism, as some labelled it, but clear judgment.'[183]

Later in the evening on 13 April, a Downing Street official sent a memo to John Major about Lady Thatcher's interview. The official said Lady Thatcher had 'gone over the top in her language, which is in places highly offensive'. They spoke of the government developing 'our counter attack' but advised against 'being dragged into a personal exchange' with Lady Thatcher. They thought that her 'more offensive allegations' were best met by the government with 'dignified silence': 'we should leave it to others to pick holes in them, or brief on these points unattributably', it said, noting that 'she has not made the error of calling for ground forces to be sent in'.[184]

The next morning, 14 April, Baroness Chalker, a Foreign Office minister, appeared on the BBC Radio 4 *Today* programme and was asked about Lady Thatcher's comments. Chalker said that though she felt no less strongly than Lady Thatcher as a minister, she had to keep her emotion under control. She also expressed concern that Lady Thatcher saw the situation in black-and-white terms.[185]

The same day, an article by Peter Riddell in *The Times*, 'Churchill's champion churns up the "level killing field"', spoke of 'Bosnia: The Thatcher intervention'. Riddell commented, 'Nothing that Margaret Thatcher has said or done since leaving Downing Street has had such a devastating impact as last night's broadside against British and European policies on Bosnia.'[186] A *Daily Mail* leader described Lady Thatcher's 'performance' as 'magnificent' but said that John Major 'would be failing in his duty if he did not ask himself those questions which she scorned' and was not 'at liberty to let his head rule his heart'.[187]

Later in the day, Lady Thatcher intervened in Parliament.[188] 'I submit that we cannot continue with a policy which says to the Moslems, "You must submit and surrender",' she said during a statement. 'In answering the question, will the noble Baroness bear in mind that there is nothing moral or right about leaving a people defenceless in the path of a determined dictator aggressor?' she went on. Responding, Lady Chalker, commented, 'My Lords, I understand fully what my noble friend Lady Thatcher said and why she put it in the terms that she did. However, it would simply do no good for Britain alone to act on the basis of the very strong emotion which every person in this House and in another place feels. Let us have no doubts about that.'

Describing Lady Thatcher as 'She Who Must Be Heard' and 'Danger Woman', the *Daily Express* journalist Paul Callan noted her handbag, 'black and sinister, lay by her side on the red leather bench'. He also said that, after speaking, she 'swept out, the aura of power still clinging like heady scent'.[189] Describing her as 'that old pyromaniac', Robert Hardman said the Lords should have known to expect trouble when Lady Thatcher walked in, as 'she was wearing the dark green dress she usually dons for Maastricht offensives'.[190]

In the Commons on 14 April, Conservative MP Harold Elletson asked Malcolm Rifkind if he would 'treat the recent comments of Baroness Thatcher with the contempt that they deserve'.[191] 'My advice to the prime minister,' another Conservative MP, Robert Adley, said, 'is that if he wants foreign policy advice from any of his predecessors, he had better listen to Lord Home and Lord Callaghan rather than this former Finchley fishwife.' On the other side, Winston Churchill MP reflected, 'For somebody who is not in government, there is nobody who speaks with greater force or greater authority.'[192]

Additionally, Lady Thatcher took her call to the United States. As she had in 1992, she attempted to influence both the American government and public opinion, taking to American television to say, 'We cannot let this evil go on.'[193] Joe Biden wrote of her attempting 'to summon the conscience of the West to accept the imperative of military intervention'.[194]

Also on 14 April, the American Embassy in London sent a telegram to the Secretary of State reporting that Lady Thatcher had 'savaged EC and Western inaction over Bosnia'. Her comments were 'scorching', representing her 'starkest attack on her successor'. She had been 'visibly shaking with fury', the telegram said, noting, however, that the government 'brushed aside her criticism'.[195]

During discussions in Cabinet the next day, it was recorded that Rifkind's statement in Parliament the previous day had elicited 'a wide measure of cross-party support' for government policy. The Cabinet also discussed that it should be emphasised publicly that while lifting the arms embargo was an option, 'it would lengthen rather than shorten the conflict in Bosnia'.[196]

On 17 April, Lady Thatcher opened the Hotel Bristol in Warsaw. 'You and I never expected to see concentration camps in our lives again,' she said at a lunch of diplomats and dignitaries. The speech was 'passionate', Julia Langdon reported: 'off the cuff about Bosnia and full of references to evil and tyranny and moral responsibility'. When Lady Thatcher went to her suite afterwards, 'she apparently withdrew privately to regain her composure'.[197]

The next day, 18 April, Labour MP Dale Campbell-Savours put to Rifkind, 'May I say to the Secretary of State what I really do believe? If Margaret Thatcher had been Prime Minister today, she would have sorted out this bloody – I use the word advisedly – nonsense one and a half years ago. At least she demanded that fascism should be stopped in its tracks in the heart of Europe, whereas this Conservative Government have ducked the issue.'[198]

In his diary on 18 April, Woodrow Wyatt wrote that he was 'terrified' of speaking to Lady Thatcher. Earlier in the day, he and Norman Lamont had discussed her 'absurd intervention over Yugoslavia'.[199] An article in *The Economist* on 24 April asked, 'Maggie, mad or magnificent?' and spoke of 'the Thatcher phenomenon' 'stirring consciences' on both sides of the Atlantic and 'shaming world leaders'. It quoted a minister – 'a sturdy admirer' of Lady Thatcher's: 'Mad old hag or one of the world's great elder statesmen? It's not all that easy to see which way she'll go.'[200]

Unlike in 1992, however, Washington was sympathetic. The Clinton administration favoured a tougher stance against the Serbian President, Slobodan Milošević, than Europe did. 'On Bosnia, the

John Major government was abysmal,' Jenonne Walker, of Clinton's National Security Council, reflected. 'Some of us on the staff muttered to each other, "If only Thatcher were still in power…".'[201] In a handwritten letter to President-Elect Clinton dated 6 November 1992, Lady Thatcher had said, 'I am so pleased to see your <u>deep concern</u> for the terrible things that are being done in <u>Bosnia</u>.'[202]

Lady Thatcher did not just direct her views at the British and American governments. She expressed them forcefully wherever she went and to whoever she met around the world.

In September 1993, she visited Malaysia. The UK's high commissioner, Duncan Slater, briefed her in August, and his meeting notes record that when Bosnia came up, 'Lady Thatcher became incandescent.' Western, particularly British, policy was 'catastrophic', she said. Slater's 'attempts to deploy counter-arguments were swept aside'. Lady Thatcher said she and Malaysia's Prime Minister, Dr Mahathir bin Mohamad, had corresponded with each other and were 'in full agreement on the action necessary'. 'When the storm had subsided somewhat', Slater said he thought it was vital that differences between the British and Malaysian governments over Bosnia should not damage their overall good relationship. 'We are going to have a problem with Lady Thatcher,' Slater concluded.[203]

His prediction proved correct. 'The Bosnian theme was dominant: she repeatedly attacked the West's perceived failure to stand up to Serbian aggression,' reported Slater's telegram after her visit. Slater also said that in her private conversations with him, Lady Thatcher was even more outspoken. She rejected his arguments that she was grossly over-simplifying the situation and left him in no doubt about 'the degree of her disenchantment' with British policy. Lady Thatcher met Dr Mahathir alone and told Slater that most of her conversation with him had been about Bosnia and that they were in complete agreement. Slater said her opinions would have been music to Dr Mahathir's ears and likely to have reinforced him in his view that Western policy was fundamentally wrong. Slater had the strong impression that Lady Thatcher was reluctant to do anything to help the government's relationship with Malaysia. He predicted that unless there were some change, Bosnia would be the most difficult issue John Major would have to deal with when he visited a couple of weeks later.[204]

Events bore out Slater's prediction again. The briefing prepared for the meeting Douglas Hurd had with Lady Thatcher on 13 October 1993 noted that Dr Mahathir's 'public outburst at the welcoming dinner for the Prime Minister on 21 September … probably owed more than a little to Lady Thatcher's endorsement of Dr Mahathir's views.'[205] At a press conference in Kuala Lumpur on 22 September, some of Lady Thatcher's comments about Bosnia were put to John Major. 'I didn't hear what may have been said on that occasion and I am not going to comment directly on remarks I didn't myself hear and haven't seen in context,' he replied.[206]

As for Slater, on his telegram an official wrote in their own hand, 'Much as expected.' It noted that their efforts to keep Lady Thatcher off 'an all out attack' on the UK's Bosnia policy was 'clearly to no avail': 'Mr Slater could not have done more,' the official concluded.[207]

It was not just in Malaysia that Lady Thatcher made her views known. Writing of her June 1994 visit to Abu Dhabi, a British official told the Foreign Office, 'Judging from comments made by Lady Thatcher, both in her formal speech and in answer to questions put to her at the lunches, her views on Bosnia would have been well received by Sheikh Zayed.' On 21 June, *Gulf News* ran a story headlined 'Maggie: It's not civil war, it's Serb aggression'.[208]

NATO eventually launched air strikes on Serb forces in

September 1995. Before that, Lady Thatcher had spoken in Parliament again. Following a Serb offensive against Srebrenica, she intervened in a ministerial statement on 12 July, concluding: 'Please will my noble friend take away the message that soft words will not do? We need stern, calmly calculated, effective action.'[209]

In June 1995 Lady Thatcher had given the *Sunday Times* a statement on the Serb hostage crisis:[210] '... the big questions about our policy in Bosnia have not gone away. Only when the Serb aggressor is defeated by a properly armed Bosnian army will peace return to the Balkans. And that must be the long-term goal.'[211]

Lady Thatcher was to have what might be termed an Indian summer on the issue of the former Yugoslavia. In September 1998 she spoke in Zagreb about 'the terror and oppression which still flow, not now into Croatia or even Bosnia, but to Kosovo, where again the ethnic cleansers are at work. And who knows where and when the madness will end.'[212]

Following the failure of diplomatic efforts to end the conflict, NATO began air strikes against Yugoslavia in March 1999. Lady Thatcher said this was 'a just and necessary war': 'I believe too that Prime Minister Tony Blair – of whom I also have many criticisms – in this case showed real determination in conducting it,' she opined.[213] Blair had called in Lady Thatcher to seek her advice,[214] which involved her visiting Downing Street, writing to him and speaking to him over the telephone.[215]

Blair also sought advice about whether to speak to John Major. 'The fact is he won't add anything useful,' one of his advisers responded, 'and it is merely a damage limitation exercise – show he is taking counsel from his predecessors and neutralising the Tories. But better done now before it becomes an issue.'[216]

As for Lady Thatcher, on 21 April 1999, *The Sun* reported that

Blair was 'extremely grateful for her unstinting support'. The article was headlined 'Maggie: War on Slobba is right'.[217] When some on the right criticised the campaign, Lady Thatcher 'considered it necessary' to express publicly the support she had given Blair privately.[218] In her speech marking the twentieth anniversary of her entering Downing Street, she set out why the campaign mattered.[219]

It was not just those on the right in the UK that Lady Thatcher was prepared to help 'neutralise'. She did so with foreign figures too. On 27 April, Blair had a telephone conversation with Lady Thatcher during which he asked her to approach the Czech opposition leader, Václav Klaus, about his lack of support for NATO operations. Lady Thatcher 'agreed immediately' to speak to him. Reporting this to the Foreign Office, a Downing Street official commented, 'It would be helpful to know if our Embassy in Prague picks up any reverberations from the [sic] Thatcher/Havel exchange.'[220]

On 30 April, she wrote a strongly worded letter to the Hungarian Prime Minister, Viktor Orbán. Commenting on the Hungarian government's statement that NATO ground forces would never be allowed to launch an attack on Serbia from Hungarian territory, she spoke of her 'astonishment' and said she was 'dismayed'. She reminded Orbán that she had 'employed all my efforts, particularly with friends in the United States, to urge the incorporation of Hungary into NATO'. Her letter ended with a plea: 'For the sake of Hungary's reputation, I do most earnestly ask you to reconsider it.' On a copy of the letter shared with Blair, the word 'wonderful' is handwritten as commentary, seemingly by Blair himself.[221]

Reflections

In a profile piece in the *Sunday Times* to mark Lady Thatcher's seventieth birthday in 1995, her friends were reported as saying that 'the biggest disappointment' of her post-Downing Street years was 'her inability to influence events in Bosnia'.[222] Perhaps this was being too harsh on Lady Thatcher, confusing 'influence' with 'change'.

While it can never be known how many lives might have been saved, or indeed how many lives might have been lost, if Lady Thatcher's recommendations had been implemented, there is no doubt she influenced the debate. In April 1993, *The Economist* said that her 'passion on the Balkans, whatever the merits of her proposals, has concentrated minds wonderfully',[223] while Peter Riddell wrote that same month: 'Lady Thatcher's interventions, whatever their flaws of diagnosis and prognosis, have forced the Bosnian issue to the centre of the political debate.'[224]

Riddell's article was entitled 'Thatcher outburst finds little support among Tory right', which helps to explain why she might not have been able to exert more influence on events. Unlike on Maastricht, for example, she did not have a group of supporters agreeing with her – or at least not in sufficient numbers for her to make more of a difference. So, on this issue, the 'numbers game' worked against her.

Ministers were not sympathetic to Lady Thatcher's arguments – rather the reverse. This showed the limits of Lady Thatcher's influence. That she had had to speak out publicly – and in the way that she did – was because she was not being listened to privately. As another premier emeritus once noted, they had most influence when it was least known publicly.[225] Lady Thatcher had no influence on government policy, and that was very much known publicly. 'She was disregarded by most of the British political class over Bosnia,' Harris stated.[226]

A disregard for Lady Thatcher's views was not confined to the British political class on this matter, either. As she wrote in *The*

Path to Power, 'the issue on which my view and that of the Western foreign policy establishments differed most was Bosnia'.[227] In his April 1993 telegram to the Foreign Office about Lady Thatcher's visit to Poland, the British ambassador commented, 'Her references to Bosnia will also have had an effect in bringing home the tragedy, but some of her listeners were aware that the issues are more complex than she suggested.'[228] Lady Thatcher's August 1992 attempt to influence the Bush administration was also not successful. 'The impact of her intervention was huge, and at one point it looked as if Bush would be shamed into changing his approach. But, having wobbled one way, he wobbled back again, under State Department pressure,' argues Harris.[229]

While Lady Thatcher may have felt disappointment at not being able to have more impact, she did make a difference – both leading and giving voice to public feeling. 'The difficulty', wrote Norman Fowler in his diary on 14 April 1993, 'is that Margaret has correctly detected the mood of the British public.'[230] More widely, as Harris noted, 'she appealed to the conscience of the world, and in the end Bosnia was saved'.[231] Aitken spoke of her being 'largely vindicated'.[232]

Lady Thatcher also received praise from some perhaps unlikely sources. Ian Gilmour, a long-time Conservative critic of Lady Thatcher's policies, said she had 'spoken eloquently and cogently on the tragedy of Bosnia',[233] while former Labour Cabinet minister and leading Liberal Democrat Shirley Williams referred to her having 'spoken with such eloquence'.[234] Lord Callaghan said, 'I agree with the noble Baroness, Lady Thatcher, that that is a real symbol of shame and frustration as regards what the West has failed to do in that situation.'[235]

In addition, we learnt more about Lady Thatcher's character from her work on Bosnia. During her visit to Singapore in September

1993, she met Lee Kuan Yew. Bosnia came up in the conversation. Lee Kuan Yew said that France, Britain and Germany had forced the UN into Bosnia. Lady Thatcher said that they were 'simply palliating their consciences'. She said the whole process had been 'futile, dishonourable and dishonest'. Reporting to the Foreign Office, Britain's high commissioner Gordon Duggan noted that at this point in the conversation, 'turning to me she said that I could report that in my telegram'.[236]

We also saw Lady Thatcher playing the character that was Margaret Thatcher. On 30 November 1994, she was interviewed by John Simpson, who asked her view of how the Foreign Office and Douglas Hurd had acted. 'The Foreign Office will not be surprised to know that I disagree with them,' she replied. When pressed about Hurd, she responded, 'Douglas, I like Douglas very much, he and I disagree on how to tackle these problems and I must say on the whole my method of tackling … aggression was quite a good one when I was in office.'[237]

'A tower of support': General Pinochet

'Lady Thatcher was a tower of support during the dark days,' said a friend of General Pinochet in March 2000.[238]

From the time of the general's arrest in October 1998 through to his return to Chile in March 2000, Lady Thatcher worked tirelessly to secure his release. She regarded his detention as 'a great injustice which should never have taken place'[239] and thought Pinochet was owed a great debt for the support he had provided Britain during the Falklands War.

When news of Pinochet's arrest broke, Lady Thatcher wrote a letter to The Times protesting it. Harris concluded, 'it was probably her single most important contribution to his release',[240] the main value of her activity after that being 'simply to keep the case on the front pages',[241] which she did in various ways. She visited Pinochet in March and June 1999, and pictures of them chatting during the earlier visit were carried live on Sky. In July, Lady Thatcher sent Pinochet some whisky: 'Scotch is one British institution which will never let you down,' she said.[242]

In her last ever parliamentary speech, Lady Thatcher spoke in the House of Lords on 6 July 1999.[243] Speeches were limited to four minutes, and as she entered her seventh minute, the Chief Whip, Lord Carter, intervened. 'My Lords, I am nearly at the end of my speech,' she responded. When she gave way, Lord Carter reminded her of the four-minute limit and asked if she could conclude her remarks. 'My Lords, I am very close to the end and I very rarely take up the time of this House,' Lady Thatcher replied. 'It will now take me longer because the noble Lord interrupted me in the middle of a sentence.'

This demonstrated Lady Thatcher's lack of understanding of House of Lords procedure, her comments about rarely speaking suggesting she had thereby accumulated extra minutes for herself. The day after the debate, the former Labour Cabinet minister, Lord Barnett, said to this author, 'Eventually, she had to be stopped. She was only allowed four minutes and she'd gone to seven minutes when our Chief Whip, historically, was willing to bring her down and stop her speaking; but she had overstepped the mark, considerably in terms of time.'

'Overstepped the mark' being, no doubt, what a lot of people (mostly men) thought Lady Thatcher did too often after 1990.

Lord Norton of Louth was also present at the debate and re-members the above exchanges. He also remembers something else, not captured in Hansard. Next to Lady Thatcher was Lord Howe of Aberavon, and Lord Norton commented to this author on how close they were sat to each other. This physical closeness was especially noteworthy given the role Lord Howe had played in her downfall and the previous souring of their relationship.

Lady Thatcher spoke at the Conservative Party conference in October 1999[244] and opened in full Margaret Thatcher character: 'My friends, it's nine years since I spoke at a Conservative Party conference. A lot has happened since then – and not much of it for the better...' She accused the government of 'collaborating in Senator Pinochet's judicial kidnap', describing him as 'this country's only political prisoner'. She spoke of 'international lynch-law', a 'show-trial': 'I never thought in my lifetime to see the honour of Britain and the reputation of British justice so demeaned as in this affair. All those responsible must be shamed, and held publicly to account,' she said. In the *Daily Telegraph* the speech was described as 'possibly the most ferocious attack made by a former Prime Minister on a serving British leader'.[245] 'The occasion seemed slightly dotty,' Moore reflected, 'an impression which the media played up.'[246] As for its impact on the Conservative Party, it was the night before William Hague's speech. 'The day was ruined,' he told Norman Lamont.[247]

Not all Lady Thatcher's activity was public. Behind the scenes she wrote to the Spanish Prime Minister[248] and to Pope John Paul II, asking the latter to 'consider making a personal and public intervention'.[249]

She also raised the case with Tony Blair, writing to him on 25 November 1998. Opening with 'My dear Prime Minister', she said that however strongly people felt about some of the abuses which had taken place while Pinochet was in power, 'the right decision now is to act swiftly to release him to return home', recalling her actions in Zimbabwe and Blair's own on the Good Friday Agreement. She recognised that what she was proposing would excite criticism in some quarters, 'But my judgement is that you are not someone to be deflected from taking the right actions by that,' she added.[250]

Pinochet was not released and Lady Thatcher 'reacted furiously' when Blair described him as 'unspeakable' at the Labour Party conference in 1999.[251] Lady Thatcher was also said to be 'furious' that William Hague 'dithered' before defending Pinochet against the government's extradition attempt.[252]

Reflections

Given the circumstances of General Pinochet's release, following medical examinations, it is difficult to assess what difference, if any, Lady Thatcher made on this issue. That said, in addition to keeping Pinochet's detention in the public eye, Lady Thatcher was also able to play the character that was Margaret Thatcher.

As the plane taking Pinochet back to Chile was on the runway in March 2000, she had a silver Armada dish sent to him. She enclosed a short note of explanation: 'These dishes were first produced in England in order to celebrate another victory over the Spanish – that of our own navy against the Spanish Armada in 1588. I am sure that you will appreciate and enjoy the symbolism!'[253] Lady Thatcher recorded that she was 'amused to learn that the Spanish, who still suffer from an inferiority complex about the Armada, were furious and the Spanish Foreign Minister apoplectic'.

She went on: 'I had clearly made my point.'[254] It is a sentence that captures so much of Lady Thatcher's character as well as the character that was Margaret Thatcher, and one applicable to Lady Thatcher's premier emeritus years, if not to her whole career and life.

'A better and stouter friend': Hong Kong and China

For Lady Thatcher, the implementation of the Joint Declaration between the UK and China for the return of Hong Kong to Chinese rule in 1997 was Britain's 'ultimate responsibility'.[255] It was also a responsibility Lady Thatcher took personally. In *Statecraft*, she wrote of feeling 'a strong moral obligation to do my best for the former colony'.[256]

Some of that moral obligation may have stemmed from feelings of regret, if not guilt. In 2007, Lady Thatcher spoke publicly for the first time of her regret about the 'impossible' situation she faced in negotiating the agreement with China for Hong Kong's handover.[257] In a March 1991 memo to John Major, Charles Powell noted, 'For the press the Government is bent on selling out Hong Kong to the Chinese without even establishing full democracy. We are constantly portrayed as grovelling to the Chinese and accepting their diktat.' 'According to that view,' Powell went on, 'your predecessor should have Hong Kong engraved on her heart, as Calais was carved on the heart of Queen Mary.'[258]

Whatever motivated Lady Thatcher's sense of moral obligation, she discharged it in three main ways up to 1997. She dealt with China, attempted to generate and maintain confidence in Hong Kong and strongly supported Chris Patten as Governor.

Lady Thatcher visited China in September 1991 and wrote about the trip in *Statecraft* under the heading, 'Hard pounding in Beijing'. She noted it had been a 'bruising visit'.[259]

As detailed in FCO files in the National Archives, Lady Thatcher met Qian Qichen, the Minister for Foreign Affairs, Rong Yiren, the Vice-Chairman of the Standing Committee of the National People's Congress, Li Peng, the Premier of the State Council, and Jiang Zemin, the Party General Secretary. She was accompanied by

John Gerson, her interpreter and personal adviser on China, who made notes of the meetings. Lady Thatcher shared these with the ambassador to China, Sir Robin McLaren, doing so 'with the injunction not to pass them on to the FCO'.[260]

Thankfully for historians of Lady Thatcher, and her post-premiership, McLaren did in fact share the notes with the FCO, albeit with a very limited distribution, as these records provide a fascinating insight into the issues Lady Thatcher raised, the way she raised them and the reaction she generated among the Chinese leadership.

During her meeting with Qian Qichen, Lady Thatcher, reflecting on the failed coup in the Soviet Union, said that in the contemporary world, tanks and guns could not overpower people's aspirations. 'Qian Qichen looked ill at ease,' Gerson noted. As for the meeting with Rong Yiren, he had appeared 'rather edgy' but 'relaxed considerably' over lunch. Gerson's note of the meeting with Jiang Zemin refers to 'a spirited debate'.

Gerson spoke to Charles Moore about the meeting with Li Peng,[261] which took place in the Ziguang Hall. Behind the principals sat about 200 Chinese high officials, and Gerson advised Lady Thatcher that they were there sitting in judgement on how well Li performed against her. She asked after Zhao Ziyang, her co-signatory of the Joint Declaration, who had been arrested on Li's orders for being too soft on the Tiananmen students. Lady Thatcher then opened her handbag and from it, she produced a tie. She then asked Li to give it to Zhao on her behalf, putting Li in 'a very awkward position' in front of his watching colleagues. Gerson said he 'held the tie as if it were a cobra', and thought Lady Thatcher had behaved in a way which the Chinese both respected and feared, considering it 'the most impressive leader-to-leader conversation' he had ever heard.

Gerson's record of the meeting notes the effect Lady Thatcher had on Li, who 'looked tired and worried'. At one point, Li was 'clearly nettled'; at another he 'looked rattled'. At a further point, Gerson noted, 'While Mr Li appeared to recover his composure, Mrs Thatcher raised the subject of human rights.' Lady Thatcher 'lightened the atmosphere' by telling Li of her efforts in support of China's Most Favoured Nation trading status with the United States, at which 'Li Peng looked very pleased indeed'. When Lady Thatcher praised China's response to a recent flood, Li 'appeared still more pleased'.

After Lady Thatcher left China, McLaren sent the FCO telegrams about the visit. In one marked 'Confidential', McLaren wrote that Lady Thatcher had 'expressed her views with her customary force and conviction', describing the meeting with Li Peng as 'vigorous and hard hitting'. At dinner, Jiang Zemin was 'at pains to be the good host', and 'Mrs Thatcher matched his knowledge of English poetry and 1940s films'.[262] (Interestingly, when McLaren accompanied Edward Heath to a meeting with Jiang in February 1993, he recorded, 'Much of the conversation was about musical matters.'[263]) In a telegram marked 'Restricted', McLaren reported that Lady Thatcher had told him she had agreed with the Chinese that she would say that 'the talks were held in a very frank and friendly atmosphere'.[264]

After Beijing, Lady Thatcher flew to Hong Kong. 'As the Prime Minister who entered into the agreement with China about Hong Kong's future,' she told business leaders, 'I have and shall always have an abiding interest in and concern for the people and events in this territory.'[265] The Governor, David Wilson, told the FCO that Lady Thatcher had given a 'generally optimistic account' and 'firmly supported the prime minister's decision to sign the memorandum of understanding on the airport and visit China', highlighting that 'she took great care with what she said in public'.[266]

Lady Thatcher's relationship with the Chinese remained bruising in the run-up to the handover. In September 1993, there was a 'high-profile publication of Deng's harsh 1982 statement to Mrs Thatcher about Hong Kong' and the British Embassy reported to the Foreign Office that there was 'no explanation given'.[267]

Nevertheless, Lady Thatcher continued engaging with China and its leadership. John Campbell noted 'a particularly sharp diplomatic crisis' in March 1995,[268] and the background to Lady Thatcher's trip that month is detailed in a file released by the National Archives in November 2023.[269] As with so many of the files in the National Archives, this one illustrates the nuanced way Lady Thatcher acted as an ex-premier, at least on occasion. Her trip had been planned since the autumn of 1994, and she had also initially planned to visit Taiwan. She took advice not to go, however, given its potential impact on relations with China.

FCO officials welcomed the visit to China as an 'opportunity to deliver key messages about Hong Kong and UK–China relations'.[270] To the FCO, the British ambassador to China, Sir Leonard Appleyard, commented in November 1994, 'I believe that, rightly handled, the visit could make a significant contribution to British interests here, particularly if Ministers are able to invest some time in discussing objectives with Lady Thatcher beforehand.' Reflecting that relations between Britain and China might not have improved by March 1995, Appleyard noted that Chinese leaders might be 'in the mood for showing their machismo by wrangling with Lady Thatcher, in the spirit of Deng Xiaoping vintage 1982'. Even so,

Appleyard thought they would be likely to 'show restraint unless Lady Thatcher decides to let them have it with some fighting talk about Tiananmen'.[271]

Earlier in November, Appleyard had told the FCO that 'Lady Thatcher would need to be very carefully briefed on what to say about the Hong Kong dimension' and this would have to be 'calibrated and implemented with great care'. 'Conversely, an energetic and free-wheeling discussion could cause us all some real problems,' he added, possibly revealing his level of understanding of Lady Thatcher and how others reacted to her.

Appleyard ended his telegram by pointing out that Edward Heath had plans to visit China in spring 1995, noting that the Chinese always gave Heath 'top-level treatment'. 'It would obviously be awkward (though intriguing) if they were both here at exactly the same time,' Appleyard went on, concluding that there was 'the risk of a comparison being made between the way in which both former Prime Ministers were treated'.[272] Sadly this was not to be, because Lady Thatcher visited in March and Heath in April.[273] This might, therefore, rank as another of the great 'what might have been' moments of British political history.

As for Lady Thatcher's visit, she wrote about it in *Statecraft*[274] and noted that there were several issues for the future of Hong Kong that needed resolving. These included the establishment of the Court of Final Appeal and the financing of the new Hong Kong airport. The Chinese also suspected that the UK intended to carry off Hong Kong's financial reserves before the handover. 'The Foreign Office and Mr Patten encouraged me to try to break the logjam,' Lady Thatcher records,[275] and she duly met Li Peng with cameras present. 'I took the opportunity of telling the press that I wished to speak about progress on Hong Kong,' she recalled, noting that 'this intrusion of substance into ceremony seemed initially to disconcert my host'.[276] This illustrates a point made by John Campbell: 'When she wanted, she still had a matchless way of cutting through diplomatic formalities.'[277] The reserves dealt with, Lady Thatcher found Li amendable on the other issues of substance.

From some of the contemporary and later commentary on Lady Thatcher's dealings with Li Peng, there is a sense of her toying with him, with Li being unsure how to respond to her. In February 1996, he even received advice from John Major on how to handle her, or rather on how to *not* handle her. In their bilateral meeting on 29 February, Li told Major that he was limited to two terms of office of five years each and that he thought that this was more democratic than the British system. 'The Prime Minister advised him not to tell Lady Thatcher that,' the Foreign Office telegram about the meeting records.[278]

Her engagement with China continued beyond 1995. In June 1996, she was reported to be on 'Hong Kong watch'. '[S]he made a speech critical of China when she was in the Philippines in January,' a former member of the entourage was quoted as saying. 'And she has given very clear support to the democratic reforms brought in by Chris Patten, despite China's opposition to what he has done.'[279] In November 1996, she told China's leaders that their persecution of dissidents had shocked the world.[280] A month earlier, in a speech in Beijing, she had set the future of Hong Kong in the wider context of the future of China itself.[281]

In addition to dealing with China, Lady Thatcher worked to generate and maintain confidence in Hong Kong, highlighting this in a Lords' speech in April 1996.[282] About various projects then underway in the colony, she commented, 'These are not new projects devised and carried out by people who are depressed and frightened about what lies ahead. Rather, they exude optimism about the future and confidence that the talents and initiative of Hong Kong's people will continue to have full rein after 1997.'

The third way Lady Thatcher discharged her responsibility to Hong Kong was by robustly backing Chris Patten as Governor. Moore writes that she did her best to support him, discounting how she might have felt about his role in her resignation as Prime Minister,[283] while Aitken records that she had been 'distinctly sniffy' about his appointment.[284] Lady Thatcher herself commented, 'I was aware that my successors had no easy task … The way in which Governor Patten went about his duties provoked a good deal of controversy. Some of the criticisms were reasonable; but many of them were not.' She went on, 'I gave full public and private support to Mr Patten. Nor do I regret doing so.'[285]

Lady Thatcher strongly supported Patten's introduction of democratic reforms, and Aitken writes that this was 'against the urgings' of Sir Percy Cradock, her former adviser.[286] Harris notes that given Cradock 'was fiercely opposed to the strategy, it was not an easy decision'.[287] 'Chris could count on the wholehearted support of Margaret Thatcher, from whom he was separated on almost every other political issue,' said Douglas Hurd.[288]

In September 1992, Patten briefed key people about his proposals, including Lady Thatcher, Edward Heath, Geoffrey Howe and his predecessors as Governor Lord Maclehose and Lord Wilson. 'None offered any criticism,' Patten recorded. Indeed, most were supportive, adding: 'Only Margaret Thatcher was to remain so in public and private, stalwartly and vigorously insisting that the Joint Declaration signed in her name should mean what it said.'[289]

Lady Thatcher's support for Patten included defending him 'robustly in the House of Lords against the old China hands'.[290] This she did in a speech on 9 December 1992. Lady Thatcher argued, 'My purpose in speaking in this debate is strongly to support the Governor of Hong Kong and to commend a policy of good relations with China. Noble Lords will detect that I do not believe there need be any contradiction between these two propositions.'[291] She also asked her only written question as an ex-premier, in support of Patten's proposals.[292]

A May 1993 telegram to the Foreign Office revealed that the press had highlighted remarks Lady Thatcher had made about Patten's proposals. She had reiterated her support for them and had noted that they did not contravene the Basic Law.[293] She also defended the proposals to the Chinese, denying they violated the Joint Agreement.[294]

Patten has reflected on Lady Thatcher's support. In 1999, he wrote, 'when I needed her help in Hong Kong she gave it unstintingly', adding: 'She was a better and stouter friend to me than she will ever know.'[295]

In comparison to Lady Thatcher, Patten described Heath as 'my biggest and most unpleasant critic'.[296] Heath's official biographer, Philip Ziegler, reports that Heath stayed with the Governor several times between 1992 and 1997 and, according to Patten, caused considerable embarrassment by criticising British policy to all and sundry. Ziegler noted that Heath never forgave Patten.[297]

An FCO memo of August 1992 identifies the problem as 'how to encourage Sir Edward Heath to take a helpful line on Hong Kong, when he visits Peking in late September'. The recommendation was that the Secretary of State should offer to brief Heath.[298] Reporting on Heath's subsequent conversation with Li Peng, Sir Robin McLaren noted that Heath commended 'the Governor in warm terms'.[299]

Things had changed by the time of Heath's visit in October 1993. He supported Michael Heseltine's objections to Patten's reforms on mercantile grounds.[300] A telegram from McLaren before Heath's visit noted, 'Sir Edward has not been particularly supportive of our approach to the 1994/95 elections in Hong Kong and I doubt whether he will speak up strongly during his visit here.'[301] During his discussion on Hong Kong with Qiao Shi, the Chairman of the National People's Congress, Heath said that he had his own views but he would not express them in the ambassador's presence. When Qiao asked Heath if he concurred that agreement between China and the UK would be in the interests of both countries as well as Hong Kong, Heath replied that he was neutral.[302]

It is also important to note that there was a third ex-premier active on Hong Kong during the 1990s. Files in the National Archives released in 2019 and 2020 detail James Callaghan's May 1993 visit to China.[303] Callaghan had sought advice from Douglas Hurd about whether to go or not, and having been, he reported on his visit to John Major, offering thoughts on how the British ambassador, Sir Robin McLaren, might be further supported. Callaghan had told McLaren that he did not think the British had handled 'the question of the elections very cleverly'. He disagreed that the Governor's proposals provided for a gradual increase in democracy, describing them as 'hardly gradual'. McLaren said it would be helpful if Callaghan could say to Jiang Zemin that progress was more likely to be made through detailed discussion than general arguments, noting that 'Lord Callaghan appeared sceptical but said he would do this'. 'Given his views, Lord Callaghan seems to have spoken on generally helpful lines,' judged McLaren.[304] In a letter dated 5 July 1993, John Major opened in his own hand with 'Dear

Jim' and ended with 'Many thanks, yours ever, John'. 'Your encouragement to the Chinese side to take a sensible approach can only be
useful in securing a successful outcome,' he wrote.[305]

Reflections

On her work between 1992 and 1997, John Campbell reflected that
Lady Thatcher 'probably devoted more time to Hong Kong and
the Far East generally than to any other subject', and that while
Maastricht and Bosnia 'made the headlines', Hong Kong was 'the
issue on which she felt she still had a responsibility and could exert
an influence'.[306] Aitken argued that due to 'the immense respect' in
which Lady Thatcher was held by the Chinese leadership, 'behind
the scenes she was a helpful influence on various difficult issues'
before the handover.[307]

Of Patten's reforms, Lady Thatcher wrote, 'they proved exces-
sively strong meat for Beijing and they have since been rescind-
ed'.[308] 'Rarely has more effort been invested with less result,' Harris
concluded.[309]

From her work on Hong Kong and China, we can learn more
about Lady Thatcher's character. In 2017, Patten revealed that she
was the only visitor who used to make her own bed, and that his
wife 'once crept in to see how well she'd done it and it looked as
though a sergeant major had been in to do it.' The *Daily Mail*
headlined the story 'The Iron Maidy'.[310] In his diaries, Patten wrote
about a visit Lady Thatcher paid in November 1996. At the end of
what Patten described as a 'diatribe' about Europe, Lady Thatcher
'rather fiercely' said to Patten's wife, Lavender: 'And you've bought a
house in France.' 'This is clearly regarded as some sort of act of trea-
son,' Patten noted. Julian Seymour pointed out to Lady Thatcher

that Peter Lilley, one of her closest political friends, had bought not only a house in France, but a château. 'She paused for a moment and then replied, "But it's in northern France."'[311]

Lady Thatcher also played the character that was Margaret Thatcher. Interviewed by CNN at the end of June 1997, Deng Xiaoping's comment was put to her that 'that woman should be bombarded out of her obstinacy'. Lady Thatcher concluded her answer with, 'Of course, I am obstinate in defending our liberties and our law. That is why I carry a big handbag.'[312]

Throughout her time as a premier emeritus, Lady Thatcher was frequently criticised for not behaving as people thought former prime ministers should. Her work on Hong Kong and China could be argued to call that criticism into question. At the very least, it could be argued that a more nuanced judgement of her work after 1990 is required. If, on the EU, the former Yugoslavia and General Pinochet, some might claim Lady Thatcher had been subversive, on Hong Kong and China she could certainly claim to have been a stateswoman.

'Tempted to talk': the things that didn't get away

'She is restricting herself to these two areas [Bosnia and Europe],' an aide of Lady Thatcher was quoted as saying in May 1993, 'because she feels most strongly about them. She believes in concentrating her fire, even if she is occasionally tempted to talk about the things that lie outside these big issues of the moment.'[313]

The final area of Lady Thatcher's policy work comprises those subjects which lie outside the 'big issues of the moment' covered above. This section is illustrative, not exhaustive. Indeed, as and when Lady Thatcher's post-prime ministerial papers at Churchill College are opened to researchers, our understanding of Lady

Thatcher's work on wider issues will expand. In terms of what is covered here, it includes policy issues Lady Thatcher spoke out on publicly as well as those she raised privately. Both demonstrate aspects of her character as well as the character that was Margaret Thatcher.

The Gulf

In *Below the Parapet*, Carol Thatcher noted that Lady Thatcher's 'demotion was brought home to her' when President Bush called her soon after her resignation. Lady Thatcher 'had carefully prepared her comments on the Gulf War, but was very disappointed and wounded when the call turned out to be less politically substantial than she'd been expecting'.[314] During the war she regularly rang the Defence Secretary, Tom King, about what she thought should be done next.[315] On 28 February 1991, Lady Thatcher made her first intervention in the House of Commons since her resignation. It was during a prime ministerial statement on the Kuwait conflict. She and John Major paid tribute to each other.[316] At an event in 2001 to mark the tenth anniversary of the liberation of Kuwait, Lady Thatcher said she wished she had been able to stay in office, 'so that we could have finished the job', adding: 'Perhaps we would not be where we are today if we had acted then.' At the same event, John Major said, 'I know of no military or political leader at the time who was for going to Baghdad.'[317]

The Kurds

In April 1991, Lady Thatcher publicly called for action to help the Kurds who were under attack from Saddam Hussein. She had been visited by some Kurdish women who, she said, 'came to beg me to speak out in order to gain relief for their compatriots bearing the brunt of Saddam Hussein's merciless attacks. Parliament was in recess and there was no minister available to see them.'[318] Not only was there no minister to see them, but President Bush was on holiday and John Major was seen at a football game.[319] Moore wrote it must have been 'irritating' for Major and Bush when she intervened while they were on holiday and made headlines such as 'Don't Leave the Kurds to Die' 'look particularly bad for them'.[320] In his memoirs, Major said Lady Thatcher 'publicly demanded help for [the Kurds] without knowing that action was already in hand',[321] while Moore records that the government was already advocating a safe havens plan and was 'privately trying to overcome American objections'. Major thought Lady Thatcher's intervention 'very un-helpful ... She really impeded the policy.'[322] Within hours of her comments, Major authorised extra funds to help the Kurds, and five days later announced his safe havens plan, which the Americans had agreed to support, albeit reluctantly.[323]

Over twenty years later, in December 2015, one of the children who visited Lady Thatcher's home in 1991, Ranj Alaaldin, wrote that 'Cameron should look to Thatcher and Major for inspiration and take the lead on stabilising the conflict in Syria'.[324] Alaaldin's article was headlined 'Cameron needs to lead like Thatcher did in Syria'.

British ambassador's residence

In his memoirs, Ken Clarke records Lady Thatcher coming to the aid of the Foreign Office, describing her as being 'outraged' when she heard that the government proposed to sell off the gardens of the British ambassador's residence in Bangkok for development.[325]

In her letter to Douglas Hurd dated 29 September 1993, about her trip to South East Asia, Lady Thatcher wrote, 'Please will you

put a stop to the nonsensical proposal to dispose of part of the British Embassy compound in Bangkok to property developers.' She
went on: 'If we want to be taken seriously as a country you do not
put highrise buildings on your front lawn.' With the nuance that
runs through her premier emeritus years, she added, 'Nothing could
be more short-sighted than taking a one-off financial gain and, at
a stroke, removing the whole "feel and presence" of our Embassy.' 'I
feel very strongly indeed about this. Appearances do matter to our
prestige,' she concluded.[326] She spoke to Hurd about it during their
meeting on 13 October, where she said the proposal was 'outrageous'
and that she would raise it in the House of Lords and 'have a go
at the Treasury'. The official taking notes of the meeting recorded
Lady Thatcher saying, 'Desecrating the Bangkok compound in this
was [*sic*] was equivalent to building sky scrapers on the green outside the Secretary of State's office!'[327]

Lady Thatcher was equally forceful with Clarke, telling him that
he was 'a philistine with no regard for our imperial heritage'. 'I re-
treated and settled for selling a strip on the road frontage only,'
Clarke commented.[328]

Defence

Malcolm Rifkind recalls briefing Lady Thatcher ahead of the Front
Line First (Defence Costs Study) statement he was giving in July
1994. He was concerned that the press might contact Lady Thatcher
and, if she had not heard the background, she might make some
critical comments. 'To see her was a wise decision,' he noted. He recorded that, at one point, Lady Thatcher commented, 'The Foreign
Office are not wet. They're drenched.' At the end of the meeting,
Lady Thatcher escorted Rifkind downstairs to see him out. He records her final comments: 'I remember that in 1939 we went to war

to save Poland. You,' she said, poking Rifkind in the chest, 'weren't even born yet.' 'That was not my fault,' he remarked. 'Lady Thatcher never made a public word of criticism of Front Line First,' Rifkind noted.[329]

Coal

In 1993, Lady Thatcher criticised the government's plans to close coal mines in Nottinghamshire, saying she had vetoed such plans when they had been put to her. She also wrote to the Energy Minister, Tim Eggar, following a 'secret meeting with the Union of Democratic Mineworkers'.[330]

Community charge/poll tax

Lady Thatcher was not happy with the government's plans to scrap the community charge/poll tax. Its abolition was 'wormwood and gall' to her, especially given that Michael Heseltine was behind it.[331]

Woodrow Wyatt recorded in his diary on 24 April 1991 that Michael Portillo, then an environment minister, had been to see Lady Thatcher to brief her on its abolition and replacement by the council tax. She was said to be 'incandescent'. On 26 April, Wyatt recorded that he had been 'dreading' calling Lady Thatcher, correctly identifying that she would 'denounce the new council tax'. He noted that 'she was in full flight' on it when he rang her at 8.30 a.m.[332]

Interviewed by the Japanese magazine *Bart* in June 1991, Lady Thatcher said the government's scheme to cut poll tax bills 'could put Britain on the road to ruin'.[333] Towards the end of 1991, she was still lamenting the tax's demise. On 9 October, Wyatt recorded that Lady Thatcher had said that 'the most terrible thing' that Major had done was go back on the community charge. It was, she said, 'letting me down. He had always been for it.'[334]

From a constituency angle, in February 1991 it was reported that Lady Thatcher had made more than one call to Robert Key, then an environment minister, complaining that the central revenue support grant to her local council was too low. The story reporting this was headlined 'Et tu, Maggie?'[335]

Reflections

Lady Thatcher also expressed wider views, and her speeches contained many suggestions of how present-day challenges could and, in her view, *should* be dealt with. *The Path to Power* and *Statecraft* included prescriptions for addressing contemporary issues. As Giles Edwards noted in 2022, 'as she travelled the world, Margaret Thatcher's speeches always pressed the case for her reforms, her view of the world'.[336]

While Lady Thatcher's energies were mainly focused on the four policy areas discussed at length above, nevertheless she spoke out on other matters too. At times, she may have given the impression – and her successors as Conservative leader especially might have felt – that she could resist everything except the temptation to talk about things that lay outside the big issues of the moment. Indeed, there was hardly a policy area on which Lady Thatcher did not comment, either publicly or privately, and sometimes both, during her premier emeritus years, at least in her siren years up to 2002.

In a note of the lunch Lady Thatcher had with President Mitterrand in June 1992, the British ambassador, Sir Ewen Fergusson, wrote, 'There was scarcely a topic of present current affairs on which Mrs Thatcher did not touch' and President Mitterrand 'visibly enjoyed seeing Mrs Thatcher again'. Mitterrand was 'often smiling at both the substance and style of Mrs Thatcher's contributions. She was in ebullient and discursive form, scarcely leaving herself time to eat her lunch. The President's interventions therefore were relatively few.' As John Major wrote on the note, 'V. interesting – a good read.'[337]

Chapter Seven

Performance

The final area of Lady Thatcher's work is performance.

As we have seen, Lady Thatcher's performance of the character that was Margaret Thatcher was central to her philosophy and party work. It also ran through her policy work. The dryness of the words on the page does not do justice to the way in which Lady Thatcher declaimed them. They also do not convey her body language and facial expressions. These forms of non-verbal communication were crucial to Lady Thatcher's (continuing) work.

That is one reason sketch writers capture so well both how Lady Thatcher went about her business in the UK after 1990 and how people responded to her. It is also why the telegrams of ambassadors and high commissioners reporting on Lady Thatcher's overseas visits are such an important source for understanding her life as a former Prime Minister. They too record the '*Carry On Maggie*' aspects of Lady Thatcher's work.

In addition, during her premier emeritus years, Lady Thatcher's performance style became of a particular type – or, at least, the style became more apparent.

All of this became key to her (emerging) legacy, for after 1990 we see Lady Thatcher almost always playing to the gallery – the gallery of history, the contemporary gallery and the gallery of the future.

Reviewing *The Iron Lady* starring Meryl Streep in November 2011, Matthew Parris wrote that Lady Thatcher 'was always a marvellous drag act'.[1] In 2001, Gyles Brandreth had picked up on something similar when he described her as 'the ultimate drag act'.[2]

This aspect of Lady Thatcher's persona was recognised throughout and beyond her political life. In 1975, one newspaper described her as 'Mike Yarwood in drag'.[3] In 1992, Sir Bernard Ingham, when reflecting on her dislike of reshuffles, denied she was 'Dracula in drag'.[4] In 2017, Bob Geldof commented, 'There's this wide anarchic streak in England, Margaret Thatcher was essentially Johnny Rotten in drag.'[5]

Interestingly, one of the first people – if not the first person – to identify this feature of Lady Thatcher's performance style was, even if unintentionally and unknowingly, Lady Thatcher herself. In a speech to Finchley Conservatives on 25 January 1975, just a few days before the first ballot in the Conservative leadership election, she reflected on who might impersonate her. Suggesting that Mike Yarwood 'might find it a little difficult to imitate me', she went on, 'but I suppose they could always bring in Danny La Rue'.[6] The *Finchley Times* reported that the line 'brought the house down'.[7] Yarwood concurred with Lady Thatcher's assessment, commenting after her election as Conservative leader, 'I had been working on Willie Whitelaw. Mrs Thatcher is going to be much more difficult. I think I'll need the help from Danny La Rue.'[8] Perhaps heeding Lady Thatcher's recommendation, La Rue did go on to impersonate her.[9]

As for Lady Thatcher, bringing the house down was a feature of her entire post-premiership. Interviewed for Brandreth's article, the present author commented, 'She's like an amazing diva on a never-ending farewell tour.'

Some twenty years on, it would probably be truer to say that during her premier emeritus years, Lady Thatcher more resembled the person who had previously lived in her house in Chester Square: Dame Shirley Bassey.[10]

Speaking of Dame Shirley in March 2023, Don Black, writer of 'Diamonds Are Forever', commented on her performance of that song: 'She acts it as much as sings it, of course, with all her customary drama. It's what I call theatrical vulgarity but I say that entirely as a compliment. She's a fantastic performer.'[11] Change 'sings' to 'speaks' and the quote could be equally applicable to Lady Thatcher after 1990, if not before, too.

'Drama', 'dramatic', 'caricature', 'icon', 'theatrical', 'theatre', 'pantomime', 'dame', 'trouper', 'actress', 'performer', 'performance', 'star', 'superstar' are all words that pepper articles and books about Lady Thatcher during her premier emeritus years. In all the areas of Lady Thatcher's (continuing) work covered above, along with the substance, there is the show. With Lady Thatcher after 1990, it was, arguably, the singer, the song *and* the singing.

That singing became of a particular type in Lady Thatcher's premier emeritus years. Or rather it became more apparent, it being magnified, as so much about Lady Thatcher was after Downing Street. Freed from the physical and mental constraints of office, Lady Thatcher was at greater liberty publicly to play the character that was Margaret Thatcher to full and seemingly ever fuller and more fulsome effect.

In 2004, Julie Burchill commented, "'First you're another sloe-eyed vamp/Then someone's mother/Then you're camp," sang Stephen Sondheim's superannuated starlet-survivor in the song "I'm Still Here", and it has even happened to the Iron Lady.'[12] In his 2011 article on *The Iron Lady*, Parris commented, '[Meryl] Streep has, to her credit, resisted the temptation to caricature or camp up her portrayal. I wish I could say that Margaret herself always resisted that temptation.'[13] In 2014, interviewed about her book *The Assassination of Margaret Thatcher*, Dame Hilary Mantel said that Lady Thatcher was 'the very stuff of drama': 'She is a fantastic character. Why did she – does she – arouse such strong reactions?'[14] A year later, Dame Hilary commented in a Radio 4 programme, *Mrs Thatcher and the Writers*, 'As a camp phenomenon, she is really under-appreciated.'[15]

As so often with Lady Thatcher, a comment possibly made to be critical, if not superior, should perhaps instead be recognised as offering a new insight. This one into the character that Margaret Thatcher was and ever more became after Downing Street.

The performance aspects of Lady Thatcher's life after 1990 were recognised by people around her. In November 2000, a member of the shadow Cabinet reflected, 'She doesn't want to disappoint people. Of course, she loves all the attention but she also believes the punters will feel let down if she doesn't turn up in all her finery. It's like a rock group doing its greatest hits at a concert.'[16]

To quote Tallulah Bankhead, 'They like me to "Tallulah". You know – dance and sing and romp and fluff my hair and play reckless parts.'[17] After 1990, it seemed that people liked Lady Thatcher to 'Margaret Thatcher' – something Lady Thatcher herself seemed to enjoy too. As part of her promotion of *The Path to Power*, she was interviewed by the Swedish journalist, Stina Dabrowski.[18] It is an illustrative, if not the most illustrative, example of Lady Thatcher 'Margaret Thatchering' after No. 10.

On occasion after 1990, Lady Thatcher's 'Margaret Thatchering' had a comedic side not always apparent during her premiership. Two examples are provided on the Thatcher Foundation website.

In November 2002, Lady Thatcher spoke to Oxford and Cambridge Conservative Students at the Carlton Club. The speech, delivered in full Margaret Thatcher character, was repeatedly inter-rupted by laughter and concluded with loud cheers and applause.[19]

In October that year, Lady Thatcher had opened the new wing of the Churchill Archives Centre which would house her papers. She commented, 'In this country, Prime Ministers only take away with them a limited – a *very* limited – *[MT gave a mock grimace; laughter]* quantity of material, unlike America.' Having brought her comments to a close, she proceeded with the cutting of the ribbon. 'Now my friends, let's get on with the business of the day. *[pauses and turns] Where are the scissors? [laughter and lengthy applause]*' There was some debate about how to cut it. Lady Thatcher commented, 'There was a battle about whether we should go to the left or to the right. *[laughter; MT cuts ribbon; applause]*' The jokes aside, Lady Thatcher also made a serious point, in line with other facets of her character. 'Our beliefs – and indeed our instincts – must anchor us firmly if we are not to capsize in the daily storms of politics. There is more to leadership than enlightened pragmatism.'[20] Writ-ing about this for *The Guardian*, Nicholas Watt commented, 'Tory central office, which used to quiver when Lady Thatcher opened her mouth, had nothing to fear yesterday as she achieved a career first – by saying nothing controversial.'[21]

Lady Thatcher's behaviour at these events illustrates an impor-tant aspect of her performance after 1990, if also not before. It was done with a purpose, and to make a point.

An illustrative example of this 'performance with a point' ap-proach is provided by Lady Thatcher's speech at the Pacific Asia Travel Association Annual Conference in Honolulu in 1993. During it, she uses a torch – a kind of 'performance with props' – when talking about a visit to Pearl Harbor. Then, in the 'spirit of have torch, will travel', Lady Thatcher offers broader thoughts about man's humanity to man.[22] One attendee said Lady Thatcher was 'stunning': 'Speaking without notes for 60 minutes and you could hear a pin drop.'[23] The performance captures perfectly what Charles Moore has described as Lady Thatcher's 'strange combination of actress and preacher'.[24]

'There was a distinct touch of *Sunset Boulevard* to her later years,' Charles Powell wrote following Lady Thatcher's death, referring to a film that had featured throughout her post-prime ministership. He added, 'But to acknowledge such frailties does not diminish the unmatched scale of her achievements as prime minister.'[25] Powell's article was headlined 'She carried an aura of excitement with her ... the atmosphere was charged'.

Equally, to highlight the performance aspects of Lady Thatcher's life after 1990 – to describe her as 'the ultimate drag act' – is in no way to diminish the work that she did in her premier emeritus years, especially during her politically active siren years. Rather, it is to offer another perspective on how she went about doing that work. A line from Marianka Swain's *Daily Telegraph* review of the satirical drag show *Margaret Thatcher: Queen of Soho* seems applicable to the whole of Lady Thatcher's post-Downing Street life: 'Despite its anarchic cabaret spirit, this production ... is incredibly thoughtful.'[26]

Reflections

If, on policy, we undertook a pathology of failure, on performance we can perhaps speak with justification of a study in success. On policy, any achievements Lady Thatcher had were essentially contingent on others being willing to be influenced by her. She was not master of her own destiny. Conversely, on performance, she was in complete control. How Lady Thatcher performed the character that was Margaret Thatcher was entirely in her gift, even if the success of that portrayal often did depend on how others responded to it. That said, responses to the performance of Margaret Thatcher the persona tended to be positive, while the responses on policy to Margaret Thatcher the person tended to be negative.

Beyond that, as argued above, the way in which Lady Thatcher performed the character that was Margaret Thatcher after Downing Street was also key to her (emerging) legacy. It impacted on how she was and is seen. It also impacted on how others were viewed in relation to her, and measured against her, including sometimes by themselves. It helps to explain why, even today, Margaret Thatcher looms large in political discourse, and it is to that subject we now turn.

Part III

Margaret Thatcher's (emerging) legacy

Robin Harris wrote that after Lady Thatcher announced her resignation, the word 'legacy' was 'incessantly on her lips'.[1] Lady Thatcher's (emerging) legacy was multifaceted, encompassing both the Conservative Party and the Labour Party, as well as Margaret Thatcher herself.

One aspect we will not focus on is the legacy of the way in which Margaret Thatcher left Downing Street. That may have been, as Charles Moore wrote, 'a disaster, from all points of view'.[2] Yet, it was mainly a disaster for the Conservative Party.

Sergeant writes of Lady Thatcher's 'fatal legacy' for her party. To Sergeant, Chris Patten said, 'She destroyed the Conservative party.'[3] 'The verdict is in, and unanimous,' Brenda Maddox concluded. 'She saved her country but ruined her party.'[4] After Lady Thatcher's death, *The Economist* spoke of 'The ghost of Mrs T', commenting that she 'is also one of the party's biggest problems'.[5] Interestingly, the sentence is in the present tense, despite Lady Thatcher not having been the leader of the Conservative Party for over twenty-two years.

The extent to which Lady Thatcher herself was to blame for this, however, it is not clear. Arguably, it was the way Lady Thatcher lost office, and those who brought that about, rather than Lady Thatcher herself, that proved to be a disaster for the Conservatives.

Lady Thatcher made this point in her August 1998 *SAGA Magazine* interview. 'The people who brought about that incident are responsible for the biggest defeat the Conservative Party has ever had … They have let the Labour Party in. And big! You won't turn *that* round in one election!'[6] It was noted that 'incident' was the word Lady Thatcher repeatedly used to describe what had happened in November 1990. Naturally, her comments generated headlines, *The Independent*,[7] *The Guardian*[8] and *The Times*[9] all running with stories that she was saying the Conservatives could not win the next election. Sir Bernard Ingham publicly criticised Lady Thatcher, again.[10]

In August 1999, Norman Tebbit commented, 'I said when Margaret Thatcher was forced out of office that it would take a generation for the party to recover from what it has done. I have no reason now to change my mind.'[11] On 22 November 2000, a *Times* leader, 'Still bleeding', judged that the Conservatives had not 'yet recovered from Thatcher's fall'.[12] It argued that the events leading to Lady Thatcher's downfall were 'an essential, probably the essential, element of the crisis' that continued to affect the Conservatives. It said they had spent ten years debating 'how best to extend, refine, redefine or repudiate Thatcherism'. *The Times* concluded no consensus had emerged and none seemed forthcoming.

In 2019, Moore wrote that as it struggled with Brexit, the Conservatives 'had still not recovered from the feelings engendered by the political assassination of its most successful peacetime leader'.[13] In 2013, John Major had said, 'Matricide is always difficult to overcome. Of course, the way in which Margaret left, rather than being defeated in a General Election, left a big scar on the Conservative

Party and no-one can deny that. And that scar continued to impact upon the party internally for a very long time.'[14] David Cameron recognised this too. 'The resentments and divisions that this act of regicide created would affect Conservative politics for the next two decades,' he said in 2019. 'In fact, they still resonate.'[15]

Beyond the Conservatives, it is not clear that the manner of Lady Thatcher's fall was a disaster for the Labour Party, even if Labour lost the 1992 election. Arguably, that defeat helped speed up and ease the changes that Tony Blair brought in when he became leader. In 2003, Tony Wright said that Lady Thatcher 'certainly helped to make Blairism possible. This may even come to be seen as her lasting legacy.'[16] Following her death, Labour MP Barry Sheerman commented, 'Mrs Thatcher transformed the Labour party. We had to reform and change and get our act together, or we would have ceased to have the presence and power of a major party in our country. We must remember what Mrs Thatcher did for parliamentary democracy.'[17]

It is also not clear that, in the longer run, or for her historical reputation, the manner of her fall was a disaster for Lady Thatcher either. Indeed, Sir Denis Thatcher reflected that 'the manner of our going could not have been better. God was good to us. We had the world's sympathy.'[18] This was recognised at the time. On 23 November 1990, Hugo Young wrote, 'For the first time in her prime ministership she provoked, while not requesting it, the human sympathy reserved for a helpless creature at bay.'[19] Joe Haines penned an article headlined 'Brought down by the pygmies',[20] also noting that 22 November was the anniversary of the assassination of President Kennedy – and Thanksgiving Day. 'They created an unforgettable, tragic spectacle of a woman's greatness overborne by the littleness of men,' Moore concluded.[21]

Even this seemed fitting. As Hugo Young commented, 'She died as she had lived, in battle. It was a quite extraordinary end, but it was in keeping with everything important that had gone before.'[22] 'Her entire life was Shakespearean,' Michael Dobbs reflected in 2013, 'at no point more dramatic than its saddest moment, leaving Downing Street for the last time, in tears, her fingernails embedded in the carpet. Yet a tragic finale was inevitable, she was never the sort to retire gracefully to the country in order to tend the roses.'[23] As John O'Sullivan put it in November 1990, 'her resignation in tranquil circumstances, with a parliamentary vote of thanks, a gold watch and a glow of bipartisan approval, would simply be a false end to such a turbulent and combative career – like a scene from *The Chiltern Hundreds* tacked on to the end of *The Duchess of Malfi*.'[24]

With that context, the (emerging) legacy we will now examine is Lady Thatcher's legacy for the Conservative Party, the Labour Party and herself.

Chapter Eight

The Conservative Party

When Lady Thatcher heard the result of the 1990 leadership election, she commented, 'My legacy has been locked in.'[1] This was true, at least in some areas of policy, if not in leadership type or performance style.

On 28 November 1990, an article entitled '"Thatcherette" in charge' recorded some of John Major's opposition colleagues' reactions to his winning the leadership election.[2] 'John Major is a Thatcherette,' said Neil Kinnock. 'That is how he sought election, that is how he has got election.' Paddy Ashdown said Major was the 'self-confessed preserver of Thatcherism'. Both men would, naturally, have their own motives for making such claims. They are not, however, claims that Major would deny.

Writing to Lady Thatcher on 26 December 1990, Major said, 'I am a little concerned at some of the press comment on a "new style".' Noting that this might imply new policies, Major went on, 'I <u>don't</u> wish to change the drift of policy. (Indeed in some areas such as Education I wish to push it further & we <u>must</u> press ahead with the Health reforms).'[3] When they met in January 1991, Major assured Lady Thatcher there was no question of backtracking on health reforms. 'In economic policy, in further privatisation, in law and order, I was no counter-revolutionary,' he wrote. 'In these policies, I led the Thatcherite march onwards with conviction – for I believed in it.'[4]

'Everyone in the government knows what the central project is,' said a minister in June 1993, 'and there's no argument about it,' while Hugo Young reflected that 'their project is the pursuit of Thatcherism by other means'.[5] In May 1995, an article by Simon Jenkins said John Major was 'a better Thatcherite' than Lady Thatcher had ever been,[6] and John Campbell concluded that Thatcherism would have continued to set the agenda for the rest of the 1990s, even if Lady Thatcher 'had gone into a nunnery on the day she left office'.[7]

During the rest of Lady Thatcher's active political life, the Conservative Party's policies continued along similar lines.

Attempts in April 1999 to move away from 'Thatcherite ideals' on health, education and welfare reform were hugely controversial.[8] The controversy demonstrated Lady Thatcher's, or at least her name's, continuing ability to generate media coverage. The coverage oozed drama, like so much of the reaction to Lady Thatcher and her name after 1990.

At the dinner to mark Lady Thatcher's twentieth anniversary of becoming Prime Minister, William Hague said it was a 'great mistake' to think that all Conservatives had to offer were free market solutions. Elsewhere on the same night, the Deputy Leader, Peter Lilley, said that belief in the free market had 'only ever been part of Conservatism'. John Campbell described this as 'extraordinary heresy'.[9] 'Was this the moment when Thatcherism died?' was the headline of a story by Boris Johnson.[10] Michael Gove and Andrew Pierce reflected, 'It was the best of nights, it was the worst of nights.'[11] A Lady Thatcher confidante said, 'She is livid. Simply livid.'[12] The story in which this quote was included was headlined '"Ballistic" Thatcher zeroes in on Hague'. The *Sunday Telegraph* reported an aide of Lady Thatcher's saying, 'She is amazed by Peter Lilley's speech – she has authorised me to tell you that.'[13] Campbell noted that instead of Hague being able to move out of Lady Thatcher's shadow, the outcry forced him to repudiate any such intention.[14]

As if to prove the point, to mark the tenth anniversary of Lady Thatcher's resignation in 2000, the then Deputy Leader and shadow Chancellor, Michael Portillo, writing in *The Times*, commented, 'I am not one of those who thinks that Margaret Thatcher's ideas are outdated.'[15] The article was headlined 'The Tories have not left Margaret behind'.

The 'extraordinary heresy' of April 1999 illustrates comments John Major and David Cameron have made about the impact of Lady Thatcher's legacy on her successors.

'There are many different Margarets,' Major said to ITV after Lady Thatcher's death, 'there is the Margaret of legend and there is the Margaret who really existed'.[16] In his memoirs, Cameron wrote, 'The *mythology* that grew and grew, particularly after her fall, was that she alone was ideologically pure.' Cameron noted the consequence, saying the problem for the party in general and its leaders in particular was 'simply put'. 'Not only were we following a hugely successful, epoch-defining leader,' he explained. 'Not only did we need to heal the divide between those who supported her to the end and those who brought about her fall. We were also being compared to the mythical Thatcher, rather than the real one.'[17]

As if to prove the point, in a speech to the Centre for Policy Studies' 'Remaking Conservatism' Margaret Thatcher Conference in March 2025, Kemi Badenoch commented that, 'For me, Margaret Thatcher wasn't just a historical figure. She shaped my entire view of politics, of leadership and of Britain itself.' She went on: 'We must be as bold as Thatcher was.'[18] In *The Spectator*, James Heale wrote of Badenoch laying 'claim to the Iron Lady's legacy'.[19] Earlier in 2025, she had reflected on this legacy for Conservative leaders, commenting, 'A tough act to follow for all her successors as Conservative party leader… and a huge responsibility'.[20]

Also in March 2025, James Graham, the playwright and writer of *Brian and Maggie*, a drama about Brian Walden's 1989 interview with Lady Thatcher, reflected on her legacy. 'No leader since has been able to reshape society in their own vision,' he said. 'As a Conservative leader, you're still defined by how close or how far away from her you are. That's incredible.'[21]

It is important to stress that this Margaret of legend, this mythical Thatcher, was not wholly based on what Lady Thatcher had done in office. It was also based on what people thought and what Lady Thatcher as 'prophet and crusader' *said* she had done in office. It is comparisons to this Margaret Thatcher – Margaret Thatcher the persona rather than Margaret Thatcher the person – that her successors as Conservative leader have been seemingly unable to escape. Sometimes because they have appeared not to want to escape them.

In July 2001, Matthew d'Ancona illustrated a practical consequence of the type of mythology that Major and Cameron identified: 'there are still those in her party who have completely misconstrued her legacy, treating Thatcherism as tablets of stone, doctrinal verities rather than guiding principles in need of constant modernisation.'[22] After Lady Thatcher's death, the Labour MP Frank Field spoke in similar terms. 'Do we see her record as though it had been brought down from Mount Sinai on tablets of stone, or would she have recognised, as I have hinted in the few conversations I have had on this specific point, that there is now a new agenda and that whatever principles one has must be applied to it?'[23]

An *Independent on Sunday* leader on 14 April 2013, 'Beware the potency of the Maggie myth', reflected on this point. It argued that too many Conservatives were 'beguiled by the simplified and my-thologised version of her beliefs' that she promoted after Downing Street, rather than by her 'pragmatism and communication skills' while she was Prime Minister. It noted the impact of this: 'Even now, 23 years on, that legacy continues to render the party almost unleadable.'[24] More than a decade later, people may wonder if any-thing is different even now.

In *Statecraft*, Lady Thatcher had herself commented, 'Com-monsense must always temper moral zeal.'[25] In *The Path to Power*, Lady Thatcher spoke of both moral and practical considerations motivating her when she intervened publicly after 1990.[26] So, even when being 'prophet and crusader', Lady Thatcher recognised, ac-knowledged and stated the need for 'guiding principles' rather than 'doctrinal verities'.

The legacy of the Margaret of legend who was still politically active was significant for her two immediate successors. She could and did highlight when she thought they had 'sinned', to adapt Douglas Hurd's phrase. Her relationship with Major is covered above. As for Hague, he described her presence as 'overpowering'.[27]

Hague was not the only person who thought that way about Lady Thatcher, both as a person and as a persona. In 1999, a Con-servative peer said to this author, 'She had a tremendous influence on people. She still has. Most people are quite nervous of her.' That she could still have this effect on people, almost a decade on from her resignation, illustrates how her personality, and people's reactions to it, were central to her continuing impact. After 1990, difficult as it might have been, people did not need to listen to or be influenced by her. This was especially the case with those in government and the wider Conservative Party. As Douglas Hurd noted, Lady Thatcher no longer had the ability to issue instructions.

When Sergeant asked Hurd whether he had to take her calls after 1990, he replied: 'Oh yes, of course. I didn't run away from her; and I'd learned how to argue with her.' As Sergeant noted, 'What is significant is that he should talk like this about arguments he had with Mrs Thatcher after she had ceased to have any direct power over his actions.'[28]

'Overpowering': William Hague

Hague felt Lady Thatcher's overpowering presence throughout his time as leader. He told Moore that she had been '90 per cent helpful' but '10 per cent disruptive'.[29] Sometimes it must have felt as if 10 per cent was an underestimate. Or that the impact of 10 per cent disruption was magnified disproportionately, Lady Thatcher's interventions giving many more bangs than the bucks invested in them.

Almost mirroring what happened with John Major, at the beginning of October 1999, the *Sunday Times* reported that Lady Thatcher had described Hague as 'wee Willie'. Major responded by saying that former Conservative leaders 'ought to support William and not get in his way'. Asked whether the same people were on Hague's back as were on his when he was leader, Major replied, 'A lot of people might say that. I couldn't possibly comment.' Staff in Lady Thatcher's office admitted that she had been 'indiscreet' at private dinner parties. 'She is behaving disgracefully,' said one senior Tory, while a member of the No Turning Back Group commented, 'Her criticism of William is the same as the criticism she made of Major: he is not me ... Nobody should pay any attention to her views on this, because she is the woman who saddled us with John Major.' A spokesman for Lady Thatcher said that relations between her and Hague had 'never been more close'.[30]

On 4 October, the day after this story was published, Lady Thatcher's *Daily Telegraph* article appeared. Hague, she said, was 'clearly one of the best leaders of the opposition our party, or any party, has had', a gifted strategist and a brilliant debater who 'regularly worsts Mr Blair at the Dispatch Box' and had 'in abundance the single most important quality in a politician: courage'.[31]

A year earlier, at the time of the first anniversary of the death of Diana, Princess of Wales, Matthew d'Ancona wrote an article headlined 'The other blonde we can't forget'. Reflecting on Lady Thatcher's interview with *SAGA Magazine*, he wrote, 'This weekend has naturally been dominated by memories of Diana, Princess of Wales, yet the Iron Lady's remarkably frank interview was a reminder that there is more than one dyed blonde female icon who can still command our attention.' He noted Lady Thatcher's 'continued psychological grip on her party. A mostly-dormant volcano, she is still able to command undivided attention among Tories with her occasional eruptions.'[32] The same day, a Trog cartoon in the *Sunday Telegraph* featured Hague holding a *Daily Telegraph* saying, 'The nation has Diana fatigue – GALLUP'. Hague's speech bubble says, '...and I have THATCHER fatigue'. The 'I' is underlined twice. Behind Hague is an oversized Lady Thatcher.

In January 2000, *The Times* reported that Hague was making weekly telephone calls to Lady Thatcher. 'She is hugely influential in the party and she maintains a keen interest in what is happening,' a Hague ally was quoted as saying. 'He talks to her to keep her up to date with what's going on in the party but also listens to what she thinks.' A friend of Lady Thatcher commented, 'There is no doubt that she enjoys being consulted.'[33]

However disruptive Lady Thatcher may have been, Hague recognised the wider help and support she gave the Conservative Party after the 1997 election defeat. Speaking to Moore, he reflected, 'In those bad times, she was brilliant at motivating our people to bother to vote.'[34] Beyond that, Lady Thatcher was also privately supportive. Sergeant wrote that Hague 'would be delighted to receive hand-written notes or cards covered on both sides with writing in blue ink'. Hague commented, 'She wasn't trying to influence any policy particularly, but she was supportive.'[35]

'I am Thatcher's heir': Iain Duncan Smith

By the time Iain Duncan Smith became leader, Lady Thatcher was approaching the end of her active political life. He did not, there-fore, have to contend with Margaret Thatcher the person in the same way as his two predecessors had done. The 2001 leadership election was Lady Thatcher's last major intervention in British pol-itics, and in September that year it was reported that she was 'to lay down her handbag'. Her friends were recorded as saying that she would retire from public life within a year, and then 'refrain from making public utterances'.[36] That said, Margaret Thatcher the persona was ever present.

In his first newspaper interview as leader, Duncan Smith told the *Daily Telegraph*, in October 2001, that Thatcherism was a 'valuable' part of our past. He went on: 'You don't reject it – you learn from it.'[37] A year later, *The Times* reported Duncan Smith as saying, 'I am Thatcher's heir'. It said that Duncan Smith would fight back against his critics by telling party members that 'the Conservatives' mission must be to complete the revolution begun by Margaret Thatcher'.[38]

'What you stood for then, we stand for now': Michael Howard

As for Michael Howard, at a dinner held in 2004 to mark the

twenty-fifth anniversary of Lady Thatcher becoming Prime Minister, he said, 'What you stood for then, we stand for now.'[39] The *Daily Telegraph* headlined its story, 'Howard returns Thatcher to Tory fold'[40] while *The Times* spoke of Howard being 'delighted to sing Thatcher's praises'.[41] 'People who are running the Conservative Party today,' said Tony Blair, 'were the arch-high priests of all those aspects of Thatcherism that people disliked most and voted to get rid of in 1997.'[42]

This was also a line that Labour proposed to use in the run-up to and during the 2005 general election. In December 2024, the National Archives released the briefs for a meeting of the Cabinet on 9 September 2004, which was followed by a political Cabinet. Among these files are pages of a memo on issues to cover at that year's Labour Party conference ahead of the next year's election. One task the memo identifies is setting out what it would mean if the Conservatives were to win the election. The memo identified a key feature of the Conservative Party as being 'a party of the past'. It went on: 'Their leader is a confirmed Thatcherite. Those are his politics and that is where his heart lies. Given a chance, that is what he would take us back to.'[43]

'I wasn't always convinced by her approach': David Cameron

'I wasn't always convinced by her approach,' David Cameron reflected on Lady Thatcher in his memoirs, 'and thought some of the rough edges needed to come off. But on the big things – trade union reform, rejecting unilateral nuclear disarmament, our alliance with Ronald Reagan's America, privatisation, Europe – she was absolutely right.'[44]

In March 2005, while the party's head of policy, Cameron had said that the Conservatives would 'offer voters practical solutions to everyday problems at the election'. This was seen as 'a clean break with Thatcherism and the ideological dogma of the past'.[45] Nevertheless, Cameron did on occasion compare himself to Lady Thatcher. In 2008, he declared, 'I'm going to be as radical a social reformer as Mrs Thatcher was an economic reformer, and radical social reform is what this country needs right now.'[46]

As Tony Blair and Gordon Brown did, Cameron entertained Lady Thatcher at Downing Street after he became Prime Minister. Her June 2010 visit to No. 10 generated extensive press coverage. 'It's great to have her back in,' Cameron said.[47] *The Sun* headlined the story, 'Maggie's den again'.[48]

Linking Lady Thatcher's visit with a Commons' debate that day, in which George Osborne was leading, Michael White wrote a story headlined 'Boy George and the Iron Lady, the new pincer movement'. 'Of the two troop movements,' White noted, 'the return of Lady Thatcher will make the most impression on jittery financial markets.' Noting that she had only been seen briefly, he went on, 'But even a glimpse will allow impressionable bankers to sleep more soundly at night. Mother is back! She will save us!'[49]

Cameron later welcomed the chance to be more Thatcherite than Thatcher. Speaking of Royal Mail privatisation in his memoirs, he reported that 'when its privatisation was proposed to Thatcher, even for her that was a step too far'. It was eventually sold off in 2013. 'For me,' Cameron concluded, 'the move had a wider symbolism. Modern, compassionate conservatism was seen by some as timid, lacking in radicalism, and just a bit too left-wing for many in the party. This would infuriate me. I would sometimes reel off a list of all the things I did that Thatcher never dared to do.' Cameron referenced increasing tuition fees in universities, reforming public-sector pensions, allowing private operators to run state schools, capping welfare, vetoing a European treaty and leaving the European People's Party as well as privatising Royal Mail.[50]

Cameron also compared his working style to Lady Thatcher's. In May 2012, he was reported as defending himself against the charge of 'chillaxing' too much by insisting he was driven like Lady Thatcher to achieve 'massive radical and structural reforms'.[51]

After Lady Thatcher's death, Cameron continued these comparisons. Speaking of the European Union in 2014, he said that Lady Thatcher had been brilliant in getting the British rebate, but that until him no one had actually cut the European budget. He also noted that Lady Thatcher had never vetoed a treaty, but that he had.[52]

So, even a Conservative leader who stated that they had always felt themselves 'more of a Thatcherist than a Thatcherite' continued, on occasion, to measure himself, and be measured by others, against Lady Thatcher's legacy.[53] In 2015, Charles Moore said Cameron was the first Conservative leader who had been 'quite good at handling the Thatcher legacy', noting that Cameron didn't feel any pressure to define himself against her. Previous leaders had had 'an agonising choice'. Were they going to 'repudiate her or suck up to her'? Moore described both as 'unsatisfactory traditions' and thought Cameron had 'quite a clever way of doing both'.[54]

No matter how Cameron had responded to Lady Thatcher's legacy, the important point was that he had not been free of it. The same could be said of his predecessors, and nor were any of his successors as they dealt with the consequences of the Brexit referendum, and more. This was equally true of Labour leaders and prime ministers too, as we shall in the next chapter.

Chapter Nine

The Labour Party

After the 1997 general election, Henry Kissinger wrote to Lady Thatcher, 'I never thought I'd congratulate you on a Labour victory in the British elections, but I cannot think of anything that would confirm your revolution more than Blair's program. It seems to me well to the Right of that which preceded yours.'[1]

On election day itself, 1 May, John O'Sullivan wrote an article in the *Daily Express* headlined 'And the winner is… Mrs T! (whatever happens today)': 'Congratulations, Lady Thatcher – it's your fifth term in office,' he said.[2] A few days earlier, the *Sunday Telegraph* produced a digest of commentary from European newspapers and stated, 'Comment on Britain's election in the European press is almost unanimous in awarding the victor's laurels to the woman who handbagged her way round the Continent in the 1980s.'[3]

The (emerging) legacy of Margaret Thatcher in relation to the Labour Party is one of the most important aspects of her premier emeritus years. It is also one of the least contested, if at all. As Philip Allmendinger argued, it is 'almost a cliché' to say that one of Lady Thatcher's biggest achievements was forcing Labour to become electable again.[4]

Lady Thatcher's (emerging) legacy to the Labour Party had two aspects: the first, in relation to her ideas, Thatcherism; the second, her leadership type. Policy aside, for both Tony Blair and Gordon Brown personally, the most important aspect of Lady Thatcher's legacy was the latter – her leadership type, against which they seemingly wished, and on occasion were claimed, to be judged, including by themselves. This also had political ramifications for the leaders of Lady Thatcher's own party, from John Major on.

'We are all "Thatcherite" now': Labour Party

On 10 June 2002, *The Times* ran a front-page news story headlined 'Mandelson tells Labour: we're all Thatcherites'. In an article in the paper that day, while qualifying his comments as being in the context of globalisation and the impact of this on the realities of the market and public finances, Peter Mandelson wrote, 'we are all "Thatcherite" now'.[5] At Prime Minister's Questions just days later, Blair appeared to distance himself from the comment, declaring, 'I am delighted that we have moved this country away from Thatcherism.'[6]

Whatever Blair's words in 2002, the Labour Party he led did in essence accept the basic premises of Thatcherism, or at least some of the policies that Lady Thatcher's government had introduced. In his memoirs, Blair argued, 'I knew the credibility of the whole New Labour project rested on accepting that much of what she wanted to do in the 1980s was inevitable, a consequence not of ideology but of social and economic change.'[7] Even if this was, to quote Lady Thatcher, 'a conversion of convenience',[8] it proved successful. As historian David Cannadine argued, 'New Labour's espousal of many Thatcherite nostrums paid enormous electoral dividends between 1997 and 2005'.[9]

After Lady Thatcher's death, Blair commented, 'I always thought my job was to build on some of the things she had done rather than reverse them.'[10] Writing in 2008, John Kampfner reflected on what Blair himself had contributed to Lady Thatcher's legacy, arguing,

'Blair not only confirmed many of her policies, but in some respects actually took them further and gave her an intellectual endorsement that went far beyond her original circle of economic monetarists and social conservatives.'[11]

This acceptance of parts of Lady Thatcher's legacy did not begin with New Labour, but started much earlier. 'Arguably, the new model Labour Party was one of her most important creations,' Hugo Young wrote the day after her resignation: 'she leaves an Opposition more anxious to retain than remove a fair amount of what she has done.'[12] Robin Oakley said the same: 'Thatcherism will leave a lasting legacy in British politics in that Mrs Thatcher's reign has forced the Labour party to change direction and swing back to the centre.'[13]

'Blair charmed her': Tony Blair

Three weeks after entering No. 10, Tony Blair hosted Lady Thatcher at Downing Street. The meeting had been planned early. The election was on 1 May, and on the 7th, Julian Seymour wrote to Jonathan Powell, Tony Blair's chief of staff. The note covers the date of the meeting, 22 May, possible press handling relating to who had instigated it, and the subjects to be covered (Europe, Asia, China and the handover of Hong Kong).[14]

The story of the visit featured on the front page of the *Sunday Times* on 25 May 1997. It was headlined 'Blair in secret talks with Thatcher; Clinton to address cabinet at No 10',[15] and the order of characters is worth noting: the then current American President *after* the former Prime Minister. 'She has strong views,' a source close to Blair said. 'She was opinionated and it was stimulating. He enjoyed the conversation. He certainly didn't find Lady Thatcher short of opinions.' A source close to Lady Thatcher said, 'She finds him extremely personable and open to ideas.' 'Blair charmed her,' John Whittingdale later claimed.[16] One of Lady Thatcher's Cabinet ministers said that Blair 'looks and talks exactly like the smooth young chaps who prospered in her court'.[17]

The meeting was just one of numerous contacts between the two prime ministers. Those relating to the former Yugoslavia, and to General Pinochet, are detailed above. In addition, in 2005 Lady Thatcher wrote to Blair about the Iraqi elections, and in 2006 about Alexander Litvinenko.[18] She had also written to him in 2002, after Blair wrote to her. In a handwritten letter dated 4 April, Lady Thatcher said she was 'very touched' by Blair's 'kind and thoughtful letter'. She went on: 'You will have found, as I did, that just as one international crisis subsides, another soon threatens. I greatly admire the resolve you are showing. You have ensured that Britain is known as a staunch defender of liberty, and as a loyal ally of America. That is the <u>very</u> <u>best</u> <u>reputation</u> our country can have.' She signed herself, 'Margaret T'.[19]

When, in January 2000, Lord Callaghan was asked about Blair consulting Lady Thatcher more than him, he replied, 'I think all it says is that he turns to somebody who won four [*sic*] elections instead of somebody who didn't win any.'[20] Interestingly, Lord Callaghan himself had been consulted not long after John Major was appointed Prime Minister. Major entered No. 10 on 28 November 1990, and his manuscript diary for 6 December 1990, released by the National Archives in June 2023, reveals a meeting with Lord Callaghan at 6.15 p.m. that day.[21]

What effectively almost became a 'love-in' between Lady Thatcher and Blair started not long after his election as Labour leader. Over the years, Lady Thatcher offered both public praise and criticism of Blair, his party and his governments. Blair did the same about Lady

Thatcher and hers. Blair was also measured against Lady Thatcher throughout his premiership, sometimes by himself.

In a *Sunday Times* interview in May 1995, Lady Thatcher said Blair was 'probably the most formidable' Labour leader since Hugh Gaitskell. 'I see a lot of socialism behind [Labour's] front bench, but not in Mr Blair. I think he genuinely has moved,' she opined. A former aide of Lady Thatcher's commented, 'This is distinctly unhelpful … Some of the things she is doing at the moment are a bit crazy.' In the same article, Edward Heath reflected, 'Tony Blair shouldn't be underestimated. He has a new face, too, and the voters like that.'[22] Yet it was Lady Thatcher's comments that seemed the most newsworthy and politically impactful. On 12 June 1995, Gyles Brandreth noted in his diary, 'Mrs T. is rocking the boat. The Baroness has been on the radio, telling us how much she admires Mr Blair.'[23]

In November 1996, Lady Thatcher used the Nicholas Ridley Memorial Lecture to deliver what was described in *The Times* as 'a ferocious attack' on New Labour and 'the continuing worldwide threat of socialism'.[24] Part of the lecture was entitled 'Don't let Labour ruin it'.[25] Lady Thatcher had also devoted a section of her Keith Joseph Memorial Lecture in January 1996 to Labour. 'The Labour Party itself may have changed many of its policies, but it hasn't changed its spots,' she argued. 'Mr Blair is not only human; he is also (as his record shows) by instinct a man of the Left.'[26]

In March 1997, Paul Johnson wrote an article for the *Sunday Telegraph*. Headlined 'Tony is the "good son" Margaret never had', it reported private conversations in which Lady Thatcher had supposedly said that Blair 'won't let Britain down'.[27] Major remembered this 'with irritation' as Lady Thatcher saying, 'People would be perfectly safe with Tony Blair.'[28] To Woodrow Wyatt, Lady Thatcher said she had no recollection of making the remark. Wyatt wondered if she had said it 'when a bit tiddly'. Lady Thatcher also told Wyatt that she thought Blair would 'do immense harm' and that she would 'vigorously campaign' for Major.[29]

During the 1997 election, Lady Thatcher was asked what she thought of it being said in America that Tony Blair was the new Margaret Thatcher. 'Well I think they have got the sex wrong for a start,' she replied, in character. 'And I think they have got the willpower wrong. I think they have got the reasoning wrong. I think they have got the strength wrong. And he is trying to take over my policy in part, it's a kind a [sic] conversion of convenience. I had to make the revolution happen by changing everything I found when I took over.'[30]

Once appointed Prime Minister, Blair's measurement against Lady Thatcher began in earnest and became a feature of his entire premiership. Not a year went by when Lady Thatcher was not a presence in Blair's life, and on occasion this could have political impact, for Blair and for Lady Thatcher's successors as Conservative leader. Sometimes the Thatcher–Blair relationship was played out in the public domain, either because they spoke about one another or because they were compared to each other, including sometimes by Blair himself, in the media. Other times, it was because they had private contact and conversation, away from the public eye. Lady Thatcher's name, and her premiership, could also appear in notes and memos that Blair received from civil servants and advisers and in correspondence he got from political actors.

Perhaps fittingly given how she was seemingly to be ever present, both as a person and as a persona, throughout his time in Downing Street, an article by Simon Jenkins in October 1997 was headlined 'To Thatcher, a son'. In it, Jenkins described Blair's conference speech as 'the best speech Baroness Thatcher never made'.[31] In October 1998, Blair compared himself to her. Dismissing claims that he had become Labour's Margaret Thatcher, he argued that she 'had no monopoly on holding firm beliefs and sticking to tough policies'.[32]

He might have added 'or having a particular style of leadership', for 1999 opened with reports of Lady Thatcher saying that she was worried about Blair 'getting awfully bossy'.[33] At the time of the Helsinki summit in December, the *Daily Telegraph* ran a leader entitled 'Blair as Thatcher'. Reflecting on an interview he had given the previous day, it commented, '"If we are isolated and we are right, then that's the correct position to be in." Vintage Thatcherite stuff; the Iron Lady standing alone against the tide of European integration. Except that the speaker was Tony Blair.'[34]

2000 appeared to be a bumper 'Thatcher Year' in Blair's life. In January, the former Liberal Democrat leader, Paddy Ashdown, sent him a letter of five sides of A4, marked 'Strictly private and confidential'. In it, he made various references to Lady Thatcher, commenting at one point, 'As I said when we last met, one of the things which drives me mad about you is that you enjoy a dominance of politics unrivalled by any other Prime Minister in this century, with the possible exception of Mrs Thatcher in her heyday – but can sometimes seem more interested in preserving this than in using it – even risking some of it – to achieve one of your aims.'[35]

In February, Blair said that Lady Thatcher did not get it all wrong in her Bruges speech.[36] A few months later, in June 2000, Jonathan Powell, Blair's chief of staff, had reported to him on a conversation he had had with Shaun Woodward, the former Conservative MP who had defected to Labour in December 1999. The memo included various references to Lady Thatcher's time as Prime Minister.[37]

By the end of the year, Blair was reported to be renouncing 'his

Thatcher inheritance'.[38] He had considered making a speech to mark the tenth anniversary of Lady Thatcher's resignation, but decided against doing so because it would distract from the government's core message.[39] That Blair even considered it is itself remarkable and illustrates Lady Thatcher's ongoing influence in British political life. While Blair did not make a speech, he did pass comment. At a Downing Street press conference on 22 November, he remarked, 'I take nothing away from those things that were done in the 1980s that we have kept, but it really is time that we move politics beyond the time of Margaret Thatcher.'[40]

A couple of days later, Simon Jenkins opened an article headlined 'The Iron Lady who made Tony Blair' with 'Wow. Tony Blair declares apostasy from Thatcher.'[41] The cartoon above the piece, by Richard Wilson, 'In the driving seat', has Blair in the front seat of a car with his hands on the steering wheel. From the back seat, an oversized Lady Thatcher reaches over the back of Blair, her much larger hands also on the steering wheel.

As for Lady Thatcher, on 22 November 2000, *The Sun* reported she had 'declared war' on Blair for supporting a European army.[42] Headlined 'Maggie rages at folly of vain Blair', the article covered almost the whole of the front page. The same edition of the paper ran a feature by Blair entitled 'Future lies in strong EU role'. A leader column, 'Who shall we trust?', commented, 'Today two Prime Ministers talk to The Sun about the European army. If we have to choose between Maggie Thatcher and Tony Blair, it's no contest.'[43]

Lady Thatcher's legacy having become 'one of the defining issues' in the June 2001 election,[44] later that month, Blair reflected on the outcome. 'The election marked Britain's desire to move beyond Thatcherism,' he said, speaking in the debate on the Queen's Speech.

'As far as I can make out from studying the positions of many of the new intake of Conservatives, the only way to resolve the leadership question is for the title to be renounced, the by-election held and the mummy to come back to the Dispatch Box.'[45]

In April 2002, Blair compared himself to Lady Thatcher again during an interview on *BBC Breakfast with Frost*. When David Frost asked him about the government's proposed health reforms, Blair replied, 'Well it's a challenge isn't it, it's a big thing. I mean it's as big as industrial restructuring was in the 1980s for the Thatcher government, to put our public services on a proper footing.'[46] The *Times* article on this was headlined 'Blair ready to follow Thatcher and confront unions on health reforms'.[47]

In December, Lady Thatcher praised Blair's leadership. Accepting the Clare Boothe Luce Award, she said, 'I am also proud that Britain stands where we must always stand – as America's surest and staunchest ally. Prime Minister Blair and I are, as is well known, political opponents. But in this vital matter I salute his strong, bold leadership.'[48]

Lady Thatcher praised Blair's leadership again in April 2003. In a short Q&A session following a pre-recorded interview for the Institute of Directors Centenary Convention, Lady Thatcher commented, 'The Prime Minister has proved a bold and effective war leader. I also think that he probably understands that business has to succeed if the country is to prosper, but that is as far as my approval goes.' She also noted 'a bit of a problem for the Conservatives; Mr Blair and the Labour Party sound too much like us!'

Asked if she was really saying the Labour government was adopting her policies, Lady Thatcher was straight back in character as Margaret Thatcher, replying: 'In many respects new Labour shows signs of reverting to old Labour with its irresponsible policies of tax and spend. Britain just cannot afford this.'[49] Alan Hamilton and Christine Buckley commented, 'like some long-retired but vividly remembered Hollywood icon, she proved yesterday that she could still raise a standing ovation'.[50]

Also in April 2003, Stephen Wall, Blair's European adviser, recommended that he meet Guy Verhofstadt, the Belgian Prime Minister, to discuss European policy. Wall ended his memo to Blair with, 'Why bother? Because, as Margaret Thatcher confided in Douglas Hurd when he asked her why she had supported John Major for the leadership if she thought so ill of him: "Because I can tell you, in confidence, that he was the best of a very poor bunch."'[51]

A year later, in April 2004, Blair said there would be a referendum on the proposed European Union constitution. 'U-turn' appeared in the media coverage. In a *Sunday Times* article, 'It took a Labour leader to win Thatcher's last battle', Michael Portillo wrote, 'The Europhobe Thatcher found no means to resist the tide that swept her along helplessly. The Europhile Blair has halted it effortlessly, with a single catastrophic blunder. She must be proud of him.'[52]

Tony Blair's attendance at Lady Thatcher's eightieth birthday in 2005 gave commentators the opportunity to reflect on his response to her legacy. Michael White and Robert Booth wrote that Blair had 'cheerfully plundered her political wardrobe to dress New Labour',[53] while Geoffrey Howe reflected, 'Her real triumph was to have transformed not just one party but two, so that when Labour did eventually return, the great bulk of Thatcherism was accepted as irreversible.'[54]

Michael Portillo wrote about Lady Thatcher and Blair again in January 2006. Describing Lady Thatcher as 'the house ghost' in 10 Downing Street during Blair's premiership, he wrote, 'What can be said for Blair, and it is saying a lot for a Labour leader, is that he preserved her legacy. But in her day her ideas were revolutionary. Britain was in the vanguard of liberal economic reform. By Blair's time such policies were commonplace. He had merely to plough along Thatcher's furrow.' Portillo claimed Blair's 'best ideas are re-heated Thatcherism'.[55]

Also in January, David Cameron said the Conservatives had to accept parts of Tony Blair's legacy or risk 'irrelevance, defeat and failure'. He argued that Blair saw New Labour's task was 'to preserve the fruits of the Thatcher revolution – the open-market economy and the end of the "us v them" mentality – whilst making progress to include the excluded minority'.[56]

When Blair resigned in 2007, Lady Thatcher wrote to him, commenting, 'Among the many challenges you faced with great courage, may I just mention two. You stayed close to our American ally in difficult times. And because of you we saw an end to the horrors of genocide in the Balkans.' Moore notes this showed how much the issue mattered to her.[57]

In September 2008, Blair was photographed supporting Lady Thatcher at a service at St Paul's Cathedral to mark the end of military operations in Northern Ireland. The *Daily Express* headlined its story, 'Helping hand for Iron Lady'.[58] In 2007, Lady Thatcher had been photographed with her arm in Blair's as they left one of the Falklands anniversary events. The front page of the *Daily Telegraph* headlined the photograph, 'Comrades in arms'.[59] *Private Eye* compared them at a Falklands event attended by the Queen, the cover of the 22 June–5 July 2007 edition featuring a photograph of Her Majesty walking by Tony and Cherie Blair and Lady Thatcher. As she passes Lady Thatcher, a speech bubble coming from the Queen's mouth reads, 'Well, at least you won your war'.[60]

For all this, it is important not to take the relationship between the two prime ministers too far. Lady Palumbo once asked Lady Thatcher what she thought of Tony Blair, to which Lady Thatcher replied, 'My dear, I do not think of him.' Lord Palumbo concluded, 'That was all.'[61]

'I am a conviction politician like her': Gordon Brown

Whatever the status of Lady Thatcher's 'love-in' with Blair, there seemed to be a similar situation with his successor, Gordon Brown, too.

The son of a preacher man and the daughter of a preacher man, Brown's relationship with Lady Thatcher had started before he became Prime Minister. Shortly after his election in 1983, Lady Thatcher had invited Brown to her room in the Commons for a whisky to discuss a speech she had heard him make.[62]

On occasion, Brown seemed more (or seemed to *want to be seen* to be more) Thatcherite than Thatcher. In 2001, William Hague commented, 'In *The Wall Street Journal* yesterday, the Chancellor said: "Margaret Thatcher rightly emphasised the importance of the enterprise culture", but that "she didn't go far enough".' Hague went on, 'Now we know what all those years of protest and Tribune group meetings were about: he wanted the Conservative Governments of the 1980s to go even further. We can all picture him with his placard: "Maggie, Maggie, Maggie, more, more, more." That is what he was asking for.'[63] In June 2003, Lady Thatcher and Brown were photographed together as they arrived at a Westminster Abbey service to mark the fiftieth anniversary of the Queen's coronation. *The Times* headlined the story, 'Iron Chancellor meets Iron Lady'.[64]

'I think Lady Thatcher saw the need for change,' Brown said in September 2007. 'I also admire the fact she is a conviction politician. I am a conviction politician like her.'[65] In response to this comparison, the Conservatives 'swiftly rushed out' some Brown quotes about Lady Thatcher that 'suggested his admiration was short-lived'.[66]

The next week, Lady Thatcher had tea at Downing Street. Brown's inner circle believed he had pulled off 'a stunning coup'.[67] The press coverage played up to Lady Thatcher's image. 'Then I saw her, or, more accurately, her never-changing candyfloss hair helmet bobbing in the back seat of the car,' Ann Treneman wrote. 'The icon had landed at No 10.'[68]

Some coverage had political implications for David Cameron. A leader in the *Daily Express* was headlined 'Cameron must show he's the true heir to Thatcher',[69] while a *Sunday Times* article was headlined 'Tories must learn the lady is for turning to their advantage'. Its author, Martin Ivens, argued that the visit highlighted a 'growing problem' for Cameron: 'How do you solve a problem like Maggie if you are Conservative leader? Even in her twilight she is too powerful a presence to ignore.'[70]

In addition to headlines, the visit also generated controversy. Labour MP John McDonnell, who had stood against Brown for the Labour leadership, said, 'I would never let her across my threshold. If this is an indication of Gordon Brown's political heroes, or his estimation of a person's character, I almost despair.'[71] Some Conservatives criticised Brown for exploiting Lady Thatcher's alleged frailty.[72] 'Only Maggie Smith's portrayal of the British ambassador's widow in *Tea with Mussolini* was as brazen as Maggie Thatcher's acceptance of tea with Gordon,' Malcolm Rifkind commented,[73] calling the invitation 'a clever stunt'.

Norman Tebbit took a different view, judging it as an example of the Prime Minister 'at his very best; a wonderful mixture of his courtesy and his political nous'. Noting that Cameron described himself as the 'heir to Blair', Tebbit said it was 'only natural' that Brown should make himself the 'heir to Thatcher'. He said that he was sure Lady Thatcher 'knew exactly what she was doing' and described her as 'too well-mannered' to turn the invitation down. Cameron, meanwhile, was at 'great pains to distance himself from her'. 'And she is, after all, a woman,' Tebbit added.[74]

Harris wrote that after Lady Thatcher's visit to No. 10, 'the Cameron camp suddenly became anxious to stage a similarly warm encounter for the cameras', describing 'a kind of competition' between the Conservative Party and Downing Street to 'offer praise or sympathy or good wishes on the slightest pretext'.[75] So, in October 2007, Lady Thatcher met David Cameron. The first time they had met one on one, it was 'a clear bid to reverse the damage caused by her photocall with Mr Brown'.[76] In September, it had been reported that Lady Thatcher had twice invited Cameron to tea and been refused each time.[77]

In September 2008, Lady Thatcher had lunch with Brown at Chequers, and she returned to Downing Street in November 2009 for the unveiling of her portrait. 'Here was a Labour prime minister thanking her for everything she had done for our country,' Michael Forsyth reflected after Lady Thatcher's death. Brown highlighted that there were only three oil paintings of past prime ministers in No. 10: Robert Walpole, the first Prime Minister; Wellington, victor over Napoleon Bonaparte; and Churchill, who had saved the country and the Continent from the Nazis. Brown said he thought it was entirely appropriate that Lady Thatcher's portrait would join their ranks. 'I was astonished by his generosity but not surprised,' Forsyth concluded. 'The times had changed.'[78]

The extent to which times had changed is the subject of the next chapter. Before that, however, it should be noted that Labour leaders after Blair and Brown have continued to reflect on Lady Thatcher's legacy.

'She was right': Ed Miliband

In his Commons' tribute to Lady Thatcher on 10 April 2013, Ed Miliband said, 'She was right to understand the sense of aspiration felt by people across the country, and she was right to recognise that our economy needed to change.' Miliband went on: 'She said in 1982, "How absurd it will seem in a few years' time that the state ran Pickfords removals and the Gleneagles Hotel." She was right. In foreign policy, she was right to defend the Falklands and bravely reach out to new leadership in the Soviet Union, and something often forgotten is that she was the first political leader in any major country to warn of the dangers of climate change.'[79] An article by Mary Riddell in the *Daily Telegraph* subsequently claimed that 'with his love of bold ideas, the Labour Party leader is a pretender to the Thatcher legacy'.[80]

'She was right': Sir Keir Starmer

In March 2023, launching Labour's law and order plan, Sir Keir Starmer commented, 'The rule of law is the foundation for everything. Margaret Thatcher called it the "first duty of government" – and she was right.'[81]

Starmer had, however, said that Lady Thatcher was wrong the year before. Interviewed in June 2022 in the *Daily Telegraph*, he argued, 'If ever there was evidence that Margaret Thatcher was wrong about there being no such thing as society, we just saw it in the pandemic.'[82]

On 2 December 2023, Starmer returned to Lady Thatcher. Writing in the *Sunday Telegraph*, he commented, 'Margaret Thatcher sought to drag Britain out of its stupor by setting loose our natural entrepreneurialism.'[83] Starmer also referenced Clement Attlee and Tony Blair, yet, as ever, it was the reference to Lady Thatcher that was the most newsworthy and controversial, and Starmer's comments were heavily criticised, including by some Labour MPs. The lead story on the front page of the *Daily Mirror* on 4 December was headlined 'Keir Starmer hit by backlash for praising Margaret Thatcher in pitch to Tory voters'.[84] Despite the backlash, a few weeks later, Tony Blair said Starmer was right, commenting, 'He was saying something that is pretty obvious – she knew where she was going.'[85]

Demonstrating the ongoing ability of Lady Thatcher, or at least the ability of her name, to generate intense reactions in others, the day after Starmer's article, the singer Billy Bragg quote tweeted the *Guardian* story about it with three words, 'Oh fuck off.'[86]

At Prime Minister's Questions on 6 December, Michael Fabricant alluded to Starmer's comments, asking Rishi Sunak, 'Does the Prime Minister share my boundless joy that on the road to Damascus and in recognition of [Margaret Thatcher's] great heritage and all that she achieved, another fanboy has joined in her great belief—the Leader of the Opposition?' When later in the exchanges, Starmer remarked, 'There was mention of Margaret Thatcher earlier', Hansard notes, [Hon. Members: "More!"] with Madam Deputy Speaker, Dame Eleanor Laing, calling, 'Order.'[87] Replying, Sunak spoke of Starmer roleplaying Lady Thatcher and also commented, 'I am always happy to welcome new Thatcherites from all sides of this House, but it says something about the Leader of the Opposition that the main strong female leader that he could praise is Margaret Thatcher, not his own fantastic deputy.' The leader of the Scottish National Party at Westminster, Stephen Flynn, asked Sunak, 'Is the Prime Minister worried that he is projected to be the first Conservative party leader to lose a general election to a fellow Thatcherite?'

The next day, 7 December, Starmer was asked if he was a fan of Lady Thatcher. He replied, 'No, absolutely not.' Speaking in Scotland, he said, 'She did terrible things, particularly here in Scotland, which everybody in this room, myself included, profoundly disagrees with.'[88]

Not long after Starmer became Prime Minister, Lady Thatcher featured in his life again. Whereas Tony Blair and Gordon Brown had invited her in, Starmer moved her out. At the end of August 2024, it was reported that he had had the 'unsettling' portrait of Lady Thatcher, which had been commissioned by Brown, removed from the room in which it was hung.[89] In September, Starmer explained that 'this is not actually about Margaret Thatcher at all', but simply because he does not 'like images and pictures of people staring down'.[90]

By way of contrast, Kemi Badenoch seemed to have no such qualms. Soon after her election as Conservative Party leader, Badenoch met Conservative councillor leaders and was photographed sat under a large portrait of Lady Thatcher. From a window ledge to Badenoch's right, a bust of Winston Churchill looks over to her.[91]

While not wanting to be looked down on by Lady Thatcher, Starmer has continued to reference her. In an article in *The Times* in January 2025 about his plans to cut regulation, he noted how the Thatcher government had deregulated financial capital in the 1980s.[92] The story in *The Times* about this was headlined 'Keir Starmer invokes Margaret Thatcher as he goes for growth'.[93]

'Part of the Thatcher legacy': Jeremy Corbyn

Sandwiched between Miliband and Starmer, Jeremy Corbyn was also not immune to Lady Thatcher's legacy. Corbyn was, however, more motivated by dismantling it, rather than building on it. In January 2016, he said he would repeal legislation introduced during Lady Thatcher's government that outlawed sympathy strikes.[94]

In 2017, Chris West asked, 'Is Jeremy Corbyn the New Margaret Thatcher?',[95] noting that both were outsiders and radicals who became party leader when an old political paradigm was collapsing. In that year's conference speech, Corbyn spoke of replacing 'the broken model forged by Margaret Thatcher many years ago'.[96] According to Robert Peston, Corbyn put the world to rights for ninety minutes, noting that the Labour leader had 'largely occupied the same political space for 50 years'. He was 'true to himself … in a way that is unusual for a politician at the top'. 'In that narrow sense – and whisper it softly – he is Thatcher's heir,' Peston concluded.[97]

In August 2019, Corbyn said that a general election would be 'a once-in-a-generation chance for a real change of direction potentially on the scale of 1945 or 1979'.[98] The *Daily Telegraph* story trailing this was headlined 'Jeremy Corbyn to promise revolution in British politics akin to Margaret Thatcher's 1979 landslide'.[99]

Whatever motivated Corbyn's reaction to Lady Thatcher's legacy, the important point is that he reacted to it at all. Lady Thatcher had been out of power for twenty-five years by the time Corbyn became leader and had died two years previously. Yet, she still mattered. In 2019, Charles Moore wrote that Corbyn was a 'part of the Thatcher legacy, a Bolshevik Bourbon who has learnt nothing and forgotten nothing from the failure of the Left's attempts to defeat her when he first entered the House of Commons in 1983'. Moore argued that Blair and Corbyn showed how Lady Thatcher had 'imprinted herself upon the consciousness of those who followed after'.[100]

The imprinting of Lady Thatcher on the consciousness of those who followed after started while she was Prime Minister. It intensified and reached its peak in her premier emeritus years, and continued even after her death, to this very day. We now turn to the explanation for that.

Chapter Ten

Margaret Thatcher

On the eve of Margaret Thatcher's eightieth birthday in October 2005, Charles Moore wrote that Lady Thatcher had 'risen above the moment and entered myth, so much so that it almost comes as a surprise that she is still flesh and blood'.[1] Moore's words capture what emerged as Lady Thatcher's legacy for and about Margaret Thatcher herself after Downing Street: her transformation from person to persona, from practising politician to political deity.

The human being that was Margaret Thatcher may have and often did cause difficulties for her successors as Conservative leader. She did not cause difficulties all the time; sometimes she was helpful. Yet the bigger difficulties her Conservative successors faced, and from which arguably her Labour successors as Prime Minister benefited, was the Margaret of legend, the mythical Thatcher. This was the Margaret Thatcher that in her premier emeritus years Lady Thatcher helped to consolidate, if not create, including by the way in which she played the character that was Margaret Thatcher after 1990. It is this version of Margaret Thatcher that remains a political force to this day.

The mythologising of Lady Thatcher started almost as soon as her resignation was announced, if not even before. 'All over the world, she meant something as a personality and as a set of ideas,' Moore wrote in 1990. 'Thatcher and Thatcherism will be words with a lasting and universal meaning. The same can probably not be said of any other peacetime Prime Minister in our history.'² As seen above, the letters Lady Thatcher received after announcing her resignation highlight all the key ingredients that make up what became her mythical status: her values, her leadership type and her style.

Lady Thatcher's performance in the no confidence debate on 22 November 1990 reinforced this. At the time, John O'Sullivan reflected that Lady Thatcher was 'a defeated woman' when she entered the Commons that afternoon. 'What followed was myth and legend in simple words and primary colours,' he went on: 'she looked like Dietrich and she spoke like La Pasionaria'. Lady Thatcher's performance was, O'Sullivan concluded, 'the triumph of a mythic heroine over political death and her rise to a greater glory'.³

If the mythologising started early, Lady Thatcher lived to see it completed. As Lesley White commented in 2004 about the fall of the Berlin Wall, in words applicable to what happened to Lady Thatcher herself after her own fall, 'she was the prophet who gets to see the second coming'.⁴ 'She is already in the pantheon of the gods,' Malcolm Rifkind wrote in 2007.⁵

While there is no such thing as the end of history, and while Lady Thatcher, and the governments she led, remain controversial and contested, during her premier emeritus years Lady Thatcher saw her historical reputation effectively settled. This was, arguably, largely in the way she would have wanted: the conviction politician, the strong leader, the powerful performer.

Lady Thatcher gave a nod and a hand to this mythmaking. 'One had to give history a bit of help,' she argued after leaving No. 10.⁶ But if Churchill helped history by writing it, Lady Thatcher did so by *acting* it. 'They tell me I have become an "ism" in my own life-time,' she said at her seventieth birthday dinner at Downing Street.[7] 'I have brought about colossal changes,' she said at the time. 'That's why I'm an ism ... It is recognition that we didn't just govern from day to day – we had principles, we had purpose, we had action, and we had perseverance.'[8]

Others recognised the mythologising was underway. 'She persists as a living symbol,' Matthew Parris wrote in June 1997, 'a portable totem, no longer required to speak, her presence alone conferring ideological benediction. Tories used to say Margaret Thatcher kept the Ark of the Covenant. These days, she *is* the Ark of the Covenant.'[9]

In 2015, Sajid Javid spoke of having received benediction himself at a Conservative fundraiser in his late twenties. He was stood in a group of five or six people, and Lady Thatcher was introduced to them all. She ignored the others, looked at Javid, took his hand in hers and stared at him. Javid takes up the story: 'And then she said, "Sajid!" and I said, "Yes", and she said, "Sajid, you will protect our great island. You will protect our great island!" And I said, "Yes I will." And then she let go of my hand and walked off.' Javid concluded, 'I couldn't believe it. It was a message. There were no hellos or goodbyes.'[10]

The bestowal of blessing by Lady Thatcher crossed party boundaries. It affected the Labour Party, under Blair and Brown, not just the Conservatives. 'Her benediction was also sought by Tony Blair and Gordon Brown,' Matthew d'Ancona wrote in 2012.[11] 'Both New Labour prime ministers had the temerity not just to embrace Thatcherism, but to invite the Iron Lady herself into her former HQ for tea,' said John Kampfner.[12] During a Commons' debate in June 2010, Labour MP David Winnick intervened in George Osborne's speech. Osborne responded, 'If the hon. Gentleman is so affronted by what Margaret Thatcher did during her premiership, perhaps he could explain why, every time there is a new Labour Prime Minister, virtually the first person they invite round for tea is Margaret Thatcher.'[13]

Further factors helped with the mythologising of Lady Thatcher – one being the change in Lady Thatcher's reputation. Moore noticed this from the beginning of the twenty-first century, citing two events: the 2001 terrorist attacks and the 2008 banking crisis.[14]

There was another factor, too, which may have helped Lady Thatcher's reputation, namely that illness had forced her to stop speaking publicly. 'She had been silenced,' Robin Harris wrote in 2013, reflecting on this. 'Was it in her best interests? Yes.'[15] 'Margaret Thatcher was,' he went on, 'quite without knowing it, well on her way to becoming a national institution – not a treasured or beloved one, perhaps, but an institution all the same.'[16] In March 2008, Moore had said something similar, writing, 'She has become, in her lifetime, a historical figure.' He said this benefited her, with people who did not like specific policies or could not stand her tone of voice now taking 'the longer view'. He reflected on a lunch he had given her a few weeks previously, when, as Lady Thatcher got up to leave, 'everyone in the restaurant started clapping this small, beautifully dressed figure in blue'. Moore concluded, 'This once most controversial leader is in real danger of becoming a national treasure.'[17]

If Lady Thatcher was in danger of becoming a national treasure in her symbol years, she also had political significance, arguably ever more political significance, after 2002. 'It is a measure of the continuing impact of Baroness Thatcher on British politics that even today,' wrote Simon Heffer in 2008, 'when they seek to introduce a controversial policy, leaders of both main parties will claim that something similar happened during the Thatcher government.' He went on, 'that they need to justify themselves in this way says it all about Lady Thatcher's continuing influence not so much as a person, but as an idea'.[18]

After 1990, Lady Thatcher became an idea of a set of values, a type of leadership, a performance style, or a combination of some or all of these. Which of these aspects people chose to invoke in relation to themselves, and others, depended on their own views and the context in which they wished to use Lady Thatcher as a 'flag of convenience'.[19]

By the time of her death, Lady Thatcher had become an all-purpose icon. People 'venerated' or were 'iconoclastic' depending on whichever part of the icon suited them best at any given moment. As Matthew d'Ancona wrote in 1998 when comparing Lady Thatcher and Diana, Princess of Wales, 'as with Diana, it is the meanings that have been imposed upon Lady Thatcher by others as much as anything she did herself which really matter'.[20]

From the time she resigned up to and beyond her death, all Lady Thatcher's successors as Prime Minister, and as leader of the Conservative Party, have been measured, sometimes by themselves, against the Margaret Thatcher persona. This has had several consequences.

First, as suggested by Cameron above, more than any other single factor, it was, arguably, the image of 'battling Maggie' that caused difficulties for her successors as Conservative Party leader. Second, it was the idea of Margaret Thatcher, rather than Margaret Thatcher herself, that ensured Lady Thatcher's continued and continuing influence in British politics. It is against the idea of Margaret

Thatcher that her successors have often been found wanting. As no doubt Prime Minister Margaret Thatcher would have been too, on occasion.

The day after Lady Thatcher died, Patrick Wintour wrote that despite her making 'no significant intervention' in public life for over ten years because of her illness, Lady Thatcher's 'influence has run through contemporary politics and politicians as if she were still today breathing defiance and conviction from a Conservative conference platform'. Wintour argued that since 1990, British politics had been 'both a reaction and an adaptation to Thatcherism', concluding: 'No subsequent PM has been able to shed her legacy.'[21]

As she had predicted in her 1992 *Newsweek* article, Lady Thatcher persisted as an idea even beyond her death. Martin Kettle had echoed this too, writing in October 1992, 'Round about 2020 the pale fanatic generation will get their turn in power and the ghost of Lady Thatcher will return to the top table.'[22]

'Competing over who gets to be crowned the true heir to Maggie': Liz Truss and Rishi Sunak

As if on cue, during the first Conservative leadership election in 2022, Liz Truss and Rishi Sunak were seen to be 'competing over who gets to be crowned the true heir to Maggie'.[23]

Truss complained about being compared with her predecessor, commenting, 'It is quite frustrating that female politicians always get compared to Margaret Thatcher, whereas male politicians don't get compared to Ted Heath.'[24] In response, Indy100 published an article, 'All the times Liz Truss has been accused of dressing like Margaret Thatcher', featuring photographs of them wearing similar outfits.[25] As for Sunak, in a *Daily Telegraph* article he declared, 'My values are Thatcherite. I believe in hard work, family and integrity.

I am a Thatcherite, I am running as a Thatcherite and I will govern as a Thatcherite.' Sunak's article was headlined 'I will be the heir to Margaret Thatcher'.[26] Ian Dunt reflected that Lady Thatcher was almost being deified: 'She's gradually morphing from a political figure to a religious one,' he said.[27]

Once elected, Truss faced even more comparisons with Lady Thatcher. Reviewing Truss' first Prime Minister's Questions as Prime Minister, a body language expert described her as a 'hybrid between Margaret Thatcher and Mavis Riley from Coronation Street'.[28]

Subsequent comparisons were almost always unfavourable. Lord Young, a former Conservative Cabinet minister, wrote an article for the *Daily Telegraph* in October 2022 headlined 'Truss has proved herself to be a poor imitation of Mrs Thatcher',[29] while the Huffington Post spoke of '"Margaret Thatcher Without The Intelligence": Voters Deliver Brutal Verdict On Liz Truss'.[30] For all the comparisons, perhaps Liz Truss' premiership might best be seen as a lesson in under-thinking Margaret Thatcher the person and over-playing Margaret Thatcher the persona.

Rishi Sunak did not escape comparisons to Lady Thatcher either, not just because he identified himself as a Thatcherite, but also because others compared him to her. In December 2022 *The Guardian* argued that 'to be more inflexible than Thatcher is a flaw', suggesting: 'The prime minister should be like his political idol and award inflation-proof pay rises to end industrial strife by key workers.'[31] In May 2023, a former Cabinet minister was quoted as saying, 'Rishi is a true fiscal Conservative, in the Thatcher mould. Like her, he believes everything must be based on sound public finances.'[32] Sunak quoted Lady Thatcher on inflation during his October 2023 party conference speech[33] and had invoked her when announcing a change to the government's net zero plans in September: 'I also believe, as I think Margaret Thatcher would have agreed with as well, that it's not right just to assert headline, chase the short-term popularity that might give without a clear and deliverable plan for how we might get there.'[34] John Rentoul set Sunak's comments in a wider context in an article entitled 'Mummy Returns: The ghost of Margaret Thatcher still haunts British politics'.[35]

'A tone that made her sound just like Margaret Thatcher': Theresa May

The ghost of Margaret Thatcher also haunted Theresa May's premiership. Like Truss, May was compared with her at her first Prime Minister's Questions. Andrew Sparrow wrote that Theresa May had 'a tone that made her sound just like Margaret Thatcher',[36] while Michael Deacon said she 'wasn't merely channelling Mrs Thatcher. She was practically doing a *Spitting Image* impression of her.'[37] The headline to Deacon's article spoke of May going 'full Thatcher'.

The comparisons with Lady Thatcher had started even before May became Conservative leader. During the 2016 leadership election, Ken Clarke was caught on mic saying to Malcolm Rifkind, 'Theresa is a bloody difficult woman. But then, you and I worked for Margaret Thatcher!'[38] 'I certainly don't think anybody can be the new Margaret Thatcher; she was absolutely unique,' May herself commented.[39]

On ConservativeHome in October 2016, James Frayne wrote, 'Theresa May is emerging as an heir to Thatcher.' She was, he said, 'demonstrating the same natural ability to speak to ordinary families across provincial England that Thatcher had'.[40] Sir Bernard Ingham wrote an article looking for 'evidence that Theresa May has a new brand of politics that spells the end of Thatcher's influence over Tory policy'. He concluded, there was not much 'to go on yet about a break with the Thatcher way of governance'.[41] The next month, another Yorkshireman, Sir Geoffrey Boycott, said, 'She'll be like Margaret Thatcher, she'll be brilliant.'[42]

On occasion, May compared her government's work with that her predecessor's. At the National Housing Federation Summit in 2018, May said, 'with the exception of one year, the last time we saw net completions this high Lady Thatcher was in Downing Street.'[43]

Asked during the 2017 election if she was abandoning Thatcherism, May replied, 'No, I'm not. I was asked that on Thursday and I said: "Margaret Thatcher was a Conservative, I'm a Conservative, this is a Conservative manifesto."'[44] 'Philosophically, there is not a blade of grass between these women of deep religious conviction,' Sir Bernard Ingham wrote, 'only language, personality and "events, dear boy, events" over the last 25 years.'[45]

On 20 May, John Prescott described May as 'a Poundland Thatcher'.[46] The next day, Damian Green said it was 'pointless' attempting to put May in 'a Thatcherite or non-Thatcherite mould', noting how much the world had moved on. He did acknowledge similarities, however, saying both prime ministers were 'tough-minded' women, seeing 'dragons to be slain', albeit 'completely different' ones.[47]

Throughout her time as Prime Minister, May was also compared unfavourably with Lady Thatcher. Whether this criticism was fair or unfair, that it was made at all is what matters.

In December 2016, David Mellor commented that when he was a minister, Lady Thatcher treated him with 'even more disrespect than my mother did', adding, however, that Lady Thatcher 'knew what she wanted to do and did it'. He said he did not think that Theresa May knew what she wanted to do, and her advisers seemed to be the ones creating the headlines. 'I think she is sitting there and she is infirm of purpose, and she needs to seize the initiative,' he concluded.[48]

In November 2018, Norman Tebbit wrote that 'the pitiful sight' of a Prime Minister being brought down by her party had 'revived memories' of Lady Thatcher's fall. He noted that some had taken it as a sign that history might be about to repeat itself, it being the same week as Lady Thatcher's resignation twenty-eight years earlier. 'But there is not much that the two events have in common and the comparison flatters Mrs May without good reason,' he added. His article was headlined 'Sorry Theresa May, but you're no Margaret Thatcher'.[49]

'The first Conservative leader since Thatcher to shake off her shadow': Boris Johnson

Theresa May's successor as Prime Minister seemed to escape being haunted by Lady Thatcher, or was initially perceived to have done. After the 2019 election, Paul Goodman said Boris Johnson was 'the first Conservative leader since Thatcher to shake off her shadow'.[50]

Yet even Johnson found himself compared with Lady Thatcher. In March 2022, the playwright David Hare said that, during the Covid pandemic, he had, for the first time in his life, found himself 'wishing for Thatcher'. 'As a scientist and a politician', he judged, she would have been across the detail and thought there would not have been as many deaths had she been in charge, saying she would have been 'a superb tank commander': 'She had a level of competence the present incumbent doesn't have in the slightest.'[51] In June 2022, David Mellor wrote an article about the rail strikes. He said that, for Boris Johnson, 'it is not just a personal imperative, but a national one, that he ends up looking like Margaret Thatcher and not Ted Heath'. The article was headlined 'I saw how Margaret Thatcher flashed her steel against the unions. Now Boris Johnson must show his mettle'.[52] The same day, Salma Shah, Sajid Javid's former special adviser, wrote, 'There is an opportunity for Thatcher 2.0. Not just as a personality or a caricature but someone with belief and courage who is going to make some tough decisions and run with them.'[53]

On occasion, Johnson himself made the comparison with Lady Thatcher. In April 2022, he commented, 'Don't forget in times of difficulty Mrs Thatcher had state spending running very, very high as a proportion of GDP … So something like Covid I think she would have dealt with in exactly the same way.'[54] He also called Lady Thatcher in aid. Defending government policies given rising inflation and interest rates in October 2021, the *Daily Telegraph* said Johnson 'channelled Margaret Thatcher' in responding, 'In a famous phrase, there is no alternative. There is no alternative.'[55]

April 2023 marked the tenth anniversary of Lady Thatcher's death. She persisted still as an idea, a measure against which people were judged, sometimes by themselves, in terms of their beliefs, their leadership type and their style, or a combination of the three.

The anniversary did not go unmarked. Professor Pete Dorey commented, 'Instead of Thatcherism being diluted and slowly downgraded in the Conservative Party since the end of her premiership in 1990 or her death in 2013, the Conservatives have actually become relentlessly more Thatcherite.'[56] Dorey's blog was entitled 'Why Conservative MPs remain under Margaret Thatcher's spell, 10 years after her death'.

If Lady Thatcher continued to cast a spell a decade after she died, this went beyond just the Conservative Party. In a *New Statesman* article on 7 April headlined 'We're still living in Margaret

Thatcher's world', George Eaton wrote, '"Will Rishi Sunak or Keir Starmer win the general election?" commentators ask animatedly. In many respects, Margaret Thatcher already has.'[57] This mirrored comments made before the 1997 election. People might be forgiven for thinking that while everything had changed in the intervening twenty-six years, so far as Lady Thatcher was concerned, nothing had.

Conclusion

Having examined Lady Thatcher's (after) life, (continuing) work and (emerging) legacy, we conclude by examining some of the judgements that have been made about her time as a former Prime Minister. To date, these have been based on three main things: how people think former prime ministers do and should behave, how Lady Thatcher compares as a premier emeritus to other ex-prime ministers, and her effect as a former Prime Minister.

In 1992 David Seymour wrote that Lady Thatcher's *Newsweek* article 'raises the old question of how former Prime Ministers should behave'.[1] Seymour's article was headlined 'Should old PMs solider on or simply fade away?'

Throughout her premier emeritus years, especially during her politically active siren years, Lady Thatcher's behaviour was compared, often unfavourably, with that of other former prime ministers. As we have seen, her conduct was contrasted with that of Lord Home of the Hirsel. It was also compared to how Edward Heath had behaved towards her.

After 1975, Heath's behaviour had also been compared with that of other former prime ministers. In February 1983, John Vincent wrote that 'a word' from Lord Home or a 'nautical observation' from James Callaghan had authority because 'its disinterestedness is assumed'. He compared Heath to Mr Rochester's wife in Jane Eyre, 'making ghostly noises from the wings'. He argued that this threatened 'injury to the valuable convention that ex-premiers are national figures above the storm'.[2]

A year later, a leader in *The Times* went further, saying that former prime ministers were 'laden with honour', 'bolstered by a princely pension' and 'warmed by a misty respect in the shortening memory of the political nation'. It argued that they retired into the chancellorships of universities, the 'writing of their version of events', and 'the occasional statesmanlike oration about the grand issues of the day as seen from a great height'. 'That is what the idealized version of the British political system prescribes; and it is to a large extent what actually happens,' *The Times* concluded.[3]

While written with Heath in mind, both these judgements are ones against which Lady Thatcher was also judged, and found wanting, after 1990. She was not seen as acting as a national figure above the storm. She was not seen as following *The Times'* idealised version.

To judge Lady Thatcher's premier emeritus years in this way would, however, be wrong. There are several reasons for this.

First, as Kevin Theakston argues, 'There is no fixed or predetermined role for former Prime Ministers in Britain.'[4] It is difficult, therefore, to judge a former Prime Minister against a job description that does not in fact exist. To adapt Herbert Henry Asquith's famous quote, perhaps even more than the Office of the Prime Minister, the Office of Prime Minister Emeritus is what its holder chooses and is able to make of it.

The second and more fundamental problem with judging Lady Thatcher against these existing notions about how former prime ministers should and do behave is that the judgements are based on flawed evidence. As our previous works have shown, few premiers emeritus have behaved as the idealised version of the British political system prescribes. This idealised version is a myth.[5] That has also been demonstrated by Theakston's *After Number 10: Former Prime Ministers in British Politics*, published in 2010, and by the behaviour of premiers emeritus since then.

The 'valuable convention that ex-premiers are national figures above the storm' does not bear scrutiny when the activity of the former prime ministers after Lady Thatcher is examined. Examples include the interventions of John Major, Tony Blair and Gordon Brown on Brexit, the roles Blair and Brown played during Jeremy Corbyn's leadership of the Labour Party, and how Theresa May has behaved, first under Boris Johnson's premiership, particularly in relation to Partygate, and since, including on the Illegal Migration Bill. Indeed, in September 2023, Labour MP Chris Bryant wrote of May's 'caustic takedowns of successive Tory prime ministers'.[6] Nor have David Cameron, Boris Johnson and Liz Truss been 'national figures above the storm' since leaving Downing Street.

Given how premiers emeritus have behaved both before and since Lady Thatcher, it is, therefore, a myth to say that she broke a convention of how a former Prime Minister should behave. There is no such convention. Even if there were a convention, it would be the opposite of the one many traditionally conceived.

Throughout British political history, where circumstances have allowed, former prime ministers have continued to be involved in the political controversies of the day, or have themselves been politically controversial. This is the case with some more than others, and some more intensely than others, but all British premiers emeritus have continued their involvement in politics to some extent, with varying degrees of controversy.

Therefore, the first new perspective we advance about Lady Thatcher's post-premiership is that she operated largely within the framework of how British ex-prime ministers behaved before and after her. She was not *sui generis* in her behaviour – it was just that her behaviour was magnified, as was people's reaction to it. As Robin Harris said, 'She didn't try to make trouble. Trouble just tended to follow her. She had this effect of magnifying everything.'[7]

Given the way her successors have themselves behaved after No. 10, Lady Thatcher has arguably acted as a 'flag of convenience' on how to be a former Prime Minister, too.

If views varied about how Lady Thatcher behaved in relation to how people think former prime ministers do and should behave, they have also differed on how she compares, as an ex-premier, to other former prime ministers.

In 1991, Robin Oakley said Lady Thatcher was 'the most powerful former prime minister we have had this century',[8] while, conversely, George Urban wrote in 1996 that 'no other democratically elected and subsequently defeated head of government left office with so little grace, or went on showing himself or herself on the stage of the world with so little modesty'.[9] In 2002, Nicholas Watt said Lady Thatcher had had 'one of the most remarkable careers of a retired prime minister in British history'.[10] In 2006, Professor Keith Middlemas said, 'She was not Mr Jefferson, to retire to Monticello, her political work done. But if I can adapt a line from Stephen Spender, "she left the vivid air signed with her brightness".'[11] In 2007, Mark Garnett claimed, 'Her retirement was less dignified than that of any predecessor,' arguing that she was 'the least dignified ex-prime minister of all time'.[12] It should be stressed, however, given events since then, that those words were written eight former prime ministers ago. In 2010, Kevin Theakston wrote, 'It had not been a quiet and serene post-premiership, nor had it been a constructive one, but it had been one impossible to ignore.'[13]

As ever with Lady Thatcher, all these views might have an element of truth. From our study, Norman Tebbit was possibly nearest to the mark when, almost on the eve of her departure from Downing Street, he said, 'There has never been a former prime minister like this one.'[14]

Perhaps the safest – most objective – perspective that can be advanced about Lady Thatcher as a premier emeritus is that never in British history has there ever been a post-prime ministerial performance like it, and, while history never ends, nor is there likely ever to be another one quite like it either.

That is the second new perspective that is necessary for understanding Lady Thatcher's life after No. 10. As a premier emeritus, Lady Thatcher was, is and is likely always to be truly herself alone.[15]

Views about Lady Thatcher's effect as an ex-Prime Minister have tended to be less contested. 'Shadow' and 'shade' are words that appear in much of the commentary.

In 2005, the BBC entitled its main programme to mark Lady Thatcher's eightieth birthday *The Shadow of Thatcher*. Reflecting on this, Charles Moore wrote, 'It strikes me that "shadow" is precisely the wrong word. What Margaret Thatcher did was to shine a fierce, bright light upon her country – an experience that was both painful and necessary for all involved.'[16]

This quote helps to refute what should be regarded as another myth about Lady Thatcher's premier emeritus years: that after Downing Street she cast a 'shadow'. This word has negative connotations and has, arguably, skewed our perspectives on Lady Thatcher's life as a former Prime Minister. It has also effectively placed responsibility almost solely on Lady Thatcher for what happened after she left office, and removed it from others in the conscious choices that they have made – and continue to make – to use or not use Lady Thatcher as a 'flag of convenience' whenever and in whatever way has suited them best. To put this another way: if Lady Thatcher were all shadow or shade, why would her successors as prime minister, and Conservative Party leader, repeatedly compare themselves to her, or call her in aid, including up to today, nearly thirty-five years after she left office? To say nothing for those Labour leaders who have done the same.

'Shadow' also implies looking back, but the story of Lady Thatcher's premier emeritus years was really one of looking forward. That was behind her desire in her siren years for continuing influence. In 1995, Sir Bernard Ingham wrote, 'the Iron Lady does not look back. She is always looking forward to the next revolution – a Conservative revolution.'[17] That looking forward continued, even if in a different way, in and beyond her symbol years, from 2002 to, well, perhaps 'To Infinity … and Beyond', to quote Buzz Lightyear, given the way in which, over three decades after her resignation, Lady Thatcher continues to have political relevance.

Another word, therefore, is needed, which more accurately describes what happened following Lady Thatcher's resignation. It is provided by Moore in the quote that opens this section: 'light'. He used the word again after Lady Thatcher's death, writing in April 2013: 'In later years, her light shone so bright that it became intolerable for those in its shade.'[18] The same month, Michael Howard said, 'The light of her legacy will shine as a beacon down the generations.'[19] As if to prove the point, to mark the fiftieth anniversary of Lady Thatcher's election as Conservative leader in February 2025, the Conservative leader, Kemi Badenoch, tweeted that when she met Lady Thatcher in 2009, she 'radiated light and authority'.[20] Some twenty-eight years earlier, *El Pais* had made a similar point: 'Both contenders do nothing but take the ex-Iron Lady as their point of reference: Major, just in case, marks a certain prudent distance so as not to be burnt by the sun of his predecessor; Blair, so as to come nearer to the star which today illuminates British reality.'[21]

The positive connotations of the word 'light' are also more in keeping with the Margaret of legend, the mythical Thatcher, the icon on which people have gazed and from which people have taken whatever suited them best at any particular moment in time since 1990. In line with some of the almost religious terminology used to describe Lady Thatcher in her premier emeritus years, it is light, not shade, that radiates out from the sacred heart.

Writing of a hustings event during the first 2022 Conservative leadership election, Will Lloyd spoke of attendees 'hallucinating' Lady Thatcher. Lloyd wrote that she was 'the sun that burns above the Conservative party, still'. Echoing Blair's words in 2001, he went on, 'It's a shame for them they can't seance her back into Westminster. On this evidence, no one else matches up.'[22] Some words from Boris Johnson's House of Commons tribute to the Queen in September 2022 also seem applicable to Lady Thatcher politically after 1990, 'so unvarying in her pole-star radiance that we have perhaps been lulled into thinking that she might be in some way eternal'.[23]

Indeed, given Lady Thatcher's continuing impact as an idea, against which politicians are still measured, including by themselves, we might be forgiven for regarding Lady Thatcher's as the premiership on which the sun has never set. As for her life after No. 10, Lady Thatcher did not cast a shadow, she shone a light. Margaret Thatcher the persona still does.

This leads us to a third new perspective on Lady Thatcher's post-premiership. It has its roots in a review Michael Gove wrote in March 1997 of Icon Books' 'Thatcher for Beginners'. Gove commented, 'Reading this book is like listening to an Abba compilation album.'[24] One of Abba's most famous songs is about a light which, when introduced in the 1950s, was the brightest in the world. Its manufacturer, Strong Lighting, states that it 'has set the standard for all other spotlights to follow. It is truly the standard by which all other follow spots are measured.'[25] The name of that light – and the name of the Abba song – is 'Super Trouper'.

So, what is that third new perspective on Lady Thatcher's life after Downing Street? Simply that, given the way in which Lady Thatcher has shone, both as a person and especially as a persona, from 1990 onwards, and given the way in which she performed the character that was Margaret Thatcher after Downing Street, it is possible to argue that in her premier emeritus years, Margaret Thatcher became the super trouper of British political history.

In light of these three new perspectives about Lady Thatcher after 1990, it is time to reframe how we view her post-prime ministership. Yes, between 1990 and 2013, there was frustration and sadness. Yes, what followed might have felt empty in relation to what had been before. Yes, there appeared little tangible difference made in the policy areas on which she concentrated. Yet, even at the time, there was triumph, just in being Margaret Thatcher.

Beyond that, we are now over ten years on since Lady Thatcher's (physical) death. We are over twenty years on from when she was effectively forced out of active political life. We are nearly thirty-five years on from her resignation. There is, therefore, enough distance between the events of 1990–2013 and the present day for us to stand back and view Lady Thatcher's premier emeritus years in a different, and more positive, light than they have been to date. It is, in fact, time to weigh the turbulence of Lady Thatcher's post-premiership, on which we have perhaps dwelt too much, against the triumph of

Lady Thatcher's life after Downing Street, up to and even beyond her death.

Whatever negativity there might have been in the period of Lady Thatcher's life that we have studied, in her centenary year we should acknowledge that for Lady Thatcher's long-term reputation, and for her continued and continuing influence after Downing Street, the negativity has, in the end, been outweighed by the positivity. Indeed, without properly understanding what happened between 1990 and 2013, both in terms of what Lady Thatcher did and was (and is), and crucially how we responded (and continue to respond) to that, it is not possible to understand British politics today. Nor is it possible to understand why Margaret Thatcher continues to have political significance three decades after she resigned as Prime Minister.

If, as Madam Deputy Speaker said some 12,061 days after Lady Thatcher left No. 10, there is understandable excitement at the mention of the name (some might think 'that bloody name'), then that is largely because of the way in which Lady Thatcher performed the character that was Margaret Thatcher from 28 November 1990 onwards. Perhaps most of all, it is because of the way in which we have reacted to, if not just accepted, the Margaret Thatcher persona, especially regarding Lady Thatcher's premiership. It is for that reason that, however small the politics may or may not have got since 1990, Margaret Thatcher is still big.

Notes

Preface

1   See Peter Just, '"I Am Big, It's the Politics That Got Small": Margaret Thatcher's premier emeritus years: her (after) life, (continuing) work, and (emerging) legacy', in Philip Norton and Matt Beech (eds), *The Companion to Margaret Thatcher* (London: Edward Elgar, forthcoming 2025).

2   https://hansard.parliament.uk/commons/2023-12-06/debates/E100CDC2-009D-4161-9443-38833C8DC25B/Engagements

3   Richard Owen and Andrew Pierce, 'Thatcher throws weight behind Berlusconi', *The Times*, 12 May 2001.

4   Tom Rhodes, 'Berlusconi's man prepares Thatcher medicine for Italy', *The Times*, 23 March 1994.

5   https://www.heritage.org/conservatism/report/what-we-can-learn-margaret-thatcher

6   Neil McLeman, 'Napoli owner makes Margaret Thatcher appeal after "thugs" hold Italian city hostage', *Daily Mirror*, 16 March 2023.

7   Dominic McGrath, 'Rishi Sunak warns migrants could "overwhelm" countries in Rome speech', www.breakingnews.ie, 16 December 2023.

8   'Iron Lady grants the Pope an audience', *Daily Mail*, 28 May 2009.

9   Charles Moore, *Margaret Thatcher: The Authorized Biography, Volume Three: Herself Alone* (London: Allen Lane, 2019), p.838.

Introduction

1   Margaret Thatcher, *The Downing Street Years* (London: HarperCollins, 1993), p.862.

2   We use Lady Thatcher throughout, rather than using Mrs Thatcher for 1990–92 and then Lady Thatcher from 1992 onwards.

3   Caroline Slocock, *People Like Us: Margaret Thatcher and Me* (London: Biteback, 2018), p.328.

4   Andy Beckett, *Margaret Thatcher* by Charles Moore; *Not for Turning* by Robin Harris, *The Guardian*, 24 April 2013.

5   Andrew Roberts, 'Happy birthday to a fearless Iron Lady', *Daily Express*, 13 October 2005.

6   Charles Moore, 'The mellowing of Margaret Thatcher', *Daily Telegraph*, 12 October 2005. Accessible at Thatcher MSS (digital collection), 110596. https://www.margaretthatcher.org/document/110596

7   http://news.bbc.co.uk/1/hi/special_report/1999/04/99/thatcher_anniversary/325148.stm

8   See, for instance, https://www.youtube.com/user/thatcheritescot, https://x.com/realmrsthatcher, https://x.com/simplysimontfa and https://www.instagram.com/the_grocersdaughter/

9   Conversation with Sir Julian Seymour, 13 March 2025.

10 Andrew Riley, correspondence with author, 23 October 2023 and 22 January 2024.

11 Matthew d'Ancona, 'Is it really ten years?', *Sunday Telegraph*, 19 November 2000.

12 Chris Patten, *East and West* (London: Pan Books, 1999), p.289.

13 Conversation with Sir Julian Seymour, 13 March 2025.
14 Moore, op. cit., p. xvii.
15 Ibid., p. xv.
16 Thatcher MSS (digital collection),109302. https://www.margaretthatcher.org/document/109302
17 For an example of where myth and reality about premiers emeritus differ (at least in relation to their parliamentary activity), see Peter Just, *Ex-Prime Ministers and Parliament: A Riposte to Mythology*, Research Papers in Legislative Studies, 1996. See also Peter Just, 'Former PMs as "double agents"', *The Times*, 10 September 1999.

Part I: Margaret Thatcher's (after) life
1 Charles Powell, 'She carried an aura of excitement with her … the atmosphere was charged', *Sunday Telegraph*, 14 April 2013.

Chapter One
1 Elisa Roche, 'Thatcher on Thatcher', *Daily Express*, 7 December 2005.
2 See, for instance, the National Archives' website: Discovery: PREM 19/4603, DEFENCE. Allegations against Mark Thatcher: Al Yamamah and others, 30 September 1994–10 November 1994, available at: https://discovery.nationalarchives.gov.uk/details/r/C16854818.
3 The National Archives, FCO 21/4831, Visit by Margaret Thatcher, former UK Prime Minister, to China, September 1991, 1 January 1991–31 December 1991, f3.
4 Ibid., f23.
5 The National Archives, FCO 8/8754, Visit by Margaret Thatcher, former Prime Minister, to the Gulf states, April–May 1992, 1 January 1992–31 December 1992, f28.
6 The National Archives' Website: Discovery: PREM 19/6222, FORMER PRIME MINISTERS. Lady Thatcher: part 2, 12 May 1993–17 March 1997, available at: https://discovery.nationalarchives.gov.uk/details/r/C17326255
7 Maureen Orth, 'Maggie's Big Problem', *Vanity Fair*, June 1991.
8 Douglas Keay, 'My children have to live their lives. I took a different life', *Daily Telegraph*, 28 August 1998.
9 Thatcher MSS (digital collection),109305. https://www.margaretthatcher.org/document/109305
10 https://www.private-eye.co.uk/covers/cover-1051
11 Tom Carlin, 'Maggie OUT!', *Sunday People*, 9 March 2008.
12 Andrew Alderson, 'The Lady Returns to Health', *Sunday Telegraph*, 9 March 2008.
13 'Maggie Maggie Maggie, Out Out Out of hospital', *Sunday Mirror*, 9 March 2008.
14 'An Iron constitution', *News of the World*, 9 March 2008.
15 'To her health', *Sunday Telegraph*, 9 March 2008.
16 Andrew Pierce, 'On the mend', *Daily Telegraph*, 30 June 2009.
17 Chris Smyth, 'Thatcher is admitted to hospital with flu infection', *The Times*, 20 October 2010.
18 'The Iron Lady returns home', *Daily Telegraph*, 2 November 2010.
19 Kevin Schofield, 'Maggie is out of hospital', *The Sun*, 2 November 2010.
20 https://hansard.parliament.uk/Commons/2010-11-01/debates/1011025000002/Aircraft Carriers#contribution-1011025000633
21 Henry Kissinger, 'Why there was only one Iron Lady', *Mail on Sunday*, 22 October 2022.
22 https://hansard.parliament.uk/commons/2013-04-10/debates/1304104000001/TributesToBaronessThatcher
23 Moore, op. cit., p.829.
24 John Sergeant, *Maggie: Her Fatal Legacy* (London: Macmillan, 2005), p.363.

Chapter Two
1 Martin Amis, 'The long kiss goodbye', *The Guardian*, 2 June 2007.
2 Matthew Parris, *Chance Witness* (London: Penguin, 2002), p.212.

3   Camilla Cavendish, 'Thatcher's spin control', *The Times*, 26 March 2003.

4   Moore, 'The mellowing of Margaret Thatcher', op. cit.

5   Hilary Alexander, 'The Iron Lady is back in style with fashion gurus', *Daily Telegraph*, 27 January 2000.

6   Lisa Armstrong, 'Style U-turn? Blame Mrs T', *The Times*, 12 May 2004.

7   Julie Burchill, 'Slimeballs always hate a strong woman', T*he Times*, 14 October 2004.

8   Vicki Woods, 'Margaret Thatcher, the Iron Lady, used her wardrobe as a weapon', *Daily Telegraph*, 12 April 2013.

9   Alistair Horne, *Macmillan 1957–1986* (London: Macmillan, 1989), p.591.

10   Moore, op. cit., p.792.

11   https://www.margaretthatcher.org/speeches

12   Thatcher MSS (digital collection), 110366. https://www.margaretthatcher.org/document/110366

13   'The Terminator meets The Iron Lady', *Sunday Telegraph*, 13 June 2004.

14   'Shoulder to shoulder: The Terminator and Lady T', *Sunday Times*, 13 June 2004.

15   https://www.youtube.com/watch?v=2ikIL_1zmNk

16   Quentin Letts, 'Who'd have thought it? After decades of vitriol, the BBC's making an honest woman of Mrs T', *Daily Mail*, 18 February 2009.

17   Matthew d'Ancona, 'Today's contenders for power are all Thatcher's children', *Evening Standard*, 4 January 2012.

18   Dominic Sandbrook, 'Blair, Brown, Major. In 100 years they will be long forgotten. But the world will still be in awe of the grocer's daughter from Grantham', *Daily Mail*, 7 January 2012.

19   Michael Dobbs, 'It's only now that I understand her', *Daily Telegraph*, 13 April 2013.

20   Valerie Grove, 'A playwright always needs a leading lady and for 16 soundbite-packed years it was Madam', *The Times*, 7 May 1993.

21   Julia Langdon, 'A treaty too farcical', *The Guardian*, 12 November 1992.

22   https://hansard.parliament.uk/commons/2013-04-10/debates/13041040000001/TributesToBaronessThatcher

23   Lady Thatcher's skill as an actress had also been seen during her premiership. For more on this aspect of Lady Thatcher's career, see Adrian Hilton, 'The Art of Margaret Thatcher', in Philip Norton and Matt Beech (eds), *The Companion to Margaret Thatcher* (London: Edward Elgar, forthcoming 2025).

24   Emily Sheffield, 'Tempered Steel', *Vogue*, July 2008.

25   https://richardstoneuk.com/portfolio/leaders/baroness-thatcher

26   Simon Walters, 'Thatcher finds a permanent home at No 10', *Mail on Sunday*, 4 January 2009.

27   John Campbell, *Margaret Thatcher, Volume Two: The Iron Lady* (London: Jonathan Cape, 2003), p.798.

28   David Charter, 'Iron Lady meets match in statue's steely gaze', *The Times*, 2 February 2002.

29   'Thatcher's back, and larger than life', *The Times*, 22 May 2002.

30   Tom Baldwin and David Charter, 'The Iron Lady loses her marble head', *The Times*, 4 July 2002.

31   Will Pavia, 'Iron Lady returns, this time in bronze', *The Times*, 22 February 2007. Accessible at Thatcher MSS (digital collection), 110913. https://www.margaretthatcher.org/document/110913

Chapter Three

1   Jonathan Freedland, 'This lovefest for Thatcher spells trouble for Cameron', *The Guardian*, 13 April 2013.

2   Kevin Theakston, *After Number 10: Former Prime Ministers in British Politics* (Basingstoke: Palgrave Macmillan, 2010).

3   Moore, op. cit., p.747.

4   Orth, 'Maggie's Big Problem', op. cit.

5   'Iron resolve', *The Times*, 16 August 1994.

6   Theakston, op. cit., p.6.

7   'Mother of the House', *The Times*, 7 March 1991.

8   Paul Johnson, 'OPEN LETTER TO AN IRON LADY', *The Spectator*, 29 June 1991.

9   Alan Travis, 'Thatcher should quit as MP, says Parkinson', *The Guardian*, 31 May 1991.

10   Michael White, 'Get a proper job or write a book, Sir Bernard advises former PM', *The Guardian*, 21 May 1991.

11   Margaret Thatcher, *The Path to Power* (London: HarperCollins, 1995), p.488.

12   Michael Spicer, *The Spicer Diaries* (London: Biteback, 2012), p.178.

13   Sarah Curtis ed., *The Journals of Woodrow Wyatt, Volume Two* (London: Macmillan, 1999), p.445.

14   Alan Travis, 'Wandering star's uncertain future', *The Guardian*, 29 June 1991.

15   'And now we can all get on', *The Guardian*, 29 June 1991.

16   https://www.youtube.com/watch?v=L9H5nGDVfQ8

17   Travis, 'Wandering star's uncertain future', op. cit.

18   Thatcher MSS (digital collection), 210255. https://www.margaretthatcher.org/document/210255

19   Janet Jones, *Labour of Love* (London: Politico's, 1999), p.138.

20   Edwina Currie, *Diaries 1987–1992* (London: Little, Brown, 2002), p.295.

21   https://hansard.parliament.uk/Lords/2013-04-10/debates/1304101000196/DeathOfA MemberBaronessThatcher

22   Ibid.

23   Sergeant, op. cit., p.294.

24   Peter Riddell, 'The Lady's farewell tour highlights Tory party differences', *The Times*, 21 October 1993.

25   https://www.private-eye.co.uk/covers/cover-831

26   Matthew Parris, 'Building up to the Iron Lady', *The Times*, 16 October 1993.

27   Thatcher, 1995, op. cit., pp.466–67.

28   Moore, op. cit., p.753.

29   Gerald Kaufman, 'She couldn't say "No"', *Sunday Telegraph*, 13 March 2005.

30   Moore, op. cit., p.xvii.

31   'Iron Lady as committed as always', *Hull Daily Mail*, 20 October 1993.

32   Moore, op. cit., pp.787–88.

33   Ibid., p.788.

34   Simon London and John Williams, 'Thatcher: The Movie', *Daily Mirror*, 20 October 1993.

35   The National Archives, PREM 19/4297/2, MEMOIRS. Policy on Ministerial memoirs: Radcliffe Report on Ministerial Memoirs, 9 May 1991–7 May 1993.

36   Ibid.

37   The National Archives, PREM 19/4827, MEMOIRS. Policy on Ministerial memoirs: Radcliffe Report on Ministerial Memoirs; part 4, 1 June 1993–4 July 1994.

38   Moore, op. cit., p.786.

39   Ibid., p.742.

40   Conversation with Sir Julian Seymour, 13 March 2025.

41   Comments by Lord Baker of Dorking at the Margaret Thatcher: life, work and legacy conference, September 2023.

42   Thomas Sutcliffe, 'Thatcher: The Frost Interview', *The Independent*, 12 June 1995.

43   Alan Hamilton, 'The lady grants her fan club an audience', *The Times*, 13 June 1995.

44   Henry Porter, 'Sometimes she thinks she is still in Number 10', *Daily Telegraph*, 12 June 1995.

45   Margaret Thatcher, *Statecraft* (London: HarperCollins, 2002), p.188.

46   https://www.gov.uk/government/publications/public-duty-cost-allowance/public-duty-costs-allowance-guidance

47   The National Archives, PREM 19/3329, EX-PRIME MINISTERS. Policy on requests by former Prime Ministers for access to papers from their administration; part 1, 1 April 1974–24 January 1991.

48 The National Archives, PREM 19/4947, FORMER PRIME MINISTERS. Policy on requests by former Prime Ministers for access to papers from their administrations; assistance to former Prime Ministers; part 2, 6 February 1991–19 January 1994.

49 TNA, PREM 19/3329, op. cit.

50 TNA, PREM 19/4947, op. cit.

51 https://api.parliament.uk/historic-hansard/written-answers/1991/mar/27/former-prime-ministers

52 Richard Ford, 'Major gives £29,000 help to former prime ministers', *The Times*, 28 March 1991.

53 Moore, op. cit., p.749.

54 Robin Harris, *Not for Turning: The Life of Margaret Thatcher* (London: Bantam Press, 2013), p.367.

55 Conversation with Sir Julian Seymour, 13 March 2025.

56 Thatcher MSS (digital collection), 108357. https://www.margaretthatcher.org/document/108357

57 Thatcher MSS (digital collection), 109302. https://www.margaretthatcher.org/document/109302

58 Andrew Roberts, 'A Churchillian blast of the truth', *Sunday Times*, 10 March 1996.

59 Records of the White House Office of Records Management (Clinton Administration), 1993–2001, https://catalog.archives.gov/id/23902864

60 TNA, PREM 19/6222, op. cit.

61 https://www.margaretthatcher.org/about

62 Tom Baldwin, 'Overlooked back home, Thatcher's legacy seeks haven in the US', *The Times*, 16 February 2006. Accessible at Thatcher MSS (digital collection), 110686. https://www.margaretthatcher.org/document/110686

63 Thatcher MSS (digital collection), 110849. https://www.margaretthatcher.org/document/110849

64 https://www.margaretthatcher.org/

65 Jonathan Aitken, *Margaret Thatcher: Power and Personality* (London: Bloomsbury, 2013), p.679.

66 TNA, PREM 19/6222, op. cit.

67 Roberts, 'Happy birthday to a fearless Iron Lady', op. cit.

68 Kevin Maguire, 'The old witch', *Daily Mirror*, 13 October 2005.

69 http://news.bbc.co.uk/1/hi/special_report/1999/04/99/thatcher_anniversary/default.stm

70 Thatcher, 1995, op. cit., p.466.

71 The National Archives' Website: Discovery: PREM 19/3213, Resignation of Margaret Thatcher as Prime Minister, 20 November 1990 – 11 November 1991, available at: https://discovery.nationalarchives.gov.uk/details/r/C16329198.

72 John Ezard, 'Port Stanley hails Thatcher as the soul of Britannia', *The Guardian*, 15 June 1992.

73 The National Archives, FCO 7/8768, Proposed visit by Margaret Thatcher, former UK Prime Minister, to the Falkland Islands in June 1992, 1 January 1991–31 December 1991, f2.

74 Ian Katz, 'Thatcher Day dawns in Falklands', *The Guardian*, 11 January 1992.

75 The National Archives, FCO 7/8729, South Georgia and the South Sandwich Islands: proposed naming of a peninsular after Margaret Thatcher, former UK Prime Minister, 1 January 1991–31 December 1991.

76 Michael Evans, 'Thatcher tribute to courage of Falklands force', *The Times*, 16 June 1997.

77 Thatcher MSS (digital collection), 109304. https://www.margaretthatcher.org/document/109304

78 Harris, op. cit., p.430.

79 'Front-line tales for Falklands' "senior veteran"', *Daily Telegraph*, 13 June 2007.

80 https://hansard.parliament.uk/commons/2013-04-10/debates/13041040000001/TributesToBaronessThatcher

81 Thatcher MSS (digital collection), 110962 and Thatcher MSS (digital collection), 110964. https://www.margaretthatcher.org/document/110962 and https://www.margaretthatcher.org/document/110964

82 Craig Woodhouse, 'Falkland victory to be celebrated thirty years on', *Evening Standard*, 14 September 2011.

83 Andrew Pierce, 'Still the Iron Lady', *Daily Mail*, 19 March 2012.

84 Kevin Meagher, 'Tony Blair's second career: explaining his first', *New Statesman*, 3 December 2015.

85 The National Archives, KF 1/24, Volume 7 – Cabinet Office Requests for evidence to and written evidence of: Sir Charles POWELL Baroness THATCHER Stephen WALL, 1996.

86 Thatcher MSS (digital collection), 110798. https://www.margaretthatcher.org/document/110798

87 Maeve Haran, 'Still Sassy at Sixty', MailOnline, 22 June 2014.

88 David Connett, 'Thatcher entangled in icy battle of wills', *The Independent*, 9 December 1993.

89 John Mortimer, 'Thatcher pursued by a smiling huntress', *Daily Telegraph*, 9 December 1993.

90 Paul Callan, 'Eye to eye with Medusa', *Daily Express*, 9 December 1993.

91 Matthew Engel, 'It is no good asking me, I was only Prime Minister', *The Guardian*, 9 December 1993.

92 Joe Joseph, 'Flying sparks shed little light', *The Times*, 9 December 1993.

93 https://hansard.parliament.uk/Lords/1996-02-26/debates/4b7a823b-200f-4fe3-84e7-ccb66a662601/ScottReport

Part II: Margaret Thatcher's (continuing) work

1   Carol Thatcher, *A Swim-On Part in the Goldfish Bowl* (London: Headline Review, 2008), p.222.

2   Campbell, op. cit., p.749.

3   Gyles Brandreth, 'From Eden to May, I've met every prime minister – and seen how they cope with crisis behind closed doors', *Daily Telegraph*, 25 May 2019.

4   Lesley White, 'The lady now: burning and still not turning', *Sunday Times*, 28 May 1995.

5   Valentine Low and Helen Rumbelow, 'Fiercely loyal old friends rallied to protect her in the last days', *The Times*, 9 April 2013.

6   Moore, op. cit., p.745.

7   Henry Porter, 'Iron Lady gleaming', *The Guardian*, 11 May 1993.

8   Matthew Parris, 'Sharpening of claws at the sound of battle', *The Times*, 8 June 1993.

9   https://hansard.parliament.uk/Lords/2013-04-10/debates/ed03d582-e113-405f-a850-856a68e08110/LordsChamber

10 Iain Dale, *Margaret Thatcher* (London: Swift, 2025), p.147.

11 Thatcher MSS (digital collection), 110849. https://www.margaretthatcher.org/document/110849

12 Orth, 'Maggie's Big Problem', op. cit.

13 Alistair McAlpine, *Once a Jolly Bagman* (London: Weidenfeld & Nicolson, 1997), p.270.

14 Anthony Clare, 'National trauma: a doctor writes', *Sunday Correspondent*, 25 November 1990.

15 TNA, PREM 19/3213, op. cit.

16 https://www.margaretthatcher.org/archive/1992TNA2

17 https://api.parliament.uk/historic-hansard/commons/1990/nov/22/prime-minister

18 TNA, PREM 19/3213, op. cit.

19 Thatcher MSS (digital collection), 111441. https://www.margaretthatcher.org/document/111441

20 Harris, op. cit., p.347.

21 *House Magazine*, 10/17 December 1990.

22 Thatcher MSS (digital collection), 108259. https://www.margaretthatcher.org/document/108259

23 Sergeant, op. cit., p.203.

24 'I still expect to turn into Downing Street for home', *The Times*, 9 March 1991.

25 Thatcher, 2008, op. cit., pp.223–4.

26 Brenda Maddox, *Maggie: The First Lady* (London: Hodder & Stoughton, 2003), p.234.

27 Moore, op. cit., p.747.

28 Private information.

29 Curtis, 1999, op. cit., p.414.

30 Porter, 'Sometimes she thinks she is still in Number 10', op. cit.

31 Sutcliffe, 'Thatcher: The Frost Interview', op. cit.

32 'The lady's all for returning', *Daily Telegraph*, 16 October 2003.

33 John Hooper, Nicholas Watt and Robert Booth, 'Lady Thatcher's final days cheered by puppy antics and tales of former PMs', *The Guardian*, 10 April 2013.

34 Keith Joseph, 'We did not go far enough; we failed her', *The Independent*, 23 November 1990.

35 Thatcher MSS (digital collection), 109483. https://www.margaretthatcher.org/document/109483

36 Peter Hennessy and Robert Shepherd, *The Complete Reflections* (London: Haus Publishing, 2020), pp.122–23.

37 Kissinger, 'Why there was only one Iron Lady', op. cit.

38 Moore, op. cit., p.747.

39 Charles Moore, 'A champion of freedom for workers, nations and the world', *Daily Telegraph*, 9 April 2013.

40 Tim Bell, *Right or Wrong* (London: Bloomsbury, 2014), p.143.

41 John O'Sullivan, 'A radical reformer who could not go gentle into the political night', *Independent on Sunday*, 25 November 1990.

42 Sally Dawson, 'The fear factor', *The House*, 18 April 2013.

43 Patrick R. H. Wright, *Behind Diplomatic Lines* (London: Biteback, 2018), p.311.

44 Ibid., p.321.

45 Ibid., p.302.

46 Ibid., p.304.

47 Ken Clarke, *Kind of Blue* (London: Macmillan, 2016), p.250.

48 'Let John get on with the job, Maggie', *The Sun*, 22 April 1992.

49 Thatcher, 1995, op. cit., p.475.

50 Carol Thatcher, *Below the Parapet* (London: HarperCollins, 1996), p.278.

51 Aitken, op. cit., p.654.

52 McAlpine, op. cit., p.272.

53 https://www.margaretthatcher.org/archive/1992TNA2

54 Bruce Anderson, 'In her dreams, she is still prime minister', *Independent on Sunday*, 24 March 2002.

55 Wright, op. cit., p.323.

56 Curtis, 1999, op. cit., p.498.

57 Allan Massie, 'Why should one withhold one's experience? Why should one be gagged?', *Daily Telegraph*, 18 October 1993.

58 Porter, 'Sometimes she thinks she is still in Number 10', op. cit.

59 George Jones, 'Thatcher backs hardline on EU', *Daily Telegraph*, 6 October 1999.

60 https://www.margaretthatcher.org/archive/1994TNA1

Chapter Four

1 Thatcher MSS (digital collection), 108263. https://www.margaretthatcher.org/document/108263

2 https://www.margaretthatcher.org/archive/1992TNA2

3 The National Archives, FCO 21/5270, Visit by Margaret Thatcher, former UK Prime Minister, to South Korea, September 1992, 1 January 1992–31 December 1992, f7.

4 Thatcher MSS (digital collection), 108302. https://www.margaretthatcher.org/document/108302

5 Thatcher, 1995, op. cit., p.468.

6 Thatcher MSS (digital collection), 111359. https://www.margaretthatcher.org/document/111359

7 Thatcher MSS (digital collection), 108353. https://www.margaretthatcher.org/document/108353

8   Simon Jenkins, 'Major on the rack', *The Times*, 13 January 1996.

9   Sergeant, op. cit., p.355.

10 Ibid., p.358.

11 Clarke, op. cit., pp.226–7.

12 Stephen Castle, 'Thatcher ready to stand in summer poll', *The Independent*, 10 March 1991.

13 Simon Heffer, 'Blair is destroying my legacy by stealth', Daily Mail, 22 May 2001.

14 Nicholas Watt, 'Bowing out: the Thatcher legacy', *The Guardian*, 23 March 2002.

15 https://www.margaretthatcher.org/archive/1994TNA1

16 The National Archives' Website: Discovery: PREM 19/4408, FORMER PRIME MINISTERS. Lady Thatcher: part 1, 9 April 1991–20 April 1993, available at: https://discovery.nationalarchives.gov.uk/details/r/C16854623.

17 Thatcher MSS (digital collection), 108272. https://www.margaretthatcher.org/document/108272

18 TNA, PREM 19/4408, op. cit.

19 Mary Dejevsky, 'Thatcher wins student cheers over Gorbachev', *The Times*, 28 May 1991.

20 'Missionary in Moscow', *The Times*, 28 May 1991.

21 Thatcher MSS (digital collection), 110849. https://www.margaretthatcher.org/document/110849

22 TNA, PREM 19/4408, op. cit.

23 Wright, op. cit., p.319.

24 Ibid.

25 Thatcher, 1995, op. cit., p.512.

26 Thatcher MSS (digital collection), 205930. https://www.margaretthatcher.org/document/205930

27 Michael Forsyth, 'She never stopped serving her country', *Daily Telegraph*, 9 April 2013.

28 Moore, op. cit., p.763.

29 Harris, op. cit., p.362.

30 David Sharrock, 'New leader takes to his limo as Russia's wheels of fortune turn', *The Guardian*, 31 January 1992.

31 The National Archives' Website: Discovery: PREM 19/3890, PRIME MINISTER. Prime Minister's meetings with Margaret Thatcher, 26 December 1990–5 February 1992, available at: https://discovery.nationalarchives.gov.uk/details/r/C16561804.

32 Thatcher MSS (digital collection), 111264. https://www.margaretthatcher.org/document/111264

33 *The Times*, 23 July 1993.

34 Mary Riddell, 'The woman at home with power', *Daily Telegraph*, 16 April 2008.

35 The National Archives' Website: Discovery: PREM 49/2202, PRIME MINISTER. Prime Minister's meetings with Lady Thatcher: part 1, 7 May 1997–17 June 1999, accessible at: https://discovery.nationalarchives.gov.uk/details/r/C17970457

36 Anders Anglesey, 'Margaret Thatcher Gave Damning Assessment of Putin in Resurfaced Clip', *Newsweek*, 9 January 2023.

37 Thatcher MSS (digital collection), 108388. https://www.margaretthatcher.org/document/108388

38 TNA, PREM 19/4408, op. cit.

39 The National Archives, FCO 15/6843, Visit by Margaret Thatcher, former UK Prime Minister, to Malaysia, Thailand and Singapore, August–September 1993, 1 January 1993–31 December 1993, f3.

40 Sergeant, op. cit., p.356.

41 TNA, PREM 19/4408, op. cit.

42 Thatcher MSS (digital collection), 108285. https://www.margaretthatcher.org/document/108285

43 The National Archives' Website: Discovery: PREM 19/4346, POLAND. UK/Polish relations: internal situation; economic assistance; part 13, 7 June 1991–29 November 1993, accessible at: https://discovery.nationalarchives.gov.uk/details/r/C16854561

44 Julian Borger, 'Excited young disciples watch as star of the West rises in the East', *The Guardian*, 17 April 1993.

45 Hugo Young, *The Guardian*, 23 November 1990.

46 Thatcher, 1995, op. cit., p.603.

47 Moore, op. cit., p.xix.

48 Harris, op. cit., p.361.

49 Thatcher MSS (digital collection),108384. https://www.margaretthatcher.org/document/108384

50 Thatcher, 2002, op. cit., p.5.

51 Thatcher MSS (digital collection),108385. https://www.margaretthatcher.org/document/108385

52 George R. Urban, *Diplomacy and Disillusion at the Court of Margaret Thatcher* (London: I. B. Tauris, 1996), p.174.

53 TNA, PREM 19/3213, op. cit.

54 The National Archives, FCO 21/4916, Visit by Margaret Thatcher, former UK Prime Minister, to Japan, September 1991, 1 January 1991–31 December 1991, f6.

55 Orth, 'Maggie's Big Problem', op. cit.

56 Urban, op. cit., pp.174–6.

57 Lady Thatcher, *Daily Telegraph*, 8 April 2013.

58 TNA, PREM 19/3213, op. cit.

59 Records of the National Security Council Records Management Office (Clinton Administration), ca. 1993–ca. 2001, https://catalog.archives.gov/id/23902871

60 Campbell, op. cit., p.783.

61 Harris, op. cit., p.392.

62 Records of the White House Office of Records Management (Clinton Administration), 1993–2001, https://catalog.archives.gov/id/23902860

63 Ibid., https://catalog.archives.gov/id/23902862?objectPage=2

64 Thatcher MSS (digital collection), 110395. https://www.margaretthatcher.org/document/110395

65 Thatcher MSS (digital collection), 110871. https://www.margaretthatcher.org/document/110871

66 Sam Coates, 'Cameron and Thatcher divided over "slavish" special relationship', *The Times*, 12 September 2006. Accessible at Thatcher MSS (digital collection), 110872. https://www.margaretthatcher.org/document/110872

67 Thatcher MSS (digital collection),110364. https://www.margaretthatcher.org/document/110364

68 Baldwin, 'Overlooked back home, Thatcher's legacy seeks haven in the US', op. cit.

69 Martin Ivens, 'Tories must learn the lady is for turning to their advantage', *Sunday Times*, 16 September 2007. Accessible at Thatcher MSS (digital collection), 110992. https://www.margaretthatcher.org/document/110992

70 Sarah Baxter, 'Rudy Giuliani mocks Hillary claim to be Iron Lady', *Sunday Times*, 16 September 2007. Accessible at Thatcher MSS (digital collection), 110996. https://www.margaretthatcher.org/document/110996

71 Andrew Roberts, 'Her determination and fortitude continue to defy the passage of time', *Sunday Telegraph*, 9 March 2008.

72 Matthew Campbell, 'Republicans vie for Thatcher blessing', *Sunday Times*, 8 August 1999.

73 Toby Harnden, 'Republicans seek Thatcher's blessing', *Daily Telegraph*, 27 July 2007.

74 Ivens, 'Tories must learn the lady is for turning to their advantage', op. cit.

75 Baxter, 'Rudy Giuliani mocks Hillary claim to be Iron Lady', op. cit.

76 'Margaret Thatcher: Mitt Romney hails former PM as "tower of strength"', *Daily Telegraph*, 14 October 2012.

77 Nick Allen,' Nikki Haley honours "ultimate Iron Lady" Margaret Thatcher to launch White House bid', *Daily Telegraph*, 15 February 2023.

78 Verity Bowman, 'From Margaret Thatcher to UFOs: 10 things you might have missed from the Republican debate', *Daily Telegraph*, 24 August 2023.

79 'Nikki Haley quotes Thatcher as she quits US presidential race', *Daily Telegraph*, 6 March 2024.

80 Emily Goodin, 'Bill Clinton reveals Democrats' biggest fail and says "Margaret Thatcher" conservative will be first woman president', *Daily Mail*, 21 November 2024.
81 TNA, FCO 21/4916, op. cit., f6 and f7.
82 The National Archives, FCO 8/9837, Visit by Baroness Thatcher, former UK Prime Minister, to the United Arab Emirates (UAE), June 1994, 1 January 1994–31 December 1994, f5.
83 Conversation with Sir Julian Seymour, 13 March 2025.
84 TNA, FCO 21/4916, op. cit., f7.
85 The National Archives, FCO 33/12683, VIP and ministerial visits from the UK to Sweden, 1 January 1993–31 December 1993, f8.
86 TNA, FCO 15/6843, op. cit., f8.
87 https://www.margaretthatcher.org/archive/1994TNA1
88 TNA, FCO 8/9837, op. cit., f7.
89 TNA, FCO 21/4831, op. cit., f7.
90 Ibid., f11.
91 The National Archives, FCO 8/8261, Visit by Margaret Thatcher, former UK Prime Minister, to the Gulf states, November 1991, 1 January 1991–31 December 1991, f9.
92 TNA, FCO 21/4916, op. cit., f24.
93 The National Archives, FCO 21/5196, Visit by Margaret Thatcher, former UK Prime Minister, to Japan, October 1992, 1 January 1992–31 December 1992, f11.
94 TNA, FCO 21/5270, op. cit., f5.
95 Ibid., f23.
96 Ibid., f55.
97 TNA, FCO 15/6843, op. cit., f14.
98 Ibid., f15.
99 TNA, FCO 21/5270, op. cit., f53.
100 TNA, FCO 8/8754, op. cit., f28.
101 TNA, FCO 8/9837, op. cit., f7.
102 The National Archives, FCO 7/10050, Proposed visit by Lady Thatcher, former UK Prime Minister, to Brazil, Chile and Mexico in March 1994, 1 January 1993–31 December 1993, f7.
103 TNA, PREM 19/4408, op. cit.
104 TNA, FCO 21/5270, f21.
105 Ibid., f22.
106 Ibid., f53.
107 The National Archives, FCO 21/4999, Visit by Edward Heath, former UK Prime Minister, to South Korea, October 1991, 1 January 1991–31 December 1991, f26.
108 TNA, FCO 21/4916, op. cit., f24.
109 TNA, FCO 8/8754, op. cit., f23.
110 TNA, FCO 15/6843, op. cit., f16.
111 TNA, FCO 7/10050, op. cit., f4.
112 TNA, FCO 21/4916, op. cit., f23.
113 TNA, PREM 19/4408, op. cit.
114 TNA, FCO 21/4916, op. cit., f24.
115 Ibid., f23.
116 TNA, FCO 21/5196, op. cit., f10.
117 Ibid., f11.
118 TNA, FCO 21/4916, op. cit., f24.
119 Joanna Pitman, 'Smitten Japan breaks gush barrier for Thatcher', *The Times*, 23 August 1991.
120 TNA, FCO 21/5196, op. cit., f11.
121 Ibid., f10.
122 Joanna Pitman, 'Thatcher star still dazzles in Japan', *The Times*, 25 November 1993.
123 TNA, FCO 8/8261, op. cit., f8.

124 TNA, FCO 21/4831, op. cit., f23.

125 TNA, FCO 21/5270, op. cit., f3.

126 TNA, FCO 15/6843, op. cit., f16.

127 TNA, FCO 8/8754, op. cit., f23.

128 TNA, FCO 21/5270, op. cit., f53.

129 Ibid.

130 The National Archives, FCO 9/7575, Possible nomination of Margaret Thatcher, UK Prime Minister, for the Ataturk International Peace Prize, 1 January 1991–31 December 1991.

131 TNA, FCO 15/6843, op. cit., f16.

132 TNA, FCO 8/8754, op. cit., f9.

133 Ibid., f19.

134 The National Archives, FCO 93/6945, Visit by Baroness Thatcher, former UK Prime Minister, to Israel, November 1992, 1 January 1992–31 December 1992, f12.

135 Ibid., f23.

136 Ibid., f22.

137 Ibid.

138 TNA, FCO 15/6843, op. cit., f17.

139 Ibid., f19.

140 William Waldegrave, *A Different Kind of Weather* (London: Constable, 2015), p.295.

141 https://www.margaretthatcher.org/archive/1994TNA1

142 Orth, 'Maggie's Big Problem', op. cit.

143 TNA, FCO 21/5196, op. cit., f11.

144 TNA, FCO 8/8754, op. cit., f23.

145 Gyles Brandreth, 'The Tory camp', *Sunday Telegraph*, 24 June 2001.

146 Conversation with Sir Julian Seymour, 13 March 2025.

147 TNA, FCO 21/4916, op. cit., f7.

148 The National Archives' Website: Discovery: PREM 19/4454, SOUTH AFRICA. Visits to UK by Nelson Mandela: meetings and conversations with Prime Minister and other politicians, 5 March 1990–15 October 1993, accessible at: https://discovery.nationalarchives.gov.uk/details/r/C16854669

149 The National Archives, PREM 19/3546, SOUTH AFRICA. UK/South Africa relations: internal situation; part 24, 9 January 1991–29 May 1991.

150 TNA, FCO 8/9837, op. cit., f7.

151 Conversation with Sir Julian Seymour, 13 March 2025.

152 Harris, op. cit., p.364.

153 Moore, op. cit., p.751.

154 TNA, FCO 15/6843, op. cit., f3a.

155 Ibid., f4.

156 TNA, FCO 21/5270, op. cit., f1.

157 TNA, FCO 93/6945, op. cit., f19.

158 The National Archives, FCO 40/3436, Visit by Margaret Thatcher, former UK Prime Minister, to Hong Kong, September 1991, 1 January 1991–31 December 1991, f11.

159 TNA, FCO 21/5196, op. cit., f10.

160 TNA, FCO 8/8754, op. cit., f.28.

161 TNA, FCO 21/5270, op. cit., f53.

162 TNA, FCO 7/10050, op. cit., f1b.

163 Conversation with Sir Julian Seymour, 13 March 2025.

164 Thatcher, 1995, op. cit., p.468.

165 TNA, FCO 8/9837, op. cit., f7.

166 TNA, FCO 21/5270, op. cit., f53.

167 Ibid., f38.

168 TNA, FCO 8/8754, op. cit., f11.

169 TNA, FCO 21/4831, op. cit., f3.
170 TNA, FCO 15/6843, op. cit., f8.
171 TNA, FCO 21/5270, op. cit., f53.

Chapter Five

1 William Hague, 'Missile with a handbag', *Sunday Telegraph*, 19 October 2003.
2 https://www.c-span.org/video/?65895-1/prime-minister-perspective
3 Moore, op. cit., p.791.
4 Robin Harris, 'John Major is the intolerable one', *Sunday Telegraph*, 15 August 1999.
5 Thatcher MSS (digital collection), 109471. https://www.margaretthatcher.org/document/109471
6 Moore, op. cit., p.792.
7 David Wastell and Tom Baldwin, 'But who has the Lady's true blessing?', *Sunday Telegraph*, 11 May 1997.
8 Harris, op. cit., p.408.
9 Jo-Anne Nadler, *William Hague In His Own Right* (London: Politico's, 2000), p.40.
10 Philip Webster and Andrew Pierce, 'Tory contenders are neck and neck', *The Times*, 19 June 1997.
11 Moore, op. cit., p.808.
12 Harris, op. cit., p.409.
13 Campbell, op. cit., p.788.
14 Robert Shrimsley, 'Maternal embrace rolls back years', *Daily Telegraph*, 19 June 1997.
15 Matthew Parris, 'Handbag swings in to bless the Young Pretender', *The Times*, 19 June 1997.
16 Hague, 'Missile with a handbag', op. cit.
17 Teresa Gorman, 'The rise of a small boy who swore at old uncles', *Sunday Times*, 22 June 1997.
18 Andrew Grice and Michael Prescott, 'Hague's battle to bind Tory wounds', *Sunday Times*, 22 June 1997.
19 Hague, 'Missile with a handbag', op. cit.
20 Harris, op. cit., p.415.
21 David Cracknell, 'Thatcher says Portillo is the right leader', *Sunday Telegraph*, 15 July 2001.
22 Moore, op. cit., p.827.
23 Andrew Pierce, 'Fatal blow was leak to newspaper', *The Times*, 18 July 2001.
24 Thatcher MSS (digital collection), 108390. https://www.margaretthatcher.org/document/108390
25 'Time to end the insanity', *Daily Mail*, 22 August 2001.
26 Moore, op. cit., p.828.
27 Nick Assinder, 'Why Thatcher still looms over politics', BBC News website, 14 October 2005.
28 David Cameron, *For the Record* (London: William Collins, 2019), p.416.
29 Sergeant, op. cit., p.10.
30 Giles Dilnot, 'Never mind the moving of a painting in No 10, the presence of Lady Thatcher subtly hangs over the leadership contest', ConservativeHome, 6 September 2024.
31 https://x.com/LeeDavidEvansUK/status/1824715580873564168
32 Zoe Crowther, 'Mel Stride Says He Will "Completely Overhaul" Tory Campaign Machine If Elected Leader', PoliticsHome, 3 August 2024.
33 Peter Walker, 'Tory gasps as Robert Jenrick reveals daughter's middle name is Thatcher', *The Guardian*, 1 October 2024.
34 'Lord Alli investigated for alleged code of conduct breach', *Daily Telegraph*, 2 October 2024.
35 https://conservativehome.com/2024/09/04/we-must-unite-if-we-want-the-british-people-to-listen-to-us-again-cleverlys-leadership-speech-full-text/
36 Andrew Roberts, 'I knew Lady Thatcher and see echoes of her in Badenoch – and the hatred she attracts from the Left', *Daily Mail*, 18 October 2024.
37 Daniel Martin, 'Kemi Badenoch has qualities of Thatcher, says minister who served under Iron Lady', *Daily Telegraph*, 17 October 2024.

38 Kemi Badenoch, email to Conservative Party members, 3 November 2024.

39 Boris Johnson, 'That nice Mr Major's been airbrushed out of history', *Daily Telegraph*, 7 October 1999.

40 Gyles Brandreth, *Breaking the Code* (London: Weidenfeld & Nicolson, 1999), p.56.

41 Currie, op. cit., p.282.

42 Moore, op. cit., p.768.

43 Charles Moore, 'Making up for lost time, or how John Major found his voice', *Daily Telegraph*, 23 March 1992.

44 Lord Whitelaw, 'Don't wreck our party, Margaret', *Daily Mail*, 8 October 1992.

45 The National Archives, PREM 19/3800, HONG KONG. Future of Hong Kong: part 28, 1 June 1992–30 October 1992.

46 Norman Fowler, *The Best of Enemies* (London: Biteback, 2023), p.409.

47 Andrew Rawnsley, 'Margaret, wish you weren't here, love and kisses, John', *The Guardian*, 9 October 1992.

48 Anthony Seldon, *Major: A Political Life* (London: Weidenfeld & Nicolson, 1997), p.328.

49 Ibid.

50 John Major, *The Autobiography* (London: HarperCollins, 1999), p.362.

51 'The Haunted Conference', *Daily Mail*, 8 October 1992.

52 Martin Kettle, 'Ghostly raging at the dying light', *The Guardian*, 10 October 1992.

53 https://www.private-eye.co.uk/covers/cover-804

54 Robert Hardman, 'Thatcher books in for a day of Blackpool illuminations', *Daily Telegraph*, 7 October 1993.

55 Philip Webster, 'Thatcher bids to defuse row over memoirs', *The Times*, 6 October 1993.

56 Philip Webster, 'Thatcher and Clarke rally round Major', *The Times*, 8 October 1993.

57 Seldon, op. cit., p.402.

58 https://www.private-eye.co.uk/covers/cover-830

59 BBC Breakfast with Frost, 17 October 1993.

60 Matthew Parris, 'Majestic vision from the deep sails serenely through media storm', *The Times*, 12 October 1994.

61 Philip Webster, Nicholas Wood and Andrew Pierce, '"Heartbroken" Thatcher denies arms deal claims', *The Times*, 11 October 1994.

62 Brandreth, op. cit., p.275.

63 Thomas Stuttaford, 'A weight on Tory minds', *The Times*, 13 October 1994.

64 Matthew Parris, 'Tories march together to a future behind bars', *The Times*, 13 October 1995.

65 Sergeant, op. cit., pp.315–6.

66 Seldon, op. cit., p.671.

67 Alice Thomson, 'Major's fortunes brighten as Thatcher swings behind him', *The Times*, 9 October 1996.

68 Sergeant, op. cit., p.320.

69 Seldon, op. cit., p.673.

70 Thomson, 'Major's fortunes brighten as Thatcher swings behind him', op. cit.

71 Seldon, op. cit., p.673.

72 Thatcher MSS (digital collection), 108366. https://www.margaretthatcher.org/document/108366

73 Philip Webster, 'Back Major, Thatcher tells Tories', *The Times*, 9 October 1996.

74 George Jones, 'Get cracking, says Thatcher', *Daily Telegraph*, 9 October 1996.

75 Damian Whitworth, 'Thatcher flies into a rage at BA logos', *The Times*, 10 October 1997.

76 Karen Pasquali Jones, 'Elizabeth Buchanan: "I learnt a lot from Margaret Thatcher"', *Great British Life*, 29 March 2022.

77 Moore, op. cit., p.810.

78 Harris, op. cit., p.409.

79 Campbell, op. cit., p.789.

80 Matthew Parris, 'A nod to the past as ailing Tories try to catch nurse's eye', *The Times*, 8 October 1998.

81 Michael Brown, 'Buddha and the grandmother face it out at the funeral', *The Independent*, 8 October 1998.

82 https://www.private-eye.co.uk/covers/cover-961

83 Ewen MacAskill, 'Not a word was exchanged for 22 years, yesterday they broke the long silence', *The Guardian*, 8 October 1998.

84 Michael McManus, *Edward Heath: A Singular Life* (London: Elliott & Thompson, 2016), p.279.

85 'You ask the questions', *The Independent*, 25 November 1998.

86 Robert Shrimsley, 'Hijacked by Iron Lady's agenda', *Daily Telegraph*, 7 October 1999.

87 Michael Prescott, 'Thatcher mocks "wee Willie" Hague', *Sunday Times*, 3 October 1999.

88 Joe Murphy and David Cracknell, 'William's winning way', *Sunday Telegraph*, 10 October 1999.

89 Margaret Thatcher, 'Well done, Tony – you've given William his chance', *Daily Telegraph*, 4 October 1999.

90 George Jones, 'Blair "tricks" denounced by Thatcher', *Daily Telegraph*, 4 October 1999.

91 Shrimsley, 'Hijacked by Iron Lady's agenda', op. cit.

92 Michael Prescott and Eben Black, 'Wee Willie's right turn', *Sunday Times*, 10 October 1999.

93 Michael White, 'Major rounds on Tory sceptics', *The Guardian*, 11 October 1999.

94 Matthew Parris, 'Answers, answers: who needs questions?', *The Times*, 4 October 2000.

95 Andrew Pierce and Tom Baldwin, 'Two pensioners try to rewrite history', *The Times*, 4 October 2000.

96 George Jones, 'Thatcher to steer clear of Tory conference', *Daily Telegraph*, 7 September 2001.

97 Dominic Kennedy, 'Warrior queen raises ancient battle standard', *The Times*, 10 April 1997.

98 Andrew Pierce, 'Iron Lady shops for Tory victory', *The Times*, 15 May 2001.

99 Fowler, 2023, op. cit., p.353.

100 TNA, PREM 19/3890, op. cit.

101 Thatcher MSS (digital collection), 108294. https://www.margaretthatcher.org/document/108294 and Thatcher MSS (digital collection), 111378. https://www.margaretthatcher.org/document/111378

102 Paul Eastham, 'Your country needs you, Maggie tells Major as she rallies Tory troops', *Daily Mail*, 23 March 1992.

103 Robert Hardman, 'Green Goddess breathes fire into Tory campaign', *Daily Telegraph*, 23 March 1992.

104 TNA, FCO 21/5270, op. cit., f5.

105 Craig Brown, 'Newspack hovers for Thatcher gaffes', *Sunday Times*, 22 March 1992.

106 Valerie Elliott, 'It's goodbye to all that', *Sunday Telegraph*, 22 March 1992.

107 Godfrey Barker, 'Major backed by a dab hand', *Daily Telegraph*, 21 March 1992.

108 Ben Fenton, 'Save my legacy says Thatcher', *Daily Telegraph*, 14 March 1992.

109 Alan Travis and Ruth Kelly, 'Thatcher hints Major gutless on tax gap', *The Guardian*, 25 March 1992.

110 David Hughes, 'Thatcher hints at a new Tory fight over Europe', *Sunday Times*, 5 April 1992.

111 Norman Fowler, *A Political Suicide* (London: Politico's, 2008), p.89.

112 https://hansard.parliament.uk/Commons/2013-04-10/debates/1304104000001/TributesToBaronessThatcher

113 Neil Syson, 'Maggie Mania', *The Sun*, 14 March 1992.

114 'Maggie-mania leaves 4 hurt', *Daily Star*, 14 March 1992.

115 'Street wise', *The Sun*, 14 March 1992.

116 Jan Disley, 'Daffed!', *Daily Mirror*, 24 March 1992.

117 'Crowds mob ex-PM', *The Guardian*, 14 March 1992.

118 Simon Hoggart, 'Lady T proves she can still get your goat', *The Observer*, 22 March 1992.

119 Alastair Campbell, 'Now what's that interfering old battleaxe up to?', *Daily Mirror*, 14 March 1992.

120 Charles Powell, 'It's not over till the Lady says so', *Sunday Telegraph*, 13 April 1997.

121 Matthew Parris, 'Lady T runs out of credit', *The Times*, 19 April 1997.

122 Thatcher MSS (digital collection), 111361. https://www.margaretthatcher.org/document/111361

123 Magnus Linklater, 'Irn Bru Lady drinks in admiration of Scottish voters', *The Times*, 22 April 1997.

124 Harris, op. cit., p.405.

125 Seldon, op. cit., p.723.

126 Brandreth, op. cit., p.483. Tim Smith, one of the MPs involved in the 'cash for questions' affair, had announced that he was standing down as a candidate.

127 Sergeant, op. cit., p.321.

128 Andrew Pierce, 'Thatcher supports revolt against single currency', *The Times*, 19 April 1997.

129 Ibid.

130 https://www.youtube.com/watch?v=4obOMntb9mo

131 Moore, op. cit., p.826.

132 Harris, op. cit., p.412.

133 Will Self, 'Brave Billie watches as the Magus weaves her strange spell', *The Independent*, 23 May 2001.

134 Brian Reade, 'Maggie Maggie Maggie In! In! In!', *Daily Mirror*, 24 May 2001.

135 Simon Hoggart, 'A noise like Omaha Beach. "Out, out, out." But she is out', *The Guardian*, 30 May 2001.

136 Quentin Letts, 'The day Lady T tore into town and apathy took to the hills', *Daily Mail*, 30 May 2001.

137 Simon Sebag Montefiore, 'Triumph of the queen of never-never land', *Sunday Times*, 3 June 2001.

138 Matthew Parris, 'Crowd goes wild as lady sings the blues', *The Times*, 30 May 2001.

139 'Out of tune', *The Independent*, 23 May 2001.

140 Martin Wainwright, 'Portillo goes Latin as Lady sings for the blues', *The Guardian*, 23 May 2001.

141 Heffer, 'Blair is destroying my legacy by stealth', op. cit.

142 Simon Walters, 'The day Portillo told Hague: You must denounce Thatcher…or face disaster', *Mail on Sunday*, 1 July 2001.

143 Ben Macintyre, 'I'm back: the Mummy returns', *The Times*, 23 May 2001.

144 Ewen MacAskill, 'Thatcher says never to single currency', *The Guardian*, 23 May 2001.

145 Thatcher MSS (digital collection), 108389. https://www.margaretthatcher.org/document/108389

146 MacAskill, 'Thatcher says never to single currency', op. cit.

147 Margaret Thatcher, 'Tony Blair is committed to the extinction of Britain', *Daily Telegraph*, 1 June 2001.

148 George Jones, 'Hague's last hurrah for Tories', *Daily Telegraph*, 6 June 2001.

149 Damian Whitworth, 'Thatcher clouds Hague's future', *The Times*, 6 June 2001.

150 Simon Carr, 'Who will Maggie Thatcher vote for? It must be Labour', *The Independent*, 30 May 2001.

151 'How Tories snubbed Maggie's offer to help on campaign', Londoner's Diary, *Evening Standard*, 6 May 2005.

152 Eddie Barnes, 'Thatcher: "Save Scotland's regiments"', *Scotland on Sunday*, 17 April 2005.

153 Ben Fenton, 'Lady Thatcher declares her support for Euro', *Daily Telegraph*, 18 March 2005.

154 Fowler, 2008, op. cit., pp.169–70.

155 Norman Fowler, 'The Truth about the Major Years', *Daily Express*, 5 May 1997.

156 Simon Hoggart, 'The less Thatcher doubted herself, the more the world applauded', *The Guardian*, 8 April 2013.

157 Nicholas Wood and Charles Bremner, 'Heath rages at Thatcher speech on EC', *The Times*, 19 June 1991.

158 Martin Fletcher, 'Thatcher aide dubs Heath an occupational hazard', *The Times*, 20 June 1991.

159 Robin Oakley, 'Heath challenges Thatcher to televised debate', *The Times*, 20 June 1991.

160 Europe's destiny, *The Times*, 19 June 1991.

161 Alan Travis, 'Major to meet head-on new onslaughts by Thatcher', *The Guardian*, 20 June 1991.

162 Sarah Hogg and Jonathan Hill, *Too Close to Call* (London: Little, Brown, 1995), p.80.

163 https://api.parliament.uk/historic-hansard/commons/1991/jun/26/european-community

164 Sergeant, op. cit., p.226.

165 Matthew Engel, 'Thatcher still a factor as Heath goes on and on', *The Guardian*, 25 March 1992.

166 https://api.parliament.uk/historic-hansard/commons/1992/may/21/european-communities-amendment-bill

167 *Hull Daily Mail*, 8 October 1992.

168 Matthew Parris, 'Stage-struck stars play bashful duet', *The Times*, 8 October 1993.

169 McManus, op. cit., p.279.

170 Ibid.

171 Ibid.

172 Thatcher MSS (digital collection), 108381. https://www.margaretthatcher.org/document/108381

173 Michael White, 'Thatcher makes her peace with Heath', *The Guardian*, 21 April 1999.

174 'WARNING', *Daily Mirror*, 21 April 1999.

175 McManus, op. cit., p.286.

176 Ibid., p.287.

177 Philip Ziegler, *Edward Heath* (London: HarperPress, 2010), p.581.

178 https://hansard.parliament.uk/Commons/2013-04-10/debates/1304104000001/TributesToBaronessThatcher

179 McManus, op. cit., p.280.

180 Thatcher MSS (digital collection), 110675. https://www.margaretthatcher.org/document/110675

181 Jack Maidment, 'Sir John Major claims Margaret Thatcher's dementia was behind her criticism of his leadership', *Daily Telegraph*, 22 June 2018.

182 https://hansard.parliament.uk/lords/1989-12-04/debates/ef33980d-7ef4-4d11-8cf2-30467d83a497/WarCrimesInquiryReport#625

183 Clarke, op. cit., p.250.

184 Patten, op. cit., p.62.

185 Fowler, 2023, op. cit., p.406.

186 Aitken, op. cit., p.667.

187 Bernard Ingham, 'Thatcher's legacy and the need to stay silent', *Daily Express*, 22 April 1992.

188 Bernard Ingham, 'Take the money and run, Maggie', *Daily Express*, 11 October 1993.

189 Harris, op. cit., p.343.

190 D. R. Thorpe ed., *Who Loses Who Wins: The Journals of Kenneth Rose, Volume Two, 1979–2014* (London: Weidenfeld & Nicolson, 2019), p.215 and p.231.

191 Maddox, op. cit., p.224.

192 Sutcliffe, 'Thatcher: The Frost Interview', op. cit.

193 Max Hastings, *Editor* (London: Macmillan, 2002), pp.259–60.

194 Ibid., p.312. Hastings also noted that his card from the Prime Minister was signed 'John Major'. Hastings commented, 'The years of "John and Norma" were over with a vengeance.' He also received a card from Tony Blair signed 'Tony'. Hastings commented, 'By such trifles did we read the runes.'

195 Seldon, op. cit., p.254.

196 Moore, op. cit., p.761.

197 Ibid.

198 https://johnmajorarchive.org.uk/1999/10/15/john-majors-contributions-in-the-the-major-years-15-october-1999/

199 Maidment, 'Sir John Major claims Margaret Thatcher's dementia was behind her criticism of his leadership', op. cit.

200 Harry Yorke, 'Margaret Thatcher's aides dispute claims her criticism of Sir John Major was due to dementia', *Daily Telegraph*, 24 June 2018.

201 Craig Simpson, 'John Major: I went easy on Margaret Thatcher because she was a woman', *Daily Telegraph*, 26 June 2023.

202 Laura Lambert, '"Mrs Thatcher was showing signs of dementia in her last year at Number 10", claims Ken Clarke', *Daily Mail*, 9 October 2017.

203 https://johnmajorarchive.org.uk/1999/10/15/john-majors-contributions-in-the-the-major-years-15-october-1999/

204 Curtis, 1999, op. cit., p.406.

205 Colin Brown, 'Thatcher backs Tory rebellion on Maastricht', *The Independent*, 29 June 1992.

206 Philip Webster, Nicholas Wood and Sheila Gunn, 'Thatcher in "get behind John" appeal to Tories', *The Times*, 15 June 1993.

207 Colin Brown and Patricia Wynn Davies, 'Thatcher supports Major leadership', *The Independent*, 15 June 1993.

208 Seldon, op. cit., p.381.

209 Brandreth, op. cit., p.186.

210 BBC Breakfast with Frost, op. cit.

211 Thatcher MSS (digital collection), 108353. https://www.margaretthatcher.org/document/108353

212 Thatcher MSS (digital collection), 111359. https://www.margaretthatcher.org/document/111359

213 Moore, op. cit., p.772.

214 Campbell, op. cit., p.766.

215 Harris, op. cit., p.344.

216 Seldon, op. cit., p.255.

217 Fowler, 2023, op. cit., p.375.

218 Seldon, op. cit., p.255.

219 Thatcher, 1995, op. cit., p.469.

220 TNA, PREM 19/6222, op. cit.

221 Michael Jones, 'Thatcher launches savage attack on Major's "misguided" policies', *Sunday Times*, 21 May 1995.

222 Sarah Curtis ed., *The Journals of Woodrow Wyatt: Volume Three, From Major to Blair* (London: Macmillan, 2000), p.513.

223 Major, op. cit., p.613.

224 TNA, PREM 19/6222, op. cit.

225 Ibid.

226 Peter Riddell, 'Major left in no doubt about his "wrong direction"', *The Times*, 12 January 1996.

227 Philip Webster and Nicholas Wood, 'Why Tories are unpopular', *The Times*, 12 January 1996.

228 Seldon, op. cit., p.628.

229 Brandreth, op. cit., p.366.

230 Moore, op. cit., p.803.

231 Brandreth, op. cit., p.398.

232 Seldon, op. cit., p.651.

233 https://johnmajorarchive.org.uk/1999/10/15/john-majors-contributions-in-the-the-major-years-15-october-1999/

234 Seldon, op. cit., p.253.

235 Harris, op. cit., p.344.

236 Moore, op. cit., p.760.

237 Ibid., pp.759–60.

238 https://www.private-eye.co.uk/covers/cover-769
239 Curtis, 1999, op. cit., p.535.
240 Curtis, 2000, op. cit., p.471.
241 Harris, 'John Major is the intolerable one', op. cit.
242 James Prior, 'A fatal lust for power', *The Observer*, 25 November 1990.
243 Peter Riddell, 'Why this Lady is not for spurning', *The Times*, 6 October 1993.
244 Forsyth, 'She never stopped serving her country', op. cit.
245 Andrew Grice, 'Heath calls Hague a no-hope leader', *Sunday Times*, 29 June 1997.
246 Andrew Pierce, 'Heath calls halt to criticism of Hague', *The Times*, 10 July 1997.
247 Robin Oakley, 'Thatcher remains the unexploded bomb in her party's heart', *The Times*, 13 June 1991.
248 Sergeant, op. cit., p.202.
249 TNA, PREM 19/4408, op. cit.
250 Sergeant, op. cit., p.307 and p.308.
251 Philip Webster, 'Major rules out single currency "in this century"', *The Times*, 26 October 1993.
252 Simpson, 'John Major: I went easy on Margaret Thatcher because she was a woman', op. cit.
253 Major, op. cit., p.215.
254 Moore, op. cit., p.759.
255 https://www.margaretthatcher.org/archive/1992TNA2
256 TNA, PREM 19/3890, op. cit.
257 Ibid.
258 Curtis, 2000, op. cit., p.444 and p.471.
259 Urban, op. cit., p.162.
260 Moore, op. cit., p.779.
261 Spicer, op. cit.
262 Seldon, op. cit., p.255.
263 Major, op. cit., p.362.
264 Hennessy and Shepherd, op. cit., p.118.
265 Steve Richards, 'Exit right: a great talker whose voice still echoed round the world stage', *The Independent*, 23 March 2002.
266 Sarah Womack, 'Thatcher forgot problems she left me, says Major', *Daily Telegraph*, 23 August 2001.
267 Seldon, op. cit., p.255.
268 Ibid., p.723.
269 TNA, PREM 19/6222, op. cit.
270 Philip Webster, 'Thatcher casts shadow over Major's visit', *The Times*, 22 September 1994.
271 https://johnmajorarchive.org.uk/1994/09/22/mr-majors-press-conference-in-pretoria-22-september-1994/
272 Philip Webster and Michael Hamlyn, 'Major heals rift with Thatcher over visit', *The Times*, 23 September 1994.
273 https://johnmajorarchive.org.uk/2013/04/08/sir-john-majors-statement-on-the-death-of-baroness-thatcher-8-april-2013/
274 https://johnmajorarchive.org.uk/2013/04/08/sir-john-majors-interview-following-the-death-of-baroness-thatcher-8-april-2013/
275 https://johnmajorarchive.org.uk/2013/04/21/sir-john-majors-itv-interview-following-the-death-of-baroness-thatcher-8-april-2013/
276 https://johnmajorarchive.org.uk/2013/05/20/sir-john-majors-statement-on-the-margaret-thatcher-scholarship-trust-20-may-2013/

Chapter Six

1 Harris, op. cit., p.376.
2 Ibid., p.403.

3   'Stateswoman – and subversive' is the title of the penultimate chapter of Moore's official biography.

4   Roland Watson and Tom Baldwin, 'Thatcher puts a bomb under Europe policy', *The Times*, 14 August 1999.

5   Harris, op. cit., p.384.

6   TNA, PREM 19/3890, op. cit.

7   Ibid.

8   'Rocks and rapids', *The Times*, 7 January 1991.

9   Major, op. cit., p.268.

10 Seldon, op. cit., p.166.

11 Nicholas Wood, 'Thatcher plans to break her silence', *The Times*, 25 January 1991.

12 Moore, op. cit., p.759.

13 Thatcher MSS (digital collection), 108275 and Thatcher MSS (digital collection), 108274. https://www.margaretthatcher.org/document/108275 and https://www.margaretthatcher. org/document/108274

14 Moore, op. cit., p.759.

15 Alan Travis, 'Tories calm Thatcher speech tremors', *The Guardian*, 19 June 1991.

16 Michael White, 'Sunset star casts a shadow', *The Guardian*, 19 June 1991.

17 'History and the pall of hindsight', *The Guardian*, 20 June 1991.

18 https://api.parliament.uk/historic-hansard/commons/1991/jun/26/european-community

19 'The blast that came out of the handbag', *The Guardian*, 27 June 1991.

20 https://api.parliament.uk/historic-hansard/commons/1991/nov/20/european-community-intergovernmental#S6CV0199P0_19911120_HOC_234

21 TNA, PREM 19/4408, op. cit.

22 https://www.margaretthatcher.org/archive/1994TNA1

23 TNA, FCO 8/8261, op. cit., f17.

24 Ibid., f17A.

25 Douglas Hurd, *Memoirs* (London: Little, Brown, 2003), p.419.

26 Moore, op. cit., p 769.

27 Major, op. cit., p.275.

28 Moore, op. cit., p.769.

29 The National Archives' Website: Discovery: CAB 128/100/14, 21 November 1991, available at: https://discovery.nationalarchives.gov.uk/details/r/C16482462

30 Curtis, 1999, op. cit., p.609.

31 Currie, op. cit., p.291.

32 Sergeant, op. cit., p.212.

33 Michael White, 'Thatcher hijacks Major's line', *The Guardian*, 21 November 1991.

34 Andrew Rawnsley, 'Ghost of Bruges applies her handbag to wobbly ministers', *The Guardian*, 21 November 1991.

35 https://api.parliament.uk/historic-hansard/commons/1991/nov/21/european-community-intergovernmental

36 Moore, op. cit., p.769.

37 'Act of disloyalty', *Daily Telegraph*, 25 November 1991.

38 Sergeant, op. cit., p.213.

39 TNA, PREM 19/3890, op. cit.

40 https://www.margaretthatcher.org/archive/1992TNA2

41 TNA, FCO 21/5270, op. cit., f7.

42 Thatcher MSS (digital collection), 108296. https://www.margaretthatcher.org/document/108296

43 The National Archives, FCO 33/11984, Parliamentary visits from the UK to the Netherlands, 1 January 1992–31 December 1992, f2.

44 Ibid., f7.

45 Thatcher, 1995, op. cit., pp.488–9.

46 Seldon, op. cit., p.292.

47 Thatcher MSS (digital collection), 108297. https://www.margaretthatcher.org/document/108297

48 George Brock, 'Gleeful gladiator puts "Euro-snobs" to the sword', *The Times*, 16 May 1992.

49 TNA, FCO 33/11984, f8.

50 Ibid.

51 'Time to accentuate the positive', *The Independent*, 16 May 1992.

52 'Thatcher's Europe', *The Times*, 16 May 1992.

53 'Entitled to her views', *Daily Telegraph*, 16 May 1992.

54 George Jones and Philip Johnston, 'Thatcher in onslaught on Europe', *Daily Telegraph*, 16 May 1992.

55 Nicholas Timmins, 'Major advised to disown Thatcher stand on Europe', *The Independent*, 16 May 1992.

56 Major, op. cit., pp.350–1.

57 Womack, 'Thatcher forgot problems she left behind, says Major', op. cit.

58 Clarke, op. cit., p.311.

59 Stephen Bates, 'Heath rounds on "rebel rouser"', *The Guardian*, 27 March 1993.

60 Moore, op. cit., p.782.

61 Major, op. cit., p.366.

62 Moore, op. cit., p.782.

63 Forsyth, 'She never stopped serving her country', op. cit.

64 Moore, op. cit., p.782.

65 Ibid., p.781.

66 https://hansard.parliament.uk/Lords/1992-07-02/debates/9ca89a9e-8907-4055-9b17-a0122ec7c68d/LordsChamber#contribution-a438109c-d00a-43a4-85e2-28d3732b74dd

67 Andrew Rawnsley, 'Lady Kraken stirs to outshout the people's Beast', *The Guardian*, 3 July 1992.

68 Matthew Parris, 'A midsummer day's dream', *The Times*, 3 July 1992.

69 Patricia Wynn Davies, 'Thatcher "bags" the attention of her peers', *The Independent*, 3 July 1992.

70 'Lady Thatcher', *Daily Telegraph*, op. cit.

71 Fowler, 2023, op. cit., p.396.

72 'Thatcher: I was right all along, Mandrake', *Sunday Telegraph*, 20 September 1992.

73 Thatcher, 1995, op. cit., p.492. It was said that after the UK left the ERM, Norman Lamont was heard singing in his bath.

74 TNA, PREM 19/4408, op. cit.

75 Thatcher MSS (digital collection), 108304. https://www.margaretthatcher.org/document/108304

76 Moore, op. cit., p.780.

77 Thatcher MSS (digital collection), 108305. https://www.margaretthatcher.org/document/108305

78 TNA, FCO 15/6843, op. cit., f1.

79 TNA, FCO 33/12683, op. cit., f8.

80 Ibid., f6.

81 Ibid., f7.

82 Ibid., f6.

83 Ibid.

84 Ibid., f8.

85 https://api.parliament.uk/historic-hansard/lords/1993/jun/07/european-communities-amendment-bill

86 TNA, FCO 33/12683, op. cit., f21.

87 https://api.parliament.uk/historic-hansard/lords/1993/jul/14/european-communities-amendment-bill

88 George Jones and Robert Shrimsley, 'Thatcher to vote against treaty', *Daily Telegraph*, 29 June 1992.

89   Andrew Rawnsley, 'Iron Peeress goes a little flat amid the ermined herd', *The Guardian*, 8 June 1993.

90   Parris, 'Sharpening of claws at the sound of battle', op. cit.

91   Anthony Bevins, 'Resolute band of followers gather in the Lords to hear Tory leader-in-exile's Maastricht rallying cry', *The Independent*, 8 June 1993.

92   'Forceful but flawed', *Daily Telegraph*, 8 June 1993.

93   https://api.parliament.uk/historic-hansard/lords/1993/jul/14/european-communities-amendment-bill

94   Thatcher MSS (digital collection), 111362. https://www.margaretthatcher.org/document/111362

95   George Jones and Charles de Lisle, 'Thatcher to vote against her party', *Daily Telegraph*, 12 July 1993.

96   Andrew Rawnsley, 'Dammit, sir, wouldn't you say it's time for a spot of dinner?', *The Guardian*, 15 July 1993.

97   Sheila Gunn and Philip Webster, 'Thatcher fails in plea to let the people vote', *The Times*, 15 July 1993.

98   George Jones and Charles de Lisle, 'Referendum rebellion crushed in Lords vote', *Daily Telegraph*, 15 July 1993.

99   Curtis, 2000, op. cit., p.258.

100 The National Archives' Website: Discovery: CAB128/106/3, 15 July 1993, available at: https://discovery.nationalarchives.gov.uk/details/r/C16748470.

101 Michael White, 'Thatcher's last stand', *The Guardian*, 15 July 1993.

102 Moore, op. cit., p.802.

103 Thatcher, 1995, op. cit., Chapter 13.

104 Harris, op. cit., p.384.

105 Major, op. cit., p.613.

106 Andrew Grice and Michael Prescott, 'Britain may have to quit EU, says Thatcher', *Sunday Times*, 22 December 1996.

107 Edward Heathcote-Amory, 'Exile of the Iron Lady', *Daily Mail*, 15 April 1999.

108 Rachel Sylvester, 'Thatcher says Britain should leave the EU', *Independent on Sunday*, 8 August 1999.

109 Polly Newton, 'Tories urged to disown Thatcher', *Daily Telegraph*, 16 August 1999.

110 Roland Watson and James Landale, 'Thatcher backs Hague on EU', *The Times*, 17 August 1999.

111 Moore, op. cit., p.824.

112 Harris, op. cit., p.384.

113 Philip Webster, 'Thatcher: Britain must start to quit EU', *The Times*, 18 March 2002.

114 Michael Gove, 'It is time for the Tories to turn away from Thatcher', *The Times*, 19 March 2002.

115 Sam Lister, Melissa Kite and Tom Baldwin, 'Thatcher wrong on Europe say Tories', *The Times*, 22 March 2002.

116 https://hansard.parliament.uk/Commons/2002-03-18/debates/d05e2481-ccea-4547-9c58-6784717db028/EuropeanCouncil(Barcelona)

117 Harris, op. cit., p.385.

118 Moore, op. cit., p.824.

119 Andrew Roberts, 'The lighter and softer side of the Iron Lady', *Sunday Telegraph*, 14 April 2013.

120 Charles Moore, 'Would Margaret Thatcher have backed Brexit?', *Daily Telegraph*, 7 February 2016.

121 Charles Moore, 'After leaving office, Margaret Thatcher believed Britain should leave the EU', *The Spectator*, 8 May 2013.

122 Harris, op. cit., p.384.

123 TNA, FCO 33/11984, f8.
124 TNA, FCO 33/12683, f6.
125 TNA, PREM 19/4408, op. cit.
126 TNA, FCO 21/5270, op. cit., f53.
127 TNA, FCO 21/5196, op. cit., f11.
128 Clarke, op. cit., p.398.
129 https://hansard.parliament.uk/commons/2013-04-10/debates/1304104000001/Tributes ToBaronessThatcher
130 The National Archives, FCO 40/3655, Visit by Sir Edward Heath, former UK Prime Minister, to China, September–October 1992: Hong Kong briefing, 1 January 1992–31 December 1992, f17.
131 TNA, FCO 21/4999, op. cit., f24.
132 Lucy Crossley, 'Very blue sky: Father-of-three photographs a cloud that looks like Margaret Thatcher over Portsmouth', *Daily Mail*, 2 June 2016.
133 Moore, op. cit., p.xx.
134 https://hansard.parliament.uk/Commons/2015-03-10/debates/15031049000003/TradingRelationshipsWithEurope
135 Jonathan Freedland, 'Labour has to get over its Tony Blair problem', *The Guardian*, 22 May 2015.
136 Jon Craig, 'Margaret Thatcher: Thirty years on from her Downing Street exit, her legacy lives on', Sky News, 28 November 2020.
137 https://hansard.parliament.uk/lords/2016-07-05/debates/D80BBB95-5A60-4084-B3DF-F83312E031C2/OutcomeOfTheEuropeanUnionReferendum
138 Nigel Lawson, 'Brexit will complete Margaret Thatcher's economic revolution', *Daily Telegraph*, 23 September 2016.
139 Andrew Sparrow, 'Margaret Thatcher would have voted to stay in EU, claims aide', *The Guardian*, 7 February 2016.
140 Moore, 'Would Margaret Thatcher have backed Brexit?', op. cit.
141 Kathy Gyngell, 'Theresa May and Margaret Thatcher – compare and despair', The Conservative Woman, 21 September 2018.
142 Matt Dathan and Nick Gutteridge, 'BOJO'S NOT FOR TURNING: Boris Johnson channels Margaret Thatcher as he vows to stand firm against France's 11th-hour Brexit demands', *The Sun*, 6 December 2020.
143 https://www.private-eye.co.uk/covers/cover-1403
144 https://www.margaretthatcher.org/archive/1994TNA1
145 Andrew Duncan interview, *Radio Times*, 16–22 October 1993.
146 Thatcher, 1995, op. cit., p.512.
147 Campbell, op. cit., p.760.
148 Thatcher MSS (digital collection), 111357. https://www.margaretthatcher.org/document/111357
149 Thatcher MSS (digital collection), 111358. https://www.margaretthatcher.org/document/111358
150 Moore, op. cit., p.775.
151 https://www.margaretthatcher.org/archive/1994TNA1
152 The National Archives' Website: Discovery: CAB128/100/15, 28 November 1991, accessible at: https://discovery.nationalarchives.gov.uk/details/r/C16482463.
153 Thatcher MSS (digital collection), 111358. https://www.margaretthatcher.org/document/111358
154 Wright, op. cit., p.311.
155 Hurd, op. cit., p.445.
156 TNA, PREM 19/3213, op. cit.
157 Harris, op. cit., p.387.
158 TNA, PREM 19/3890, op. cit.
159 TNA, FCO 33/11984, f8.
160 https://www.margaretthatcher.org/archive/1994TNA1

161 TNA, PREM 19/4408, op. cit.
162 https://www.margaretthatcher.org/archive/1994TNA1
163 TNA, PREM 19/4408, op. cit.
164 Ibid.
165 https://www.margaretthatcher.org/archive/1994TNA1
166 The National Archives, PREM 19/3992/1, YUGOSLAVIA. Internal situation: UK/Yugoslavia relations: part 5, 1 July 1992–31 July 1992, accessible at Thatcher MSS (digital collection), 210278. https://www.margaretthatcher.org/document/210278
167 The National Archives, PREM 19/3993, YUGOSLAVIA. Internal situation: UK/Yugoslavia relations: part 6, 1 August 1992–11 August 1992, accessible at Thatcher MSS (digital collection), 210310. https://www.margaretthatcher.org/document/210310
168 Ibid., accessible at Thatcher MSS (digital collection), 210279. https://www.margaretthatcher.org/document/210279
169 Thatcher, 1995, op. cit., p.514.
170 Thatcher MSS (digital collection), 108299. https://www.margaretthatcher.org/document/108299
171 Thatcher, 1995, op. cit., p.514.
172 https://www.youtube.com/watch?v=RTwONspMxXw
173 Moore, op. cit., p.776.
174 The National Archives, PREM 19/3993, YUGOSLAVIA. Internal situation: UK/Yugoslavia relations: part 6, 1 August 1992–11 August 1992.
175 Seldon, op. cit., p.306.
176 Thatcher MSS (digital collection), 109355. https://www.margaretthatcher.org/document/109355
177 Thatcher MSS (digital collection), 110821. https://www.margaretthatcher.org/document/110821
178 The National Archives, PREM 19/4508, YUGOSLAVIA. Internal situation: UK/Yugoslavia relations: part 18, 1 April 1993–19 April 1993.
179 'Taking Bosnia seriously', *The Times*, 15 April 1993.
180 Malcolm Rifkind, *Power and Pragmatism* (London: Biteback, 2016), p.320.
181 Hurd, op. cit., p.460.
182 TNA, PREM 19/4508, op. cit.
183 Records of the National Security Council European Affairs Office (Clinton Administration), ca. 1993–ca. 2001, https://catalog.archives.gov/id/40482309
184 TNA, PREM 19/4508, op. cit.
185 Ibid.
186 Peter Riddell, 'Churchill's champion churns up the "level killing field"', *The Times*, 14 April 1993.
187 'Bosnia: Should the heart rule the head?', *Daily Mail*, 14 April 1993.
188 https://api.parliament.uk/historic-hansard/lords/1993/apr/14/bosnia
189 Paul Callan, 'Danger Woman switches her swoop into a gentle glide', *Daily Express*, 15 April 1993.
190 Robert Hardman, 'The Lady's all for burning', *Daily Telegraph*, 15 April 1993.
191 https://api.parliament.uk/historic-hansard/commons/1993/apr/14/bosnia-1
192 Philip Webster and Martin Fletcher, 'Thatcher takes Bosnia campaign to America', *The Times*, 15 April 1993.
193 Jon Craig, 'Maggie warned of all-out war', *Daily Express*, 15 April 1993.
194 Records of the National Security Council European Affairs Office (Clinton Administration), ca. 1993–ca. 2001, https://catalog.archives.gov/id/40482309
195 Telegram accessible at Thatcher MSS (digital collection), 109355. https://www.margaretthatcher.org/document/109355
196 The National Archives' Website: Discovery: CAB128/105/13, 15 April 1993, accessible at: https://discovery.nationalarchives.gov.uk/details/r/C16748460
197 Julia Langdon, 'Lady Thatcher rides again', *The Guardian*, 19 April 1993.
198 https://api.parliament.uk/historic-hansard/commons/1994/apr/18/bosnia

199 Curtis, 2000, op. cit., p.209.
200 'Maggie, mad or magnificent?', *The Economist*, 24 April 1993.
201 Moore, op. cit., p.777.
202 Records of the National Security Council Records Management Office (Clinton Administration), ca. 1993–ca. 2001, https://catalog.archives.gov/id/23902871
203 TNA, FCO 15/6843, op. cit., f12.
204 Ibid., f14.
205 Ibid., f18.
206 https://johnmajorarchive.org.uk/1993/09/22/mr-majors-press-conference-in-kuala-lumpur-22-september-1993/
207 TNA, FCO 15/6843, op. cit., f14.
208 TNA, FCO 8/9837, op. cit., f7.
209 https://api.parliament.uk/historic-hansard/lords/1995/jul/12/srebrenica
210 The Bosnian Serbs had been holding over 300 United Nations troops hostage.
211 Thatcher MSS (digital collection), 110823. https://www.margaretthatcher.org/document/110823
212 Thatcher MSS (digital collection), 108378. https://www.margaretthatcher.org/document/108378
213 Thatcher, 2002, op. cit., p.309.
214 Tom Baldwin, Andrew Gilligan and David Wastell, 'Blair enlists Thatcher for advice on war', *Sunday Telegraph*, 25 April 1999.
215 Harris, op. cit., p.394.
216 The National Archives' Website: Discovery: PREM 49/785, FORMER YUGOSLAVIA. Internal situation: UK/Yugoslavia relations; part 25, 27 April 1999–28 April 1999, available at: https://discovery.nationalarchives.gov.uk/details/r/C17515796
217 Trevor Kavanagh, 'Maggie: War on Slobba is right', *The Sun*, 21 April 1999.
218 Thatcher, 2002, op. cit., p.309.
219 Thatcher MSS (digital collection), 108381. https://www.margaretthatcher.org/document/108381
220 TNA, PREM 49/785, op. cit.
221 The National Archives, PREM 49/786, FORMER YUGOSLAVIA. Internal situation: UK/Yugoslavia relations; part 26, 29 April 1999–30 April 1999. Accessible at Thatcher MSS (digital collection), 243044. https://www.margaretthatcher.org/document/243044
222 Russell Miller, 'We are happy', *Sunday Times*, 22 October 1995.
223 'Maggie, mad or magnificent?', *The Economist*, op. cit.
224 Peter Riddell, 'Thatcher outburst finds little support among Tory right', *The Times*, 15 April 1993.
225 Private information.
226 Harris, op. cit., p.403.
227 Thatcher, 1995, op. cit., p.514.
228 TNA, PREM 19/4408, op. cit.
229 Harris, op. cit., p.390.
230 Fowler, 2023, op. cit., p.429.
231 Harris, op. cit., p.403.
232 Aitken, op. cit., p.664.
233 https://api.parliament.uk/historic-hansard/lords/1993/jun/07/european-communities-amendment-bill
234 Ibid.
235 https://api.parliament.uk/historic-hansard/lords/1993/jun/08/european-communities-amendment-bill
236 TNA, FCO 15/6843, op. cit., f16.
237 Thatcher MSS (digital collection), 110580. https://www.margaretthatcher.org/document/110580
238 David Graves, 'General delighted with Thatcher "victory" gift', *Daily Telegraph*, 6 March 2000.
239 Thatcher MSS (digital collection), 109296. https://www.margaretthatcher.org/document/109296
240 Harris, op. cit., p.398.

241 Ibid., p.401.

242 Moore, op. cit., p.822.

243 https://api.parliament.uk/historic-hansard/lords/1999/jul/06/general-pinochet

244 Thatcher MSS (digital collection), 108383. https://www.margaretthatcher.org/document/108383

245 Robert Shrimsley and David Graves, 'Thatcher condemns "kidnap" of Pinochet', *Daily Telegraph*, 7 October 1999.

246 Moore, op. cit., p.823.

247 Ibid.

248 Harris, op. cit., p.402.

249 Moore, op. cit., p.822.

250 The National Archives' Website: Discovery: PREM 49/212, CHILE. UK/Chilean relations: internal situation; part 1, 2 January 1998–18 December 1998, available at: https://discovery.nationalarchives.gov.uk/details/r/C17515223.

251 David Cracknell, 'Thatcher to make Pinochet speech', *Sunday Telegraph*, 3 October 1999.

252 Prescott, 'Thatcher mocks "wee Willie" Hague', op. cit.

253 Thatcher MSS (digital collection), 109296. https://www.margaretthatcher.org/document/109296

254 Thatcher, 2002, op. cit., p.272.

255 The National Archives, PREM 19/4230, HONG KONG. Future of Hong Kong: part 31, 1 May 1993–1 December 1993.

256 Thatcher, 2002, op. cit., p.190.

257 Miles Goslett, 'My regrets over Hong Kong handover, by Lady Thatcher', *Sunday Telegraph*, 10 June 2007.

258 The National Archives, PREM 19/3386, HONG KONG. Future of Hong Kong: part 24, 1 April 1990–28 March 1991.

259 Thatcher, 2002, op. cit., p.151 and p.190.

260 TNA, FCO 21/4831, op. cit., f27.

261 Moore, op. cit., pp.764–66.

262 TNA, FCO 21/4831, op. cit., f21.

263 The National Archives, FCO 21/5388, Official and private visits to China: visit by Sir Edward Heath, former UK Prime Minister, to China and Hong Kong, October 1993, 1 January 1993–31 December 1993, f11.

264 TNA, FCO 21/4831, op. cit., f19.

265 Thatcher MSS (digital collection), 108281. https://www.margaretthatcher.org/document/108281

266 TNA, FCO 40/3436, op. cit., f11.

267 TNA, PREM 19/4230, op. cit.

268 Campbell, op. cit., p.774.

269 The National Archives, FCO 21/5661, Visit by Lady Thatcher, former UK Prime Minister, to China, March 1995, 1 January 1994–31 December 1994.

270 Ibid., f13.

271 Ibid., f8.

272 Ibid., f5.

273 The National Archives, PREM 19/5561, CHINA. UK/Chinese relations: part 8, 10 January 1995–5 February 1996.

274 Thatcher, 2002, op. cit., pp.190–3.

275 Ibid., p.191.

276 Ibid.

277 Campbell, op. cit., p.774.

278 TNA, PREM 19/5561, op. cit.

279 Michael Jones and Michael Prescott, 'Thatcher goes on Hong Kong watch', *Sunday Times*, 30 June 1996.

280 Jonathan Mirsky, 'Thatcher attacks China's treatment of activists', *The Times*, 15 November 1996.

281 Thatcher MSS (digital collection), 108367. https://www.margaretthatcher.org/document/108367

282 https://api.parliament.uk/historic-hansard/lords/1996/apr/24/hong-kong

283 Moore, op. cit., p.766.

284 Aitken, op. cit., p.657.

285 Thatcher, 2002, op. cit., p.190.

286 Aitken, op. cit., p.657.

287 Harris, op. cit., p.357.

288 Hurd, op. cit., p.484.

289 Patten, op. cit., p.61.

290 Harris, op. cit., p.357.

291 https://api.parliament.uk/historic-hansard/lords/1992/dec/09/hong-kong-and-china-1

292 https://api.parliament.uk/historic-hansard/written-answers/1992/dec/14/hong-kong-governors-proposals

293 TNA, PREM 19/4230, op. cit.

294 Thatcher, 2002, op. cit., p.192.

295 Patten, op. cit., p.62.

296 Moore, op. cit., p.766.

297 Ziegler, op. cit., p.570.

298 TNA, FCO 40/3655, op. cit., f5.

299 Ibid., f16.

300 Hurd, op. cit., p.484.

301 TNA, FCO 21/5388, op. cit., f40.

302 Ibid., f42.

303 The National Archives, FCO 21/5390, Visit by Lord Callaghan, former UK Prime Minister, to China, May 1993, 1 January 1993–31 December 1993, and FCO 40/4049, Visit by Lord Callaghan, former UK Prime Minister, to China and Hong Kong, May 1993, 1 January 1993–31 December 1993.

304 TNA, FCO 40/4049, op. cit., f24.

305 Ibid., f28.

306 Campbell, op. cit., pp.773–4.

307 Aitken, op. cit., p.657.

308 Thatcher, 2002, op. cit., p.190.

309 Harris, op. cit., p.357.

310 Jim Norton, 'The Iron Maidy: How Mrs Thatcher was the only guest to make her own bed during diplomatic trips to Hong Kong', *Daily Mail*, 28 June 2017.

311 Chris Patten, 'As I looked at these clapped-out Chinese tyrants, I thought "Why do we allow ourselves to be bullied by them?"', *Daily Telegraph*, 29 May 2022.

312 Thatcher MSS (digital collection), 109211. https://www.margaretthatcher.org/document/109211

313 Porter, 'Iron Lady gleaming', op. cit.

314 Thatcher, 1996, op. cit., p.275.

315 Seldon, op. cit., p.253.

316 https://api.parliament.uk/historic-hansard/commons/1991/feb/28/the-gulf

317 Richard Beeston, 'We should have finished job, says Thatcher', *The Times*, 26 February 2001. Accessible at Thatcher MSS (digital collection), 143718. https://www.margaretthatcher.org/document/143718

318 Thatcher, 1995, op. cit., p.512.

319 Orth, 'Maggie's Big Problem', op. cit.

320 Moore, op. cit., p.740.

321 Major, op. cit., p.242.

322 Moore, op. cit., p.740.

323 Ibid.

324 Ranj Alaaldin, 'Cameron needs to lead like Thatcher did in Syria', *The Independent*, 3 December 2015.

325 Clarke, op. cit., p.331.

326 TNA, FCO 15/6843, op. cit., f17.

327 Ibid., f19.

328 Clarke, op. cit., p.331.

329 Rifkind, op. cit., pp.301–302.

330 David Hencke, 'Thatcher's secret move to get coal mines reopened', *The Guardian*, 1 October 1993.

331 Moore, op. cit., p.738.

332 Curtis, 1999, op. cit., pp.501–2.

333 Nicholas Wood, 'Thatcher scorns Major's cut in poll-tax bills', *The Times*, 7 June 1991.

334 Curtis, 1999, op. cit., p.588.

335 'Et tu, Maggie?', *The Times*, 22 February 1991.

336 Giles Edwards, 'How to be a former prime minister', BBC, 10 December 2022.

337 TNA, PREM 19/4408, op. cit.

Chapter Seven

1   Matthew Parris, 'You turn away if you want to – but this gets my vote', *The Times*, 15 November 2011.

2   Brandreth, 'The Tory camp', op. cit.

3   Sandbrook, 'Blair, Brown, Major. In 100 years they will be long forgotten. But the world will still be in awe of the grocer's daughter from Grantham', op. cit.

4   *Hull Daily Mail*, 19 September 1992.

5   'Londoner's Diary: Bob Geldof is riled up at The Convention', *Evening Standard*, 15 May 2017.

6   Thatcher MSS (digital collection), 102450. https://www.margaretthatcher.org/document/102450

7   Thatcher MSS (digital collection), 102471. https://www.margaretthatcher.org/document/102471

8   https://bsky.app/profile/whyoutloud.bsky.social/post/3llhwewudj7724 The author is grateful to Matthew Bailey for the details of this quote.

9   Nosheen Iqbal, 'Drag queen Danny La Rue dies aged 81', *The Guardian*, 1 June 2009.

10 Moore, op. cit., p.748.

11 Richard Barber, '"I'll work until the fat lady sings" – Don Black is determined to carry on composing', *Daily Express*, 4 March 2023.

12 Burchill, 'Slimeballs always hate a strong woman', op. cit.

13 Parris, 'You turn away if you want to – but this gets my vote', op. cit.

14 Damian Barr, 'Hilary Mantel on Margaret Thatcher: "I can still feel that boiling detestation"', *The Guardian*, 19 September 2014.

15 Chris Hastings, 'She's at it again. Now Wolf Hall author attacks Maggie's "camp" dress sense: Tory anger as Hilary Mantel launches new broadside against ex-PM', *Mail on Sunday*, 7 June 2015.

16 d'Ancona, 'Is it really ten years?', op. cit.

17 Kaufman, 'She couldn't say "No"', op. cit.

18 https://www.youtube.com/watch?v=p_gnhy7eT1s

19 Thatcher MSS (digital collection), 110367. https://www.margaretthatcher.org/document/110367

20 Thatcher MSS (digital collection), 109441. https://www.margaretthatcher.org/document/109441

21 Nicholas Watt, 'Mummy returns…again', *The Guardian*, 31 October 2002.

22 https://x.com/realmrsthatcher/status/1745343534595703178?s=20 The author is very grateful to Jared Towers (@realMrsThatcher) for providing the details of this speech.

23 https://www.pata.org/blog/pata-70th-anniversary-looking-back-from-the-eyes-of-michael-paulin

24 Charles Moore, 'Why Theresa May, a good MP, should never have been prime minister', *Daily Telegraph*, 8 March 2024.

25 Powell, 'She carried an aura of excitement with her … the atmosphere was charged', op. cit.

26 Marianka Swain, 'Margaret Thatcher: Queen of Soho is fantastically entertaining and surprisingly sympathetic', *Daily Telegraph*, 22 August 2021. *Margaret Thatcher: Queen of Soho* debuted at the Edinburgh Festival in 2013. It had a West End run in 2021. Its premise is Prime Minister Thatcher stumbling into a Soho gay club on the eve of the vote on Section 28.

Part III: Margaret Thatcher's (emerging) legacy

1 Harris, op. cit., p.340.

2 Moore, op. cit., p.733.

3 Sergeant, op. cit., p.11.

4 Maddox, op. cit., p.233.

5 *The Economist*, 13–19 April 2013.

6 Keay, 'My children have to live their lives. I took a different life', op. cit.

7 Paul Waugh, 'Thatcher predicts Tories will lose', *The Independent*, 28 August 1998.

8 Michael White, 'Tories will lose again – Thatcher', *The Guardian*, 28 August 1998.

9 Philip Webster, 'Tories cannot win next time says Thatcher', *The Times*, 28 August 1998.

10 Colin Brown, 'Ingham rebuke for Thatcher', *The Independent*, 29 August 1998.

11 Watson and Baldwin, 'Thatcher puts a bomb under Europe policy', op. cit.

12 'Still bleeding', *The Times*, 22 November 2000.

13 Moore, op. cit., p.733.

14 https://johnmajorarchive.org.uk/2013/04/08/sir-john-majors-interview-following-the-death-of-baroness-thatcher-8-april-2013/

15 Cameron, op. cit., p.37.

16 Tony Wright, 'How Mrs Thatcher Saved the Labour Party (and Destroyed the Conservative Party)', in Stanislao Pugliese ed., *The Political Legacy of Margaret Thatcher* (London: Politico's, 2003), p.366.

17 https://hansard.parliament.uk/Commons/2013-04-10/debates/1304104000001/TributesTo BaronessThatcher#contribution-13041020000026

18 Thatcher, 1996, p.278.

19 Young, *The Guardian*, 23 November 1990, op. cit.

20 Joe Haines, 'Brought down by the pygmies', *Daily Mirror*, 23 November 1990.

21 Moore, op. cit., p.733.

22 Young, *The Guardian*, 23 November 1990, op. cit.

23 Dobbs, 'It's only now that I understand her', op. cit.

24 O'Sullivan, 'A radical reformer who could not go gentle into the political night', op. cit.

Chapter Eight

1 Moore, op. cit., p.737.

2 Nikki Knewstub, '"Thatcherette" in charge', *The Guardian*, 28 November 1990.

3 TNA, PREM 19/3890, op. cit.

4 Major, op. cit., p.215.

5 Hugo Young, 'You clap, I'll sing', *The Guardian*, 12 June 1993.

6 Simon Jenkins, 'The posthumous years', *The Times*, 24 May 1995.

7 Campbell, op. cit., p.750.

8 Philip Webster, 'Hague backs Lilley as Tory revolt erupts', *The Times*, 21 April 1999.

9 Campbell, op. cit., p.790.

10 Boris Johnson, 'Was this the moment when Thatcherism died?', *Daily Telegraph*, 21 April 1999.

11 Michael Gove and Andrew Pierce, 'Hague's party turn falls flat', *The Times*, 24 April 1999.

12 Andrew Pierce, '"Ballistic" Thatcher zeroes in on Hague', *The Times*, 24 April 1999.

13 Tom Baldwin, 'New Hague reforms outrage old guard', *Sunday Telegraph*, 25 April 1999.

14 Campbell, op. cit., p.790.

15 Michael Portillo, 'The Tories have not left Margaret behind', *The Times*, 22 November 2000.

16 https://johnmajorarchive.org.uk/2013/04/21/sir-john-majors-itv-interview-following-the-death-of-baroness-thatcher-8-april-2013/

17 Cameron, op. cit., p.37.

18 https://capx.co/you-need-courage-to-change-a-country

19 James Heale, 'Badenoch lays claim to Thatcher's legacy', *The Spectator*, 17 March 2025.

20 https://x.com/KemiBadenoch/status/1889292437392155096

21 Guy Kelly, 'James Graham: "No leader since Thatcher has been able to reshape society in their own vision"', *Daily Telegraph*, 2 March 2025.

22 Matthew d'Ancona, 'Thatcher and Blair get it – so why don't Tory MPs?', *Sunday Telegraph*, 15 July 2001.

23 https://hansard.parliament.uk/commons/2013-04-10/debates/13041040000001/TributesTo BaronessThatcher

24 'Beware the potency of the Maggie myth', *Independent on Sunday*, 14 April 2013.

25 Thatcher, 2002, op. cit., p.xxii.

26 Thatcher, 1995, op. cit., p.512.

27 Moore, op. cit., p.809.

28 Sergeant, op. cit., p.187.

29 Moore, op. cit., p.809.

30 Prescott, 'Thatcher mocks "wee Willie" Hague', op. cit.

31 Thatcher, 'Well done, Tony – you've given William his chance', op. cit.

32 Matthew d'Ancona, 'The other blonde we can't forget', *Sunday Telegraph*, 30 August 1998.

33 James Landale, 'William's weekly call to "Mother"', *The Times*, 29 January 2000.

34 Moore, op. cit., p.825.

35 Sergeant, op. cit., p.331.

36 Jasper Gerard, 'Lady T takes a vow of silence to help the party go with a swing', *Sunday Times*, 9 September 2001.

37 George Jones and Rachel Sylvester, 'Thatcher is the past, says new Tory leader', *Daily Telegraph*, 6 October 2001.

38 Philip Webster and Melissa Kite, 'I am Thatcher's heir, says Duncan Smith', *The Times*, 7 October 2002.

39 Harris, op. cit., p.416.

40 George Jones, 'Howard returns Thatcher to Tory fold', *Daily Telegraph*, 5 May 2004.

41 Tom Baldwin and Helen Rumbelow, 'Howard delighted to sing Thatcher's praises', *The Times*, 1 May 2004.

42 Toby Helm and George Jones, 'Blair attacks Howard as a relic of Thatcherism', *Daily Telegraph*, 5 May 2004.

43 The National Archives, PREM 49/3402, CABINET. Cabinet briefs: part 6, 30 June 2004–10 November 2004, accessible at https://discovery.nationalarchives.gov.uk/details/r/C19388169

44 Cameron, op. cit., p.416.

45 Rosemary Bennett, 'Make a clean break with Thatcher, party is told', *The Times*, 10 March 2005.

46 James Chapman, 'Cameron: I want to be the Thatcher of social reform', *Daily Mail*, 18 August 2008.

47 'And guess who popped in to offer support', *Daily Mail*, 9 June 2010.

48 'Maggie's den again', *The Sun*, 9 June 2010.

49 Michael White, 'Boy George and the Iron Lady, the new pincer movement', *The Guardian*, 9 June 2010.

50 Cameron, op. cit., p.473.

51 Patrick Wintour, 'David Cameron says he is driven like Margaret Thatcher', *The Observer*, 20 May 2012.

52 Peter Dominiczak and Bruno Waterfield, 'Cameron styles himself as the heir to Thatcher', *Daily Telegraph*, 27 June 2014.

53 Cameron, op. cit., p.416.

54 Joy Lo Dico, 'Charles Moore: David Cameron is the first PM who can handle Thatcher's legacy', *Evening Standard*, 6 October 2015.

Chapter Nine

1 Moore, op. cit., p.805.

2 John O'Sullivan, 'And the winner is … Mrs T! (whatever happens today)', *Daily Express*, 1 May 1997.

3 'Thatcher has already won, says Europe', *Sunday Telegraph*, 27 April 1997.

4 Philip Allmendinger, 'Myth and Reality: The Impact and Legacy of Margaret Thatcher', in Pugliese, op. cit., p.352.

5 David Charter, 'Mandelson tells Labour: we're all Thatcherites', *The Times*, 10 June 2002.

6 https://publications.parliament.uk/pa/cm200102/cmhansrd/vo020612/debtext/20612-02.htm#20612-02_spmin2

7 Tony Blair, *A Journey* (London: Hutchinson, 2010), p.99.

8 Thatcher MSS (digital collection), 111361. https://www.margaretthatcher.org/document/111361

9 David Cannadine, *Margaret Thatcher: A Life and Legacy* (Oxford: Oxford University Press, 2017), p.125.

10 Gordon Rayner, 'Thatcher sent handwritten note to Blair praising his "resolve" after invasion of Afghanistan', *Daily Telegraph*, 19 July 2023.

11 John Kampfner, 'Ogre to the Left, inspiration to New Labour', *Daily Telegraph*, 17 April 2008.

12 Young, *The Guardian*, 23 November 1990, op. cit.

13 Robin Oakley, 'Thatcherism: a style or a philosophy?', *The Times*, 23 November 1990.

14 TNA, PREM 49/2202, op. cit.

15 Andrew Grice and James Adams, 'Blair in secret talks with Thatcher; Clinton to address cabinet at No 10', *Sunday Times*, 25 May 1997.

16 Sergeant, op. cit., p.332.

17 Matthew d'Ancona, 'Introducing the real Maggie in Tony's life', *Sunday Telegraph*, 13 April 1997.

18 Harris, op. cit., p.420 and p.363.

19 The National Archives' Website: Discovery: PREM 49/2774, PRIME MINISTER. Prime Minister's meetings with Opposition Parties: part 1, 3 July 2001–11 April 2002, accessible at: https://discovery.nationalarchives.gov.uk/details/r/C18252068

20 Nicholas Watt, 'Build loyalty or face revolt, Callaghan warns Blair', *The Guardian*, 3 January 2000.

21 The National Archives, PREM 32/26, John Major 1990 manuscript diary, 22 November 1990–2 January 1991, accessible at: https://discovery.nationalarchives.gov.uk/details/r/C18188775

22 Andrew Grice and Michael Prescott, 'Thatcher: Blair best Labour leader for 30 years', *Sunday Times*, 28 May 1995.

23 Brandreth, op. cit., p.325.

24 Philip Webster, Arthur Leathley and Andrew Pierce, 'New Labour will ruin it, says Thatcher', *The Times*, 23 November 1996.

25 Thatcher MSS (digital collection), 108368. https://www.margaretthatcher.org/document/108368

26 Thatcher MSS (digital collection), 108353. https://www.margaretthatcher.org/document/108353

27 Paul Johnson, 'Tony is the "good son" Margaret never had', *Sunday Telegraph*, 16 March 1997.

28 Moore, op. cit., p.801.

29 Curtis, 2000, op. cit., p.721.

30 Thatcher MSS (digital collection), 111361. https://www.margaretthatcher.org/document/111361

31 Simon Jenkins, 'To Thatcher, a son', *The Times*, 1 October 1997.

32 Jill Sherman, 'Blair dismisses Thatcher gibe as an "absurdity"', *The Times*, 3 October 1998.

33 Michael Prescott, 'Thatcher calls Blair "bossy"', *Sunday Times*, 31 January 1999.

34 'Blair as Thatcher', *Daily Telegraph*, 11 December 1999.

35 The National Archives, PREM 49/2205, PRIME MINISTER. Prime Minister's meetings with Opposition leaders: part 3, 1 January 2000–7 June 2001.

36 Philip Webster, 'Blair admits Thatcher "not all wrong" on EU', *The Times*, 23 February 2000.

37 The National Archives, PREM 49/3352, GENERAL ELECTIONS. General Election policy: part 1, 7 September 1999–20 October 2000, accessible at: https://discovery. nationalarchives.gov.uk/details/r/C18508686

38 Andy McSmith, 'Blair renounces his Thatcher inheritance', *Daily Telegraph*, 23 November 2000.

39 Tom Baldwin, 'No tears for Thatcher ten years on', *The Times*, 21 November 2000.

40 Philip Webster and Tom Baldwin, 'Blair severs ties with Thatcher', *The Times*, 23 November 2000.

41 Simon Jenkins, 'The Iron Lady who made Tony Blair', *The Times*, 24 November 2000.

42 Trevor Kavanagh, 'Maggie rages at folly of vain Blair', *The Sun*, 22 November 2000.

43 'Who shall we trust?', *The Sun*, 22 November 2000.

44 Jones, 'Hague's last hurrah for Tories', op. cit.

45 https://publications.parliament.uk/pa/cm200102/cmhansrd/vo010620/debtext/10620-05. htm#10620-05_spmino

46 http://news.bbc.co.uk/1/hi/programmes/breakfast_with_frost/1942222.stm

47 Tom Baldwin and Nigel Hawkes, 'Blair ready to follow Thatcher and confront unions on health reforms', *The Times*, 22 April 2002.

48 Thatcher MSS (digital collection), 110687. https://www.margaretthatcher.org/document/110687

49 Thatcher MSS (digital collection), 109483. https://www.margaretthatcher.org/document/109483

50 Alan Hamilton and Christine Buckley, 'Thatcher's greatest hits replay', *The Times*, 1 May 2003.

51 The National Archives, PREM 49/3037, EUROPEAN POLICY. The future of Europe: part 11, 5 March 2003–16 May 2003, accessible at: https://discovery.nationalarchives.gov.uk/ details/r/C18508371

52 Michael Portillo, 'It took a Labour leader to win Thatcher's last battle', *Sunday Times*, 2 May 2004.

53 Michael White and Robert Booth, 'Thatcher's old foes left out in the cold', *The Guardian*, 14 October 2005.

54 Andrew Pierce, 'The ultimate Eighties revival night', *The Times*, 14 October 2005. Accessible at Thatcher MSS (digital collection), 110597. https://www.margaretthatcher.org/ document/110597

55 Michael Portillo, 'Blair is fading away to a dubious place in history', *Sunday Times*, 1 January 2006. Accessible at Thatcher MSS (digital collection), 110868. https://www.margaretthatcher. org/document/110868

56 Rosemary Bennett, 'Win centre ground or failure is inevitable, Tories told', *The Times*, 31 January 2006. Accessible at Thatcher MSS (digital collection), 110693. https://www. margaretthatcher.org/document/110693

57 Moore, op. cit., p.778.

58 'Helping hand for Iron Lady', *Daily Express*, 11 September 2008.

59 'Comrades in arms', *Daily Telegraph*, 18 June 2007.

60 https://www.private-eye.co.uk/covers/cover-1187

61 https://hansard.parliament.uk/Lords/2013-04-10/debates/1304101000196/DeathOfA MemberBaronessThatcher

62 Philip Webster, 'Revealed: Thatcher's unlikely admirer', *The Times*, 5 September 2007. Accessible at Thatcher MSS (digital collection), 110990. https://www.margaretthatcher.org/ document/110990

63 https://publications.parliament.uk/pa/cm200102/cmhansrd/vo010620/debtext/10620-04. htm

64 Sam Lister, 'Iron Chancellor meets Iron Lady', *The Times*, 3 June 2003.

65 Kampfner, 'Ogre to the Left, inspiration to New Labour', op. cit.

66 Webster, 'Revealed: Thatcher's unlikely admirer', op. cit.

67 Kampfner, 'Ogre to the Left, inspiration to New Labour', op. cit.

68 Ann Treneman, 'Iron Lady on the doorstep as Tories launch a doorstopper', *The Times*, 14 September 2007. Accessible at Thatcher MSS (digital collection), 110991. https://www. margaretthatcher.org/document/110991

69 'Cameron must show he's the true heir to Thatcher', *Daily Express*, 14 September 2007.

70 Ivens, 'Tories must learn the lady is for turning to their advantage', op. cit.

71 Kampfner, 'Ogre to the Left, inspiration to New Labour', op. cit.

72 Philip Webster, 'Tebbit hits out at Tories and names Brown as Thatcher's natural heir', *The Times*, 26 September 2007. Accessible at Thatcher MSS (digital collection), 111063. https:// www.margaretthatcher.org/document/111063

73 Malcolm Rifkind, 'So why that red dress and those TV cameras, Margaret?', *The Observer*, 16 September 2007.

74 Webster, 'Tebbit hits out at Tories and names Brown as Thatcher's natural heir', op. cit.

75 Harris, op. cit., p.417.

76 Paul Waugh, 'Cameron: We'll be the party to wipe out poverty in Britain', *Evening Standard*, 16 October 2007.

77 Ivens, 'Tories must learn the lady is for turning to their advantage', op. cit.

78 Forsyth, 'She never stopped serving her country', op. cit.

79 https://publications.parliament.uk/pa/cm201213/cmhansrd/cm130410/debtext/130410-0001. htm#1304104000001

80 Mary Riddell, 'What Titanium Ed and the Iron Lady have in common', *Daily Telegraph*, 16 April 2013.

81 Sir Keir Starmer speech at Port Vale FC, 23 March 2023.

82 Ben Wright, 'Keir Starmer: "Thatcher was wrong about British society"', *Daily Telegraph*, 10 June 2022.

83 Keir Starmer, 'Voters have been betrayed on Brexit and immigration. I stand ready to deliver', *Sunday Telegraph*, 2 December 2023.

84 Lizzy Buchan, 'Keir Starmer hit by backlash for praising Margaret Thatcher in pitch to Tory voters', *Daily Mirror*, 4 December 2023.

85 George Parker and Jim Pickard, 'Tony Blair think-tank revenues hit $140mn as governments pay for advice', *Financial Times*, 22 December 2023.

86 https://twitter.com/billybragg/status/1731257312575168700?t=Gc6Llio j1dWcplokr VVyLQ&s=03

87 https://hansard.parliament.uk/Commons/2023-12-06/debates/0C37F592-2EBD-4421-BCF4-B7355EBD6440/PrimeMinister

88 Amy Gibbons, 'Thatcher did terrible things, Starmer insists after backlash against praise', *Daily Telegraph*, 8 December 2023.

89 Nadeem Badshah, 'Keir Starmer "gets rid of" 10 Downing Street's Thatcher portrait', *The Guardian*, 30 August 2024.

90 Peter Walker, 'Starmer removed Thatcher portrait as he dislikes "pictures of people staring down at him"', *The Guardian*, 8 September 2024.

91 https://x.com/KemiBadenoch/status/1854593617463063009

92 Keir Starmer, 'We'll cut the weeds of regulation and let growth bloom', *The Times*, 28 January 2025.

93 Chris Smyth, 'Keir Starmer invokes Margaret Thatcher as he goes for growth', *The Times*, 28 January 2025.

94 Rowena Mason, 'Jeremy Corbyn says he would repeal Thatcher's sympathy strikes ban', *The Guardian*, 17 January 2016.

95 Chris West, 'Is Jeremy Corbyn The New Margaret Thatcher?', Huffington Post, 3 July 2017.

96 Loulla-Mae Eleftheriou-Smith, 'Labour Party conference: Read Jeremy Corbyn's speech in full', *The Independent*, 27 September 2017.

97 Robert Peston, 'Why Corbyn is Thatcher's heir', ITV News, 27 September 2017.

98 '"The country faces a fundamental choice"– Corbyn's full speech in Corby', LabourList, 19 August 2019.

99 Christopher Hope, 'Jeremy Corbyn to promise revolution in British politics akin to Margaret Thatcher's 1979 landslide', *Daily Telegraph*, 18 August 2019.

100 Charles Moore, 'A nation in crisis needs vision and leadership. That's exactly what Mrs Thatcher provided', *Daily Telegraph*, 27 September 2019.

Chapter Ten

1 Moore, 'The mellowing of Margaret Thatcher', op. cit.

2 Charles Moore, 'A farewell to a great prime minister', *Daily Telegraph*, 23 November 1990.

3 O'Sullivan, 'A radical reformer who could not go gentle into the political night', op. cit.

4 Lesley White, 'Far from the madding crowd', *Sunday Times*, 21 March 2004.

5 Rifkind, 'So why that red dress and those TV cameras, Margaret?', op. cit.

6 Moore, op. cit., p.745.

7 Thatcher MSS (digital collection), 109299. https://www.margaretthatcher.org/document/109299

8 Sergeant, op. cit., p.348.

9 Parris, 'Handbag swings in to bless the Young Pretender', op. cit.

10 James Chapman, 'Mrs T gave me her blessing, says Tory star Javid: She told me "you'll protect our great island", Muslim minister reveals', *Daily Mail*, 6 May 2015.

11 d'Ancona, 'Today's contenders for power are all Thatcher's children', op. cit.

12 Kampfner, 'Ogre to the Left, inspiration to New Labour', op. cit.

13 https://hansard.parliament.uk/Commons/2010-06-08/debates/beec9d97-061c-411d-90ac-1ad4d1cadbff/CommonsChamber

14 Moore, op. cit., p.xix.

15 Harris, op. cit., p.423.

16 Ibid., p.417.

17 Charles Moore, 'This once most controversial figure is at risk of becoming a national treasure', *Sunday Telegraph*, 9 March 2008.

18 Simon Heffer, 'Radical visionary who rescued Britain', *Daily Telegraph*, 10 April 2008.

19 Moore argues that when Major claimed to the true heir to Thatcher 'he was using her as a flag of convenience'. Moore, op. cit., p.759.

20 d'Ancona, 'The other blonde we can't forget', op. cit.

21 Patrick Wintour, 'Thatcherism holds sway for politicians to this day', *The Guardian*, 9 April 2013.

22 Kettle, 'Ghostly raging at the dying light', op. cit.

23 Eleni Courea, 'Margaret Thatcher's ghost looms over Liz Truss and Rishi Sunak', Politico, 4 August 2022.

24 Dominic McGrath, 'Liz Truss rejects Margaret Thatcher comparisons: "I am my own person"', *Evening Standard*, 21 July 2022.

25 Kate Plummer, 'All the times Liz Truss has been accused of dressing like Margaret Thatcher', Indy100, 27 July 2022.

26 Rishi Sunak, 'I will be the heir to Margaret Thatcher', *Daily Telegraph*, 20 July 2022.

27 Ian Dunt, 'The Tory party is losing itself in a haze of Thatcher worship', iNews, 24 August 2022.

28 Aden-Jay Wood, 'Liz Truss' body language a "hybrid between Margaret Thatcher and Mavis Riley from Coronation Street"', GB News, 7 September 2022.

29 Lord Young, 'Truss has proved herself to be a poor imitation of Mrs Thatcher', *Daily Telegraph*, 17 October 2022.

30 Kevin Schofield, '"Margaret Thatcher Without The Intelligence": Voters Deliver Brutal Verdict On Liz Truss', Huffington Post, 11 October 2022.

31 'The Guardian view on Sunak's strikes: to be more inflexible than Thatcher is a flaw', *The Guardian*, 12 December 2022.

32 Dominic Lawson, 'Far from being the closet Lefty his critics claim, Rishi is the most true-blue of the bunch', *Daily Mail*, 14 May 2023.

33 Rishi Sunak, speech to Conservative Party conference, 4 October 2023.

34 'Rishi Sunak latest: Net zero changes can win Tories next election, says Jacob Rees-Mogg', *Daily Telegraph*, 21 September 2023.

35 John Rentoul, 'Mummy Returns: The ghost of Margaret Thatcher still haunts British politics', *The Independent*, 21 September 2023.

36 Andrew Sparrow, 'PMQs verdict: May mimics Maggie – and surprises with jokes', *The Guardian*, 20 July 2016.

37 Michael Deacon, 'Remind you of anybody? At her first PMQs, Theresa May goes full Thatcher', *Daily Telegraph*, 20 July 2016.

38 Michael Deacon, 'Ken Clarke's takedown of the Tory hopefuls is glorious. Give him my job', *Daily Telegraph*, 5 July 2016.

39 Judith Woods, 'Theresa May is the Bloody Serious Woman that Britain needs for prime minister', *Daily Telegraph*, 11 July 2016.

40 James Frayne, 'May is emerging as the true heir to Thatcher', ConservativeHome, 6 October 2016.

41 Bernard Ingham, 'Has PM May come to bury Margaret Thatcher or to praise her?', *Yorkshire Post*, 19 October 2016.

42 Jason Farrell, 'Theresa May is "like Thatcher" says ex-cricketer Geoffrey Boycott', Sky News, 7 November 2016.

43 Theresa May, speech to the National Housing Federation summit, 19 September 2018.

44 Ben Riley-Smith, 'Theresa May exclusive interview: "I'm not abandoning Thatcherism"', *Daily Telegraph*, 20 May 2017.

45 Bernard Ingham, 'Thatcherism is in save [sic] hands with Theresa May', *Yorkshire Post*, 24 May 2017.

46 John Prescott, 'Theresa May is a Poundland Margaret Thatcher peddling the same old Tory lies and broken promises', *Daily Mirror*, 20 May 2017.

47 Toby Helm and Andrew Rawnsley, 'Mrs Thatcher saw dragons to be slain. Theresa is tough, too, but the dragons are very different', *The Observer*, 21 May 2017.

48 Christopher Hope, 'Theresa May is "no Margaret Thatcher", says ex-minister David Mellor who served her for four years', *Daily Telegraph*, 18 December 2016.

49 Norman Tebbit, 'Sorry Theresa May, but you're no Margaret Thatcher', *Daily Telegraph*, 19 November 2018.

50 Paul Goodman, 'The election in which the Conservatives finally waved farewell to Thatcher's ghost', ConservativeHome, 13 December 2019.

51 Dominic Cavendish, 'David Hare: If Thatcher had been in charge during Covid, "I don't think so many people would be dead"', *Daily Telegraph*, 12 March 2022.

52 David Mellor, 'I saw how Margaret Thatcher flashed her steel against the unions. Now Boris Johnson must show his mettle', *Daily Mail*, 22 June 2022.

53 Salma Shah, 'The Conservative Party in its current form is flailing – it's time for Thatcher 2.0', *The Independent*, 22 June 2022.

54 Jamie Micklethwaite, 'Boris Johnson compares himself to Margaret Thatcher: "She would have dealt with Covid in same way"', GB News, 8 April 2022.

55 Catherine Neilan and Dominic Penna, 'Boris Johnson channels Thatcher in defence of post-Brexit transition', *Daily Telegraph*, 5 October 2021.

56 https://blogs.lse.ac.uk/politicsandpolicy/why-conservative-mps-remain-under-margaret-thatchers-spell-10-years-after-her-death/

57 George Eaton, 'We're still living in Margaret Thatcher's world', *New Statesman*, 7 April 2023.

Conclusion

1   David Seymour, 'Should old PMs solider on or simply fade away?', *Today*, 22 April 1992.

2   John Vincent, 'Will the real Ted Heath speak up?', *The Times*, 2 February 1983.

3   'After Downing Street', *The Times*, 1 December 1984.

4   https://history.blog.gov.uk/2012/11/01/former-prime-ministers/

5   See Peter Just, 'United Kingdom: life after number 10 – premiers emeritus and parliament', *Journal of Legislative Studies*, Volume 10, 2004, Issue 2–3: Legislatures and Executives: An Investigation into the Relationship at the Heart of Government. See also Just, 1996, and Just, 1999, op. cit.

6   Chris Bryant, '*The Abuse of Power* by Theresa May review – rewriting history', *The Guardian*, 28 September 2023.

7   Moore, op. cit., p.758.

8   Oakley, 'Thatcher remains the unexploded bomb in her party's heart', op. cit.

9   Urban, op. cit., p.160.

10 Watt, 'Bowing out: the Thatcher legacy', op. cit.

11 https://www.gresham.ac.uk/watch-now/leadership-and-change-prime-ministers-post-war-world-thatcher

12 Mark Garnett, 'Banality in Politics: Margaret Thatcher and the Biographers', *Political Studies Review*, vol. 5, 2007.

13 Theakston, op. cit., p.205.

14 Philip Webster, 'Life begins at 65, Thatcher tells staff', *The Times*, 27 November 1990. Accessible at Thatcher MSS (digital collection), 107870. https://www.margaretthatcher.org/document/107870

15 Not only is 'Herself Alone' the title of Charles Moore's third and final volume of Lady Thatcher's authorised biography, it is also the title of the last chapter of the final edition of Hugo Young's *One of Us*, published in 1991, part of which covered the first period of Lady Thatcher's life after Downing Street.

16 Moore, 'The mellowing of Margaret Thatcher', op. cit.

17 Bernard Ingham, 'The right way to grasp victory', *Daily Express*, 12 June 1995.

18 Moore, 'A champion of freedom for workers, nations and the world', op. cit.

19 https://hansard.parliament.uk/Lords/2013-04-10/debates/1304101000196/DeathOfAMemberBaronessThatcher

20 https://x.com/KemiBadenoch/status/1889292437392155096

21 'Thatcher has already won, says Europe', op. cit.

22 Will Lloyd, 'Thatcher burns bright at "Conservative Way Forward" event', UnHerd, 11 July 2022.

23 https://hansard.parliament.uk/commons/2022-09-09/debates/7E1BA553-600D-41B4-BAB9-849A02B254C3/TributesToHerLateMajestyTheQueen

24 Michael Gove, 'Now the lady is for learning', *The Times*, 15 March 1997.

25 https://web.archive.org/web/20180830132730/ and http://strong.lighting/portfolio/super-trouper/

Bibliography

Archives

Margaret Thatcher Foundation https://www.margaretthatcher.org/

John Major Archive https://johnmajorarchive.org.uk/

The UK National Archives https://www.nationalarchives.gov.uk/

The USA National Archives

Books

Aitken, Jonathan, *Margaret Thatcher: Power and Personality* (London: Bloomsbury, 2013)

Bell, Tim, *Right or Wrong* (London: Bloomsbury, 2014)

Blair, Tony, *A Journey* (London: Hutchinson, 2010)

Brandreth, Gyles, *Breaking the Code* (London: Weidenfeld & Nicolson, 1999)

Cameron, David, *For the Record* (London: William Collins, 2019)

Campbell, John, *Margaret Thatcher, Volume Two: The Iron Lady* (London: Jonathan Cape, 2003)

Cannadine, David, *Margaret Thatcher: A Life and Legacy* (Oxford: Oxford University Press, 2017)

Clarke, Ken, *Kind of Blue* (London: Macmillan, 2016)

Currie, Edwina, *Diaries 1987–1992* (London: Little, Brown, 2002)

Curtis, Sarah, ed., *The Journals of Woodrow Wyatt, Volume Two* (London: Macmillan, 1999)

Curtis, Sarah, ed., *The Journals of Woodrow Wyatt, Volume Three* (London: Macmillan, 2000)

Dale, Iain, *Margaret Thatcher* (London: Swift, 2025)

Fowler, Norman, *A Political Suicide* (London: Politico's, 2008)

Fowler, Norman, *The Best of Enemies* (London: Biteback, 2023)

Harris, Robin, *Not for Turning: The Life of Margaret Thatcher* (London: Bantam Press, 2013)

Hastings, Max, *Editor* (London: Macmillan, 2002)

Hennessy, Peter and Shepherd, Robert, *The Complete Reflections* (London: Haus Publishing, 2020)

Hogg, Sarah and Hill, Jonathan, *Too Close to Call* (London: Little, Brown 1995)

Horne, Alistair, *Macmillan, 1957–1986* (London: Macmillan, 1989)

Hurd, Douglas, *Memoirs* (London: Little, Brown, 2003)

Maddox, Brenda, *Maggie: The First Lady* (London: Hodder & Stoughton, 2003)

Major, John, *The Autobiography* (London: HarperCollins, 1999)

McAlpine, Alistair, *Once a Jolly Bagman* (London: Weidenfeld & Nicolson, 1997)

McManus, Michael, *Edward Heath: A Singular Life* (London: Elliott and Thompson, 2016)

Moore, Charles, *Margaret Thatcher: The Authorized Biography, Volume Three: Herself Alone* (London: Allen Lane, 2019)

Nadler, Jo-Anne, *William Hague In His Own Right* (London: Politico's, 2000)

Norton, Philip and Beech, Matt, eds, *The Companion to Margaret Thatcher* (London: Edward Elgar, forthcoming 2025)

Parris, Matthew, *Chance Witness* (London: Penguin, 2002)

Patten, Chris, *East and West* (London: Pan Books, 1999)

Pugliese, Stanislao, ed., *The Political Legacy of Margaret Thatcher* (London: Politico's, 2003)

Rifkind, Malcolm, *Power and Pragmatism* (London: Biteback, 2016)

Seldon, Anthony, *Major: A Political Life* (London: Weidenfeld & Nicolson, 1997)

Sergeant, John, *Maggie: Her Fatal Legacy* (London: Macmillan, 2005)

Slocock, Caroline, *People Like Us: Margaret Thatcher and Me* (London: Biteback, 2018)

Spicer, Michael, *The Spicer Diaries* (London: Biteback, 2012)

Thatcher, Carol, *Below the Parapet* (London: HarperCollins, 1996)

Thatcher, Carol, *A Swim-On Part in the Goldfish Bowl* (London: Headline Review, 2008)

Thatcher, Margaret, *The Downing Street Years* (London: HarperCollins, 1993)

Thatcher, Margaret, *The Path to Power* (London: HarperCollins, 1995)

Thatcher, Margaret, *Statecraft* (London: HarperCollins, 2002)

Theakston, Kevin, *After Number 10: Former Prime Ministers in British Politics* (Basingstoke: Palgrave Macmillan, 2010)

Thorpe, D. R., ed., *Who Loses Who Wins, The Journals of Kenneth Rose, Volume Two 1979–2014* (London: Weidenfeld & Nicolson, 2019)

Urban, George R., *Diplomacy and Disillusion at the Court of Margaret Thatcher* (London: I. B. Tauris, 1996)

Waldegrave, William, *A Different Kind of Weather* (London: Constable, 2015)

Wright, Patrick R. H., *Behind Diplomatic Lines* (London: Biteback, 2018)

Young, Hugo, *One of Us* (London: Macmillan, 1991)

Ziegler, Philip, *Edward Heath* (London: HarperPress, 2010)

Interviews, conversations and correspondence

Lord Barnett

Lord Carr of Hadley

Earl Ferrers

Sir David Knox

Sir Michael Marshall

Lord McIntosh of Haringey

Lord Merlyn-Rees

Lord Norton of Louth

Lord Rawlinson

Lord Richard

Andrew Riley

Sir Julian Seymour

Lord Shore of Stepney

Baroness Young

Former members of Lady Thatcher's governments

Former Labour Cabinet ministers and junior ministers

Acknowledgements

In writing this book, and in the many years of it coming to fruition, I have accumulated many debts.

First, I owe a debt of gratitude to my former supervisor, Professor The Lord Norton of Louth, for suggesting that I submit an abstract to the Margaret Thatcher life, work and legacy conference he organised in September 2023. The initial draft of the 10,000-word paper I had to present at the conference came out at 80,000 words. That's Margaret Thatcher for you. Given that initial draft, Lord Norton suggested I write this book. Over and above that, I am grateful for all the advice, support, encouragement and friendship that Lord Norton has given me since first I became one of his students in the early 1990s.

I also owe a debt to Iain Dale, both for employing me at Politico's bookstore and for giving me the opportunity to meet the subject of this work during the period of her life that it covers. The impressions I gained of Lady Thatcher from those meetings, few and brief though they were, underpin much of what I have written. I also owe Iain thanks for his kindness about and endorsement of this book.

Similarly, thanks are also due to the other people who have provided endorsements: Matthew Parris, Andrew Roberts and Anthony Seldon. I am very grateful.

I am especially grateful to Richard Stone for allowing us to use his first portrait of Lady Thatcher for the cover. I am deeply honoured that this is also the first time that he has given permission for one of his portraits of her to be used in this way.

I also owe thanks to James Stephens at Biteback for commissioning the book and particular thanks to my editor, Olivia Beattie, for all her advice, help and support, all much appreciated especially as a first-time author. I am also grateful to Namkwan Cho for designing the fantastic cover that captures so brilliantly the story this book tells, and Suzanne Sangster and Nell Whitaker for their PR and marketing advice and support.

I am grateful to Christopher Collins of the Margaret Thatcher Foundation and Andrew Riley, the archivist of Lady Thatcher's papers, for responding to my queries and for arranging the copyright permissions. Copyright from the Thatcher Estate is republished with permission. As I said in the introduction, the Margaret Thatcher Foundation website is an incredible achievement, not just in relation to Lady Thatcher's prime ministership, but also in relation to her post-prime ministership, and her pre-prime ministership. A model of how to provide access to prime ministerial papers, students of former prime ministers can live in hope that one day Lady Thatcher's successors will follow her example in this area too and do so successfully this time. I owe particular thanks to Andrew Riley for giving me a tour of the archives at Churchill College in January 2025 and for allowing me to see The Handbag and to meet Stanley, the cat who guarded the door to Lady Thatcher's Downing Street flat during the Falklands War.

Like anyone interested in or who is a student of Margaret Thatcher, I am indebted to Jared Towers for his outstanding work on the Twitter (now X) account @realMrsThatcher. It is an invaluable resource, including about Lady Thatcher's life after Downing

Street. It provides many examples of what this book has shown: person and persona, substance and show.

Particular thanks are owed to those people who shared their reflections on former prime ministers, including Lady Thatcher, with me when I was undertaking my postgraduate research. The ones quoted here include Lord Barnett, Lord Carr of Hadley, Earl Ferrers, Sir David Knox, Sir Michael Marshall, Lord McIntosh of Haringey, Lord Merlyn-Rees, Lord Rawlinson, Lord Richard, Lord Shore of Stepney, Baroness Young, other members of Lady Thatcher's governments, and former Conservative and Labour ministers, opposition spokespeople, MPs and peers.

I am also very grateful to Sir Julian Seymour for meeting with me shortly before he died in March 2025 to discuss the book and Lady Thatcher's post-prime ministership more generally, and for allowing me to quote from our conversation. With Sir Julian's death, an invaluable witness of and participant in Lady Thatcher's ex-premiership has been lost. I am pleased that some of his reflections are included here.

More general acknowledgement is due to four groups of people. First, the journalists, sketch writers, leader-writers and other authors who have chronicled Lady Thatcher's life after Downing Street. They have helped to reveal one of the certainties of British politics over the last thirty-five years: while up to 2002 Lady Thatcher never stopped talking to (if not at) us, since 1990 we have never stopped talking about her. Second, special recognition should be given to the aides and officials who worked within government, especially from 1990 to 1997. They helped navigate the ship of state through some of the turbulence generated by Lady Thatcher and people's reactions to her after 1990 and deserve more credit than they have perhaps had to date. Third, the ambassadors, high commissioners and other staff in embassies and high commissions around the world who reported on Lady Thatcher's visits also deserve acknowledgement. Through their letters, memos, minutes, records and telegrams we have learnt more about Lady Thatcher, her life as an ex-premier and the Office of Prime Minister Emeritus. Whatever Lady Thatcher's views of the Foreign Office, as a former Prime Minister she has been well served by it. Fourth, and perhaps most importantly, Lady Thatcher's staff and advisers, especially her two knights, Sir Julian Seymour and Sir Mark Worthington. The triumph of Lady Thatcher's life after Downing Street would not have been possible without them. Whatever people's views of her aides over the years, Lady Thatcher's staff served her exceptionally well and are among the unsung heroes of the story of her post-prime ministership.

While any errors in this work are my responsibility, for commenting on an earlier draft, I am most grateful to Ken Batty. It is better than it was because of Ken's comments.

For their encouragement, I am very grateful to Diana Evans and Professor Jois Stansfield. I owe Mary ('The Baroness') Whitticase and Alexander Harrison thanks for sharing their observations of Lady Thatcher with me, as I do to Stephen Kingdom for alerting me to various 'flag of convenience' moments.

Beyond that, huge thanks are due to my family, especially my father, Derrick (who died while this was being written), my mother, Jean, and my brother, Steven. They have lived with Margaret Thatcher, or rather they have lived with my interest in her, for forty years and more. They deserve a medal. As do my friends, particularly my comrades-in-arms at Politico's Aileen Butler, Colin MacArthur, Rebecca Milton, Katy Payne, Dorothy Rogers, Carol Smith, Joanne Swales and Andrew (Syb) Thompson. My colleagues Dilnaz

Gorwala and Caroline Wright deserve thanks too, for putting up with it.

Deep thanks are owed to Norma Webster. For almost the entire duration of Lady Thatcher's life after No. 10, Norma regularly sent me newspaper clippings about her. Without them, I would not have had the amount – or the richness – of material I have.

My debt to those people who make up my Italian life is incalculable. First, to The Roman, La Nostra Guida, Alessandro, who broke the news to me that Lady Thatcher had died. Then to Gloria, Sonia and Daniele and Sara, Ema, Sheena and Domenico, and Gianfranco, Linda, Vittoria and Lorenzo, to name the fewest number possible. *Grazie, per tutto, per sempre.* Most of all, thank you for teaching me the one essential life lesson: when you are in Rome, the world is another place.

Finally, the most important acknowledgement and the biggest debt is to one of the people to whom this book is dedicated, my late grandmother, Ivy Mary Just. Thanks, Grandma. This is for you.

Index